Introduction

May the grace of the Lord Jesus Christ,
and the love of God,
and the fellowship of the Holy Spirit
be with you all.

2 CORINTHIANS 13:14 NIV

WHAT A PRIVILEGE it is to take time with the Lord, to enjoy talking with and listening to Him, our best and dearest Friend. During our busy and often challenging days, we can call on Him and be blessed as He whispers encouragement and direction to our hearts.

Join with me and be uplifted by these inspirational daily devotions. May each entry help you to focus on how God sheds His love and grace on each of us during the different situations of life.

There's also ample space to write in your own special thoughts, thank-you notes to God, and prayer requests. At the bottom of each page, you'll find room to date and record your faith-building answers to prayers.

My prayer is that God will bless and encourage you during your twelve-month journey with Him—and that you will experience His surprising, amazing mercy and grace.

ANITA CORRINE DONIHUE

Better Than Any Map

Jesus said to him, "I am the way...." JOHN 14:6 NKJV

MANY OF US have a sense of adventure when it comes to traveling. If someone says "Let's go," we drop what we're doing (whenever possible) and head out the door. My mother was like that, more than the average person. Whenever she came upon a back road, she couldn't resist taking it for another adventure. Most of the time it was fun. But when one back road led to another, we'd occasionally get lost and have to make multiple turnarounds so we could find the main road.

Perhaps I inherited my mother's trait. I don't take unknown back roads, but I love traveling. Whenever Bob and I take a trip, I feel my blood pumping the moment we climb in the car. We often take our electronic map with the lady's lovely voice guiding us along the way. However, there are times even she gets us lost.

During life's journeys, we may decide to head out on our own. Perhaps we press the limits, stray from the directions God gives, and lose our bearings. The farther we stray, the more we get lost.

Soon confusion and fear take over. Sometimes we get into so much trouble that we simply don't know what to do next. It is often then that we cry out to God to rescue us from whatever desperate situations we find ourselves in. We frantically turn to His map (the Bible) and allow Him, step-by-step, to lead us where we're supposed to be.

What a comfort to know that the way Jesus clearly directs our paths is far better than any earthly map or influence we may be tempted to follow. When we listen to and obey Him, He faithfully guides us along the roads of life that are sure and true.

Jesus said to him, "I am...the truth." JOHN 14:6 NKJV

LORD, THERE ARE numerous beliefs that people are following these days. Show me how to search Your Scriptures to discover what's absolutely true. As I glance through Grandmother's Bible and see the timeless verses she marked, I recognize what a treasure I have. I love reading from it. Thank you for this Book.

I read in Genesis how You created the earth, the sea, the animals, and human beings.

Then I read farther and realize the marvelous way You, Lord Jesus, Your Father, and the Holy Spirit had a unified part in creating everything: "In the beginning was the Word, and the Word was with God, and the Word was God" (John 1:1 NKJV).

I go on to read how You became a man. You lived here on earth, and You died so I could be one of Your children: "For you are all sons [and daughters] of God through faith in Christ Jesus" (Galatians 3:26 NKJV).

I think of how You made me in Your image. How strange it is that when I look at myself in the mirror, I only see a simple, searching face staring at me. How can I know that You really did live, die, and continue to live for me?

But in Grandma's Bible, before my eyes, is a picture of You, Jesus, praying in the Garden of Gethsemane shortly before You were crucified. On the next page I discover the truth You are showing me! While You were kneeling in the garden, You prayed for me...a prayer that lasts through eternity. "[Jesus prayed, Holy Father,] 'I pray for...those you have given me, for they are yours'" (John 17:9 NIV).

You *are* the everlasting truth, dear Lord. I really am one of Yours. Thank You for how You are praying for me even still today.

"For He is good, for His mercy endures forever..." EZRA 3:11 NKJV

WHEN WE CROSS paths with great Christian leaders serving in various fields, we often think of them as having always been the ideal Christians—even from the time they were very young. How surprised we are when we hear the stories of what they were like while growing up.

I knew one pastor who decided, when he was a boy, that he wanted to get the attention of everyone in the church...and he shaved his head. Another Christian, who is a leader in her community, liked to play every practical joke she could think of as a teenager. Some, by the way, got a little out of hand.

One great man was a handful during his early years in school, often misbehaving. Even though he was smart, his attitude about education caused him to receive poor grades. But a Sunday school teacher led him to the Lord, and when he grew up, D. L. Moody became one of the greatest evangelists of his time.

Many people during their younger years rebelled and made disastrous decisions. Yet God saw worth in them and gave them new lives. Now they are leading others to the altar of grace. In one form or another, we are all works in progress. The Bible promises us that God gives us brand-new lives every single day. Jesus said, "I am...life" (John 14:6 NKJV).

We aren't who we used to be. Neither are we today what we will be tomorrow. Because of God's gracious, loving hand, we can trust Him to help us develop into what we shall become.

Is God ever finished with us? Ask a Christian grandfather or grandmother. Most will tell you that they are still a work in progress. Take heart, dear reader. God isn't finished with you yet.

Look at our future Christian leaders...They often carry Bibles in their hands and bubble gum in their pockets!

"Yes, I'm listening." 1 SAMUEL 3:10 TLB

ISN'T IT WONDERFUL to know that our Lord is as close to us as the very air we breathe? When our minds are occupied with different things, we may be unaware of His presence. Yet we can still recognize His being with us all the time.

The Lord makes His awesome presence known to us in different ways. He frequently places everyday blessings on our pathway. He helps us to sense His nearness through various loving, comforting ways. During our times of prayer, when we pour out our deepest needs and feelings to the Lord, He helps us to know that He is patiently listening to our every word.

Now and then He firmly nudges us to help with important or perhaps even urgent needs. He may pierce our consciences with imperative warnings, helping us to avoid saying or doing things against His will. In similar ways He cautions us against danger and threatening forces of evil.

He may gently whisper to us in our dreams. When we wrestle with a problem during the night and cry out to Him for help, He can speak tender words of comfort, assuring us that He's taking care of things and will work everything together for good.

God also speaks to us through His Word. When He does, we can claim His sure, true promises for our lives, right here, right now: "And the Lord came and called as before, 'Samuel! Samuel!' And Samuel replied, 'Yes, I'm listening'" (1 Samuel 3:10 TLB). "For his Holy Spirit speaks to us deep in our hearts, and tells us that we really are God's children" (Romans 8:16 TLB).

As we go to the Lord in prayer, let's ask Him to speak to our hearts. He's never too busy to talk with us about our cares, hopes, and dreams.

I will praise you, my God and King, and bless your name each day and forever. PSALM 145:1–2 TLB

DO YOU EVER feel as if your prayers are becoming stagnant and they aren't going anywhere? No matter how much you pray, do they seem to bounce off the walls and ceiling rather than reaching the ears of the One you love most? If so, you need not feel alone. Now and again most everyone encounters this problem.

Distractions, cares, busy schedules, depression, or weariness can hinder our communication with God. Other causes might be wrong choices, anger, or resentment. However, our Lord hasn't gone anywhere. His presence is constantly with us. He loves us with an unconditional love. His mercy is immeasurable. The Bible tells us that neither one thing nor one person can separate us from God's love. Even when we're so weak we don't know how to pray, the Holy Spirit intercedes for us to our heavenly Father (Romans 8:26–27).

Shawn struggled with his prayer life while going through a hurtful, stressful time. No matter how much he prayed, he missed feeling God's presence. Then while reading the Psalms, Shawn noticed how David found the answer. Despite what was happening, David worshipped and praised God. And when he made wrong choices, David sought the Lord's forgiveness.

Shawn decided that whether he felt God's presence or not, he would tell the Lord he loved Him and thank Him for His compassion and grace. Shawn also asked God to forgive his wrong choices and to help him forgive those who had caused pain.

Soon Shawn saw a difference in his prayer life. He learned to forget about himself and focus on the Lord's wonderful ways. The barriers were gone. Once again Shawn felt God's encouraging presence in his prayers.

Praise breaks down barriers that hinder our prayers and opens wide the doors to the holy presence of God.

For He Himself is our peace. EPHESIANS 2:14 NKJV

LORD, THANK YOU for helping me to lay my responsibilities and concerns aside, relax, and focus on Your loving presence. Thank You for using those who care about me to help me recognize my need for peace and rest. May I continue to be sensitive to their advice.

How grateful I am that You called me from a world of hurry. Even when my mind has been going ninety miles an hour, You somehow manage to get through to me. It's time to take a break, time to get away and recharge my batteries. You certainly know, Lord, that I've been getting low on the power You are so willing to give me.

When I allow You to restore my soul, my energy grows; my thoughts become clear. I'm discovering that this can't be a quick time away, but one where I must slow down and rest, share my thoughts with You, and be willing to remain with You for a while. It is then that I listen as You gently talk to my heart.

As I search for peace, I pray for Your wisdom and direction. Show me the way You want me to go, O Lord. Keep my paths right and true. Guide me with Your wisdom and righteousness.

Ah, the peace I sense coming from You. How sweet and certain it is. As I rest and we commune with each other, I sense Your loving care and the graciousness of Your Holy presence overshadowing me, cleansing, nurturing, restoring, filling me. Now my soul becomes one with You.

You indeed are my Shepherd, O Lord. I praise You for leading me beside Your quiet waters and kindly granting me peace.

Oh, this river of peace
Makes me perfect and whole;
And its blessings increase,
Flowing deep in my soul.
—DANIEL S. WARNER

He has shown you, O man [and woman], what is good; and what does the LORD require of you but to do justly, to love mercy, and to walk humbly with your God? MICAH 6:8 NKJV

HEARING GOD CALLING us to serve Him can be exciting, but when we consider the whole picture, we might wonder if we're worthy of His calling. When God calls, *He* determines our capabilities and will give us all the help we need to serve Him.

It wasn't long after Dave earned his college degree that he felt God's call to the ministry. Although he studied hard, he never held a four-point grade average. He knew he had numerous faults. His singing voice wasn't that great. How could he measure up to the perfect example he felt was required of a minister? He studied the Scriptures, asking God to lead him. The closer he drew to God, the more he felt concerned about his weaknesses.

One morning as Dave sat deep in thought at the open kitchen window, he heard birds chirping and glanced outside at the bird feeder. He noticed one feathered creature singing louder than the others. The bird enthusiastically puffed out its chest, and delightful melodies filled the air. Dave was surprised when he discovered that the bird was missing a leg. Still, it shuffled about, appeared happy, and kept singing.

Dave prayed, "God, You must not care if I'm weak or strong, talented or average. Only through You am I worthy to be Your loyal servant. You've promised me that Your grace is sufficient; Your power is made perfect in my weaknesses. I trust You to provide me with confidence and strength."

God honored Dave's faith. Now he's a dynamic youth minister for needy teens.

God has a calling for each of us. When we answer, He shows us mercy. Where we were once weak, He makes us strong through His powerful Spirit.

But they that wait upon the LORD shall renew their strength; they shall mount up with wings as eagles; they shall run, and not be weary; and they shall walk, and not faint. ISAIAH 40:31 KJV

JUST AS IT is important to repair or maintain our homes and belongings, it is also important to renew and maintain our physical and spiritual health.

Last spring I suffered from a serious case of pneumonia that lasted close to three months. I was unable to sit in front of a fan or open window without choking. As much as I love the outdoors, I couldn't even handle being exposed to a breeze, and I had to drop out of my water aerobics class at the YMCA.

When I finally recovered, I found that the muscle tone in my body had deteriorated. I knew I must renew my physical strength through a regular routine of walking outdoors and returning to the water aerobics. Now I'm learning to vigorously rebuild and maintain my strength on a regular basis.

It didn't take me long to discover that I couldn't allow myself to coast regarding physical exercise. The same goes for not letting myself become lax in my relationship with the Lord.

We are often bombarded with worries and distractions that drain our spiritual health. How good the Lord is to give us a nudge to get back into reading His Word and drawing closer to Him so He can renew and maintain our spiritual strength. How grateful we can be that the Lord helps us by intervening in all these areas of our lives so we can maintain a healthy balance in Him. He's our compassionate Counselor, our Refuge in times of trouble, our Trainer, our greatest Source of strength.

Your strength shall be renewed day by day like morning dew. PSALM 110:3 TLB

I WATCH THE early morning sun peek over the horizon. It slivers its way between spring rain clouds and enters our living room window. It seems to reflect God's light. Birds chirp outside, heralding a welcome to scattered showers—a promise of a new day.

How dear You are, Lord, how attentive to my thoughts and needs. I get to have a good visit with You, my best Friend. What could be any better than this? Thank You for Your Word and Your empathetic presence. Above all, You are my best promise for a new day!

I flip open my recliner, draw up my knees for a type of table, and reach for the Bible kept near to my chair. Its once-crisp pages are dog-eared and worn from use. I turn to the Lord's promise of peace and assurance in Psalm 112: "Blessed is the man [or woman] who fears the LORD, who finds great delight in His commands" (NIV).

I find a note I wrote years ago in the margin. Its prayer still applies today: "Lord, please help my family to always love and obey You." A stain covers a corner of that page. I remember that my note had been mingled with my tears.

I lay my Bible down and open my heart to Him. I share my frustrations and my faith, my pain and my pleasures. I talk and talk and tell Him how much I love Him. I share with Him my deepest secrets and my greatest joys. How kind He is.

When I'm finished, I close my eyes. I lean my head back and listen—not to the birds, just to Him speaking to me. He pours infinite wisdom and understanding into my spiritual cup. I hear Him gently whisper to my heart, "Oh, taste and see that the Lord is good."

Have mercy on me, O God, according to Your unfailing love. PSALM 51:1 NIV

HOW GRATEFUL WE can be that God patiently urges us to give our lives to Him. No matter what wrongs we've done, it's never too late to ask Him for forgiveness and help.

Rahab the harlot most likely knew everything happening in her city. No doubt she'd heard about the intimidating Israelites camped across the Jordan River. Perhaps she heard how God had rescued them from the Egyptians, parted the Red Sea, and led them to safety.

Did Rahab feel God tugging at her heart? Had the Israelites' God given these intruders the land where she lived? What did she think when two strangers slipped through the city gate and came to her home? Was God encouraging her to protect these Israelite spies?

Rahab hid the men under stalks of flax drying on the roof. Concealing her fear, she sent the king's men pursuing the spies in a false direction. By saving the strangers, she endangered herself and her family.

Darkness fell. The king's searchers left. Jericho's city gate was shut for the night...but the spies never left their hiding place. When all appeared to be safe, she went to the roof and told them they could come out.

Rahab told the men about the city's fear of the Israelites and their God, begging them to be kind to her and her family. The men agreed to protect them as long as she kept their identities a secret. (See Joshua 2:9–12.)

How could God have had any use for Rahab? In spite of her faults, He gave her His mercy and grace.

Whatever our past or present, God can change everything. He wants us to give Him our hearts. When we do, He forgives us and graciously gives us new life through Him.

When someone becomes a Christian he [or she] becomes a brand new person inside. He [or she] is not the same any more. A new life has begun! 2 CORINTHIANS 5:17 TLB

AS WE EXPERIENCE God's grace, our hearts begin to draw closer to Him. Though we're undeserving, He rescues us from sin and wrong and makes us His own.

Rahab lowered the men down an outside city wall to the ground with a scarlet cord after directing them to a nearby mountain, where they hid for three days until the search for them ended. Then they returned to the Israelite camp.

Rahab hung the scarlet cord in her window for the Israelites to see. Had Rahab's belief in God intensified when she heard what happened at the Jordan River? Rahab must have waited in fear while God's people camped outside Jericho. The city gates slammed shut; no one could enter or leave its confines. Rahab could hear the rams' horns blowing and the marching feet. Around the city they went before returning to their camp. For six days, the rams' horns sounded. The marching continued, one time around, each day.

On the seventh day, the Israelites marched around the entire city six times and kept going! Tension must have filled the air as they circled. Suddenly, with the seventh time, there were deafening trumpet blasts and triumphant shouts.

Everything shook. Walls tumbled all around Rahab's house, but she kept her family inside her home as instructed. They could only wait.

Joshua's spies honored their word and rescued Rahab and her family. Quickly the men led them to the Israelites' camp. That day, Rahab experienced God's mercy when He offered her a new life.

When *we* turn our hearts to God, He sheds His mercy on us and gives us a new beginning with Him.

[Jesus said,] "My grace is sufficient for you, for my power is made perfect in weakness."
2 Corinthians 12:9 RSV

ISN'T IT AMAZING how God mercifully provided Rahab with a brand-new life in Him!

The book of James tells that "She was saved because of what she did when she hid those messengers and sent them safely away by a different road" (James 2:25 TLB).

Rahab's actions left their mark on history. And some Bible scholars say she left an even greater legacy by marrying an Israelite named Salmon and giving birth to Boaz. Boaz was the great-grandfather of King David, whose lineage came to include Joseph, the husband of Mary who was the mother of Jesus.

When Rahab was confronted with a need, her fear of God and the Israelites caused her to hide the spies from Jericho's king and then guide them to safety. She did something immediately. Not only did she have faith in the Israelites and their God, but she put her faith into action. Although her background was undesirable, God obviously saw something priceless in this woman.

God calls all kinds of people. Some are highly educated and come from "fine" backgrounds. Others, like Rahab, are easy to ignore. Yet the latter are equally valuable in His sight. Rahab is best remembered not for having been a harlot, but for being a woman willing to step out in faith in her newly found Lord and God.

No situation exists that someone hasn't faced before. God loves us right where we are. As we turn to Him and take each step of faith, He's already with us, working through our situations, transforming our lives, and giving us a victorious future with Him.

When God calls us to do something for Him, we must put our faith into action and follow His direction—for He may ask us to pass on His mercy and grace.

Grace is not sought, nor bought, nor wrought. It is a free gift of Almighty God to needy mankind.
—BILLY GRAHAM

[Jesus said,] "and lo, I am with you always, even to the end of the age." MATTHEW 28:20 NKJV

IT IS BEYOND my comprehension, Lord, how You are and were and ever shall be. You were there before the beginning of time. You in all Your wisdom were there before the earth was even formed. You were there before fountains abounded with water. Before the mountains and hills, You were there.

You, my holy God, orchestrated the preparations of the heavens. It was You who methodically drew a circle and separated the deep waters. You placed rain-filled clouds in the sky. You assigned boundaries and gave rhythm to the rolling seas. It was as though You took Your hand, Lord, and formed the earth's foundations. Then, in all, You were pleased.

You, Lord, made plants and trees that brought forth fruit with seeds. You stretched out the expanse of the sky and separated the day from night. It was You, Lord, who marked the seasons, the days, and the years. It was You who ordered the sun and moon into their places and flung the stars across the heavens.

You fashioned sea creatures and released them into the waters. You made birds to fly across the vast sky. You created livestock and wild animals, each one of its kind.

And then, in all your wisdom, You made man. In Your own image and resemblance You made him. Then, over the span of time, You exercised Your unique wisdom and planning and made me.

You were always there, Lord. Even now, You are still with me. How great is Your wisdom! How marvelous is the way You fashioned all this miraculous beauty for your people to enjoy. How thankful I am that You took the time and care to create me. In You, Lord, I live and move and have my being. To You, I bring all glory and praise.

As God has said: "I will dwell in them.... I will be a Father to you, and you shall be My sons and daughters." 2 CORINTHIANS 6:16, 18 NKJV

ONE OF THE most exciting and miraculous events in our lives is when we accept Jesus as our Lord and Savior. For some period of time, the Lord patiently knocked at our heart's door, asking us to invite Him in. Then we finally opened that door and welcomed Jesus into our hearts, asking Him to forgive our sins. He forgave us and adopted us as His children. Soon we discovered a brand-new life with Him.

From that moment on we were never alone again. God has promised us that He will never leave us or forsake us—that He is continually with us day and night, wherever we are. The Comforter known as the Holy Spirit is not only with us; He dwells in our hearts. He's here, loving, comforting, directing. Along with this, we are now a part of God's family—a family of born-again believers. A family God chooses for us to share our joys and sorrows. A family that will last for an eternity.

A memory planted indelibly in my mind begins when a young man in our church had only been a Christian for a few days. My husband, Bob, noticed him sitting quietly in the back row of the church with his wife and children. Bob announced that we had a birthday to celebrate. It was the birthday of a new member being born into the family of God.

Bob strode down the aisle to where the young man sat and reached out his hand in fellowship. "Welcome to the family of God," he happily said. The man's face glowed as he clasped Bob's hand in return.

If you, too, have recently accepted the Lord, welcome to the family of God! May the Lord richly bless you in your new life in Him!

He helps me do what honors him the most. PSALM 23:3 TLB

DISAGREEMENTS ARE UNPLEASANT and can be painful, whether we are coworkers or we volunteer in a community or church. After praying, we're often able to find solutions to our problems, but occasionally, no matter how we try, we may not reach an agreement. When we experience this, we wonder what God wants us to do next. Let me tell you about men named Barney and Paul who went through this very thing.

Barney and Paul were close friends—like brothers. They went to church, prayed, and felt God calling them to serve on the mission field together.

Still, the two men's personalities were completely opposite. Barney had a loving, caring way, always trying to encourage people to seek God. Paul told people about Jesus with vigor and drive. He focused on the most efficient way to spread the gospel and reach as many souls as possible.

On one of their mission trips, Barney brought his cousin Mark along. Partway through the trip, Mark told the other two he wanted to go back home. Barney and Paul continued their work of winning souls for the Lord without Mark.

A new mission trip was planned. Barney wanted to encourage Mark by including him. Paul reminded Barney how Mark had abandoned them before, and he gave a firm no to the request. Tempers rose, harsh words were spoken, and Barney and Paul decided to go their separate ways.

As you can probably guess, this story is the story of Paul, Barnabas, and Mark from the Bible (see Acts 15:36–41). Hurt feelings must have been deep. Yet, in time, God softened the hearts of Paul and Barnabas and worked circumstances together, bringing forth forgiveness and grace—much like He does when He softens and heals our hearts and teaches us to forgive others.

"Forgive, and you will be forgiven." LUKE 6:37 RSV

NONE OF US know what God's will was for Paul or Barnabas when they disagreed. God certainly must have hurt for them. In spite of it all, God blessed each of their ministries. In time, their wounds healed.

Sometimes Christians disagree, many feeling they are led of God in their opinions or decisions. After struggling to work things out, they give up and go their separate ways. They may try to make things right, but the hurts go too deep.

When this happens, our concerns must be brought to God and left for Him to handle. God can help us forgive even if the other person isn't sorry. Not forgiving is destructive. When we allow Him to, God creates a new work within us, making a pure heart, free from bitterness and acceptable to Him. This can be done only when we call upon God for His graciousness and love. We wait on Him while He patiently deals with us and those who hurt us. We realize we must change where we're wrong. We must forgive, let the faults of others go, and pray for those people. It may take time to heal. However, God has an amazing way of turning around our bungles and poor attitudes. He does remarkable things in our lives when we trust Him.

In spite of everything, God has the love and compassion to bless those who long to serve Him. He works things out simultaneously, achieving what is best for all, when we obey Him. Paul later wrote, in Colossians 4:10 NIV: "My fellow prisoner Aristarchus sends you his greetings, as does Mark, the cousin of Barnabas. (You have received instructions about him; if he comes to you, welcome him.)"

He will help us to let go and be merciful as we press forward with Him.

The LORD is my strength and my song; he has become my salvation. He is my God, and I will praise Him. EXODUS 15:2 NIV

NEW GOALS AND accomplishments can be good, but they can also wear us out. Instead of trying to improve our own lives, listening to God is much better.

He encourages us to think of our bodies as His temples and reminds us to care for them. Exercise increases our energy levels, reduces stress and fatigue, and gets our blood circulating better than caffeine. What about junk food? I have a sweet tooth. When I don't eat right, my body complains. Soon I sense the Lord lovingly, graciously calling me back to better habits.

Time crunches can be frustrating. Schedules help. Praying for His perceptive, positive advice each day helps everything to fall into place.

Enjoying family and friends often adds zest and joy to our lives. When our days end and we have a lot on our minds, we can bring everything to our gracious, understanding Lord and rest, knowing He has the answers. After we sleep, we can usually think more clearly and can make sound decisions.

Taking off one day a week recharges our physical and spiritual batteries. Going to church helps us to focus on the Lord's graciousness and kindness. After reading the Scriptures of His steadfast faithfulness, we know that the lessons He patiently teaches us will provide all the direction and wisdom that we need.

I love opening the windows and doors of our home and letting in sunlight and fresh air. Even better is when we open our hearts to the Lord and allow the light of His presence to flow in. God cares about what's happening to us. When we listen, He gives us the needed strength, fulfillment, and joy for each day.

But Jesus said, "Let the little children come to me, and don't prevent them. For of such is the Kingdom of Heaven." And he put his hands on their heads and blessed them before he left.
MATTHEW 19:14–15 TLB

THOSE OF US who are parents or work with children might feel at times that we want to give up. But God wants us to stick out the calling He has given until He directs us otherwise. When the days (or weeks) are bumpy, ask Him to shed His mercy on those active children.

Years ago, a humble, dedicated Sunday school teacher named Edward Kimball taught a bunch of rambunctious ten- and eleven-year-old boys. Kimball often invited them to become Christians, and several youngsters accepted the Lord. However, one student named Dwight, being an independent thinker, didn't respond. But since Dwight walked a long way in order to go to church, he obviously wanted to come.

Kimball kept praying for young Dwight. One day during the week, the teacher felt compelled to talk with the boy at the store where he stocked shoes. Kimball walked in the door and straight back to where Dwight worked.

Dwight appeared surprised to see him and asked why he came. Kimball didn't hesitate. He firmly yet lovingly told Dwight how much God loved him and that he needed to make a commitment for Jesus. The teacher most likely rejoiced when Dwight accept the Lord in response! Unbeknownst to Kimball, God set Dwight's course that day on a journey of faith with Him.

The Lord raised up Dwight L. Moody to be one of the greatest evangelists of our time. Countless souls were won to God. To think, it began with a regular Sunday school teacher who helped to change the course of some exuberant boys' lives.

If you lead children, be encouraged. You also are taking a journey of faith with God. Don't ever give up.

The Lord sees promise in our rough-hewn youngsters. He wants to raise them up so that they can one day lead the way for the next generation.

[Jesus said,] "Behold, I stand at the door and knock; if any one hears my voice and opens the door, I will come in to him and eat with him, and he with me." REVELATION 3:20 RSV

HOW MANY TIMES have we put off going to the Lord in prayer? Perhaps we've been too busy, or something in our lives has caused us to shy away from His presence. Whatever the situation we're in, we can be assured that He's waiting for us to come to Him and trust Him with our concerns and needs.

At times, my various responsibilities and substituting as a paraeducator keeps me extremely busy. Because of this, I have to be conscious of the Lord's being near each day. Sometimes I'm tempted to say a quick prayer and ask for His help while running out the door. But when I do this, I feel drained.

One day I answered an assignment to substitute in an elementary school "Structured Learning Special Education" class. The teacher warned me that one of the students, whom I'll call Pamela, was autistic. Whenever a substitute was present, Pamela would begin screaming nonstop from anxiety. The teacher instructed me not to approach Pamela, try to talk with her, or even make eye contact. After a few hours, she said, Pamela might warm up to me. I was concerned about doing the right things regarding Pamela, so I paused and asked God to give me grace and understanding. I carefully respected Pamela's space. Then I followed each of the teacher's instructions. In less than an hour, Pamela joined me and the rest of my study group. By the end of the day, I was surprised at how Pamela trusted me and stayed by my side.

That night, I thanked God for helping me through my day. While I kept the door of my weary heart open to Him, He guided me each step of the way.

For as he thinks in his heart, so is he [or she]. PROVERBS 23:7 NKJV

I LOVE IT when God brings to mind the good things He has blessed me with. Every day I try to shove out the negative and dwell on what's positive. Here are some ideas I've come up with for keeping God's joy:

1. Take a smile and pass it on. Frogs are my favorite little critters. Each time I see one, I can't help chuckling at its funny grin. I have a ceramic frog on my windowsill that I named TASAPIO. Its name comes from a favorite saying of mine: "*Take A Smile And Pass It On.*"

2. Curl up the face muscles. Medical research shows that when we smile, we tell our brains to function more positively.

3. Enjoy good belly laughs. First-rate clean movies, books, and funny stories we hear from family and friends can revitalize our days.

4. Look on the bright side. Researchers say it isn't what's happening that dictates our outlook. It's the way we view it. While telling about an event, mention only the good things.

5. Thank God for who we are. Don't worry about whether someone else is thinner or fatter, younger or older. Be thankful that we are all children of a King. He made us; He loves us our personal strengths and weaknesses.

6. Make grape jelly. When someone has a sour-grape attitude around us, let's not allow it to spoil our mindset. Instead, let's ask our Lord to fill us with His gracious presence, take those sour grapes, and stir them into a sweet, delectable grape jelly.

7. Spread the joy. When we come across a good thing, let's share it. A note, phone call, e-mail, or kind word can change someone's entire day.

Ever-living joy in Christ produces a victorious life, everlasting and free.

A friend loves at all times.... PROVERBS 17:17 NIV

LIFE FOR ME gets pretty hectic at times. I look at other people who have busy schedules and appear to be so "together," and I wonder how they do it. I can manage the daily juggling act for a month or so, but then everything has a way of catching up with me. That's when I have to back off and ask the Lord to help me find a way to enjoy some quiet time.

My friend Jan has an intuitive way of keeping a close watch on how I'm doing. She always seems to know when I'm about to fall apart because I've once again taken on more responsibilities than I should. I have a bad habit of going and going like a battery-operated toy until my physical, emotional, and spiritual batteries seriously need recharging.

Perhaps it's a tone in my voice or my deer-in-the-headlights look or my body weakening to the point where my fingers are almost touching my toes when I walk. At any rate, Jan just knows. This is about the time I hear her say, "Grab your overnight case. Plan to spend several days at my home away from the telephone. Bring your laptop. And come share some homemade soup with me."

My body starts to relax as I near her driveway. While I'm there, we read, we write, we pray together, and we walk. Then we talk and laugh about everything and nothing while sipping nice bowls of hot soup. Her kind spirit reflects God's graciousness to me.

Let's pray that we, too, can learn to become more thoughtful to our friends by sharing a pot of soup, or providing a getaway together, and especially having a listening ear.

A friend is God's graciousness in the form of smiles and hugs.

Then Jesus called the children over to him and said to the disciples, "Let the little children come to me! Never send them away! For the Kingdom of God belongs to men [and women] who have hearts as trusting as these little children's." LUKE 18:16 TLB

THIS MORNING I e-mailed a smiley face. Just a smiley face. That was all. It was in response to a brief reply I had received from my son Dan during a busy time in both our lives. His message? It simply said, "I love you too, Mom."

Five little words, yet they said it all. It represented the countless times we enjoyed sitting out on his patio or mine, talking about important and unimportant things. It represented trust and appreciation, believing in each other. A love and trust that sprung up years ago when Dan was little continues to endure and will remain for an eternity. That little click of a message helps to fill a longing for us to be with each other, this son and me.

Numerous times during our days, we may send small prayers of love and gratitude to our heavenly Father. A quick reply from His Holy Spirit warms our hearts and most likely His. Even though this earthly life is a blessing from our Father, there is occasionally something within us that causes us to long to be home in heaven with Him. When we feel this way, frequent messages of love received from our Father can help fill the longing in our hearts. How grateful we can be that He is only a prayer away.

What makes God glad? That we come to Him now the same way we did when we were children, expressing total faith and confidence in His love, wisdom, and care. It's also good to know that as we are faithful to Him, our Father can place His trust in us as well.

The angel of the LORD encamps all around those who fear Him, and delivers them. PSALM 34:7 NKJV

ONE OF THE greatest kinds of love is that which a father or mother has for his or her child. During one afternoon several years ago, I saw an example of this while eating dinner in a small sandwich shop. I noticed a father, a mother, and two small girls sitting at a table in a corner. Everything appeared to be calm until I glanced up and saw a gang of teenage boys with baseball bats fighting just outside the shop's door.

Someone called the police—and the father stepped up to the inside of the door. There, feet spread apart and arms folded, he stood tall without saying a word, facing the battle outside. No one would get past him and threaten his wife and children. And there he remained until the police arrived.

Our Lord God possesses a far greater love for us. He protects us more times than we are aware. I recently heard of a mother and her little boy who went for a walk along a country trail. The scenery was beautiful. Trees and large rocks lined both sides of the trail.

At one point, the mother asked her son to stop a couple of feet ahead so she could take his picture. Later the mother had the pictures developed, and she was shocked when she looked at that particular picture on the trail. Just above the boy's head, on a large rock, crouched a mountain lion ready to pounce.

Could there have been a guardian angel with them that day? Could there have been unseen angels posted in front of the father outside the shop's door? The Father protects us countless times from evil and harm, whether we realize it later or not. How grateful I am for His watchful love.

Be glad for all God is planning for you. Be patient in trouble, and prayerful always.
ROMANS 12:12 TLB

LORD, LIFE'S CIRCUMSTANCES have changed for me recently. Because of all that's happened, I feel displaced and confused. Things don't seem to be fitting together anymore. What used to motivate me and give me vision and hope is no longer a part of what I can focus on. I feel tired and apathetic. Right now I have no purpose or goals to pursue. Please help me.

Take away my apathy and replace it with zeal for whatever You are calling me to do. Help me to get my mind off myself and center my thoughts on You, Your Word, and others.

I know that the zeal You offer doesn't come from whatever limited knowledge I have regarding my purpose and goals. You can give me an infinite zeal that comes through seeking first You and Your righteousness.

Even though I don't see the whole picture of what You have planned for me, I will love and trust You for whatever You have in store each day. Help me not to think only about myself and my needs. Instead, I want to change my focus to caring about those around me with a true Christian love—and to put their concerns and needs above my own.

How comforting to know, Lord, that only You are the One who understands everything You have planned. Thank You for urging me to hold onto the zeal You freely give. I pray that You will provide me with a Spirit-filled drive to serve You. Once again, please help me to put You first so I may love and obey You with all my heart, soul, and mind.

Even though I don't know Your plans for me, I will try to be patient. As I trust in You, I'm already excited about whatever lies ahead.

But they that wait upon the LORD shall renew their strength; they shall mount up with wings as eagles; they shall run, and not be weary; and they shall walk, and not faint. ISAIAH 40:31 KJV

LIVING FOR THE Lord is seldom boring. When we hear God's call, we are often thrilled at what He wants us to do. Sometimes we get so excited that we want to jump in and change the world without waiting for His direction. (I know I've been guilty of that.) Before long, we look around and wonder why everything is going wrong and where God is in the process.

God doesn't just call us. He carefully prepares us for what He wants us to do. It's important for us to stop and wait for further instructions from Him. It may take a few hours, days, months, or even years. Remember, Jesus patiently waited thirty years for God's plan to be fulfilled.

It's as important to wait and allow God to groom us for His work as it is to answer His call in the first place. As we learn to patiently listen, pray, and study the Bible, we'll be able to serve Him in a far better way than if we were to rush out on our own.

There may be times we're serving in His name when we think we've figured it all out. Too often, though, we may make a wrong turn. That's the time to stop and once again pull out God's Word, pray for a calm heart, and listen for His guidance.

Linger with Him as long as needed, and be patient while waiting. After a time, He'll restore your strength.

He causes us to ascend on His wings like baby eagles. Our surety and stamina will increase, and our racing minds and hearts will be more careful and sure. Then when He gives us the go-ahead, we can run and not be weary. We can walk and not faint.

"Listen to Me, O Jacob, and Israel, My called: I am He, I am the First, I am also the Last."
ISAIAH 48:12 NKJV

AS WE LOOK back over our lives, we may marvel at the mighty ways God's hand has been upon us. Before we were born, He formed us and watched over us. During our childhood He was there. When we invited Him into our hearts, He welcomed us as His own. Through our bumpy, irresponsible years, He rescued us from wrong circumstances. Even now He's still with us, constantly helping and guiding.

When times are difficult and our souls feel dry, we can be assured that God is near, ready to pour out His Holy Spirit upon us. When all is well, He still remains—counseling, leading us all the way.

May God bestow His blessings not only upon us but upon the lives of our offspring. May He teach them His marvelous lessons. May they spring up like grass in the field—like sturdy poplar trees growing near flowing streams. May our children and children's children come to say, "I belong to the Lord. He is my all in all!"

It was His hand that laid the foundations of the earth. He spread out the heavens. All of His creation is subject to bow down to Him.

He is our Lord, our gracious, mighty God. Day after day He directs us. If we stray, He helps us back to the right paths. His righteousness is like a cleansing ocean spray. When we obey Him, He gives us peace that's like a smoothly flowing river.

Though our lives are constantly changing, we need not fear. Our past was in His faithful hands; let us trust our present and future to Him. He is our wonderful, gracious Lord. He is our beginning, our present, our future, and our eternity.

Jesus said to them, "You are truly my disciples if you live as I tell you to, and you will know the truth, and the truth will set you free." JOHN 8:31–32 TLB

IT'S HEARTWARMING TO see someone return money to a clerk who gives too much change. We are pleased to hear a child tell the truth about a wrong act in spite of facing a punishment. Truth clears doubts, builds trust, and sets the spirit free.

My friend Vera had an experience while doing jury duty that still makes me smile. After waiting in the jury room, Vera and other jurors were called to the courtroom for a criminal case. The defendant fidgeted in his chair. Vera felt she should pray for the Lord to help him.

In the courtroom, attorneys began questioning each jury member while the defendant looked on. The prosecuting attorney's remarks were precise and easily understood. The defense attorney, however, used flamboyant words far above the jurors' heads.

Vera hoped she wouldn't be put on the case. When she heard her name called, Vera reluctantly stepped forward.

The prosecution's questions went well. But when the defense suggested it may be acceptable to withhold some of the truth, a phrase came to mind: "The truth is always best."

When asked what she would do if she were the defendant, Vera said that the truth was best. When the lawyer rephrased his question, she replied, "I'd think about the advice and would consider getting a different lawyer!"

Vera was dropped from the case. But she kept praying for God to help the defendant to do right. Vera said she was grateful that God gave her courage to speak for truth. She hoped that what she said would cause others to stop and think about the truth!

What measure is truth? An honest word speaks volumes.

Test me, O LORD, and try me, examine my heart and my mind; for your love is ever before me, and I walk continually in your truth. PSALM 26:2–3 NIV

HOW OFTEN ARE we caught up with time-consuming demands and forget to take care of the little yet important things? My friend Jan and her brother Richard experienced this when they purchased their country home.

All looked good, except that no one could find the septic tank. The previous owners finally discovered the tank buried under a pile of topsoil with a spruce tree planted over it, so they removed the tree. Jan and Richard felt certain their only problem had been solved.

About three years later, they noticed rainwater cascading over the roof's gutters. They discovered that the drain spouts were *also* buried beneath layers of topsoil. They were clogged, and the gutters had pulled away from the sides of the house.

Since neither Richard nor Jan could correct the problem, Jan called her son Jon to help. Although the problem had been present for three years, there was no damage to the house's walls and Jon was able to make the repairs.

This causes me to think of how God is always on call for us when we ask Him to search our lives for the little things that need correcting. When we allow Him to work, He can help us find whatever is clogging things in our lives. Then the living water of His Holy Spirit can run freely and keep us pure in Him.

David's prayer in Psalm 139:23–24 can become our own: "Search me, O God, and know my heart; test me and know my anxious thoughts. See if there is any offensive way in me, and lead me in the way everlasting" (NIV).

Not only does our Lord help to make things right, He teaches us to avoid catastrophes before they happen.

Exactness in little duties is a wonderful source of cheerfulness.
—FREDERICK W. FABER

Don't let anyone look down on you because you are young, but set an example for the believers in speech, in life, in love, in faith and in purity. 1 TIMOTHY 4:12 NIV

WERE YOU EVER told you were too young to be used of God? I was. But I refused to let it discourage me. No matter how young or old we are, God can use us to be a blessing and bring honor to Him.

We have a marvelous mix in our church, where children, teenagers, young adults, and elderly mingle, loving and serving the Lord. They sing together on the worship team, share their concerns during prayer time, and hold each other up in special prayer.

There's a mutual respect between the ages, and each one encourages the other. The youth turn to the elderly for encouragement and advice. The adults are gracious and compassionate toward the younger ones going through struggles and insecurities—purposefully remembering what it was like when they were "that age."

During service last Sunday morning, one of my Sunday school students sat next to me. It was obvious she had some important things on her mind. When it came time to go to the altar for prayer, she asked me to go forward with her and pray about her needs.

We kneeled at the altar, prayed, and talked. She asked me how she could gain wisdom and strength. I explained to her that wisdom is reserved for those who seek God with an open heart and listen to the elderly who are wise. I told her she was never too young to learn wisdom and be a blessing for Him.

Already, I see God's special hand on our children and youth. Already, He's preparing them to one day step into the roles of Christian leadership. Like Samuel, they are sensing God's presence and recognizing His voice as He patiently prepares them for the plans He has for their futures.

I have much more to say to you, more than you can now bear. But when he, the Spirit of truth, comes, he will guide you into all truth. JOHN 16:12–13 NIV

DURING OUR WALK with the Lord, we can feel compelled to help others around us. At times we enjoy every minute of it...yet we occasionally become overwhelmed when seeing the tremendous amount of help that's needed.

Do you ever feel burned-out to the point where you can barely put one foot in front of the other? Although you love serving the Lord, do you occasionally become weary and just want to get away from everything? If so, take comfort; you are not alone.

In spite of the needs that crush in from all sides, there is a way of escape. We must with unyielding purpose take time away with the Lord again and again.

The very essence of our physical and spiritual well-being depends on our frequently breaking away and entering the compassionate presence of God. There, we can pour out from the depths of our souls our every feeling, anxiety, and need. Take as long as you need for His Holy Spirit to fill and refill your soul.

The Bible tells how Jesus was pressed in on every side. Yet He purposely broke away from responsibilities to be with His heavenly Father. He knew the Father and Holy Spirit could be with those in need even when He was away.

We must accept that we aren't the answer to people's problems. God is. Where we aren't able to be, what we aren't able to do, God can.

Let us dip into His storehouse of love and mercy. There before Him, let us ask Him to fill and refill our souls to overflowing and meet our needs—to rejuvenate, empower, and direct us. One day at a time, every single day.

The LORD himself goes before you and will be with you; he will never leave you nor forsake you. Do not be afraid; do not be discouraged. DEUTERONOMY 31:8 NIV

MANY OF US are surrounded by wonderful, caring family and friends. We most likely enjoy being with them. We often appreciate the blessings we get by watching out for each other. Yet no matter how dear our loved ones and friends are, there are times we might feel let down or possibly even deserted.

As we well know, we all have our share of shortcomings. No matter how hard we try to be there for each other, we can only do so much. It is then that we realize we certainly aren't God and can't be the answer to all of life's problems. Neither must we expect those around us to always be able do so. We can gain strength and comfort by knowing above all else that Christ is the lifeline we are always able to depend upon. He has promised that He will never leave us nor forsake us.

Not long ago, I watched an old movie that told about a homesteading family trying to survive the fierce South Dakota winters. In order to do their outdoor chores during whiteout snowstorms, they strung a rope from the outside of the house to the different places where they had to go. They knew they would probably be all right while holding onto the lifeline with one hand and carrying a bucket or any other needed object in the other.

When the whiteout storms of life crash in on us so severely that we can't see any hope of help around us, we can be sure we are safe when we hold onto Christ, our unfailing lifeline. Know for certain, dear reader: He patiently solves any struggles we go through and any uncertainties we have to deal with. In Him, we will never, ever be alone.

Give ear to my words, O LORD, consider my meditation. Give heed to the voice of my cry, my King and my God, for to You I will pray. My voice You shall hear in the morning, O LORD; in the morning I will direct it to You, and I will look up. PSALM 5:1–3 NKJV

DO YOU EVER feel life is going way too fast and you need a sliver of time to tell your best Friend, the Lord, everything that's going on? If you need to, let someone know you have an appointment on the way home and then find a quiet spot for your appointment with God, even if it's a supermarket parking lot.

Allow the world to stop around you. Tell the Lord everything that's on your mind and heart. You can be free to laugh, cry, or stomp your feet in frustration. Nothing else around you matters. After you're finished talking, take a few more minutes to listen to Him.

Sometimes we feel like all we need is a good listener to whom we can vent our feelings and concerns. We *do* have Someone who listens. He's with us all the time. After we talk with Him, we're better prepared to face the next part of our day. What a difference a good venting to the Lord makes.

≥♣

This has been an especially busy week, Lord. As You know, I just phoned home to let everyone know I would be a few minutes late after running my morning errands, that I would be taking time out with You in a nearby park. It is so good to simply bask in Your peaceful presence. Thank You for listening while I share with You everything going on this week. Big and little things in my life seem to be equally important to You. I'm grateful for how You take my needs on Your shoulders even before I ask. I'm ready to go now, Lord, with You by my side.

[Jesus said,] "If you obey my commands, you will remain in my love.... I have told you this so that my joy may be in you and that your joy may be complete." JOHN 15:10–11 NIV

EVERYTHING I'VE EVER needed, Lord, I have now found in You. I used to wonder why I didn't have a deep, inner joy that I saw in those who knew You as their Savior. I was happy most of the time, but it was a conditional happiness that depended more on how good or bad my days were.

I couldn't understand what was missing until I read Galatians 5:22 in the Bible and discovered the answers. I needed to commit my life to You and to ask Your Spirit to dwell within me.

But the fruit of the Spirit is love.... Although I love my family and friends, Lord, I've longed for Your holy love. It is flawless—a love without limit or condition. Fill me with Your unselfish love.

The fruit of the Spirit is joy.... This inner joy I searched for comes when I put You before everything else in my life. It's a joy that springs forth no matter what life's circumstances bring.

The fruit of the Spirit is peace.... In this turbulent world, I find myself yearning for a peace of heart and mind. Cleanse my heart, Lord, and give me a peace that passes all understanding.

The fruit of the Spirit is patience.... Lord, when I get tired, my patience is sometimes stretched to the limit. It's only through Your Spirit that I can obtain the patience I need. Thank You for being gracious to me.

The fruit of the Spirit is kindness and goodness.... How kind and good You are to me, Lord. Help me to pass Your thoughtfulness on to others, whether or not they are kind to me.

I'm so grateful for Your being in my life, Lord, and allowing me to remain in Your love. In You, my life is now complete.

But Naomi said, "Turn back, my daughters; why will you go with me? Are there still sons in my womb, that they may be your husbands?" Then they lifted up their voices and wept again; and Orpah kissed her mother-in-law, but Ruth clung to her. RUTH 1:11, 14 NKJV

HAVE YOU EVER had to make an unwanted move? The book of Ruth tells of a woman named Naomi who felt sorrow from having to leave a land she held dear.

Naomi made her home in Bethlehem, Judah, with her husband and sons. But because of a famine, they'd been forced to move to Moab where they could find food and water. If we were to put ourselves in Naomi's place, we too would have experienced sorrow. She had to leave a familiar home, her extended family, and her friends. But Naomi knew that uniting with her husband in this difficult move was what God wanted.

After some time, Naomi's husband died. By then her sons were old enough to marry. As far as we know, there were no other people in Moab who believed in the one true God, so the sons married Orpah and Ruth. Both women were of a different faith. In spite of her grieving for the loss of her husband, God must have given Naomi an extra measure of grace to love her two daughters-in-law as though they were her own.

Ten years passed, and Naomi's sons also died. How much sorrow could one woman take? Even though she loved Orpah and Ruth dearly, she had no one near her from her direct family. She must have longed to be with them again.

Naomi heard there was food in her homeland once more. She made the decision to return to Bethlehem and encouraged Orpah and Ruth to go back to their mothers.

We can be confident that when God leads, His grace remains with us all of the time. It's amazing how He makes a way and provides for our needs.

You have made known to me the ways of life; You will make me full of joy in Your presence.
ACTS 2:28 NKJV

TEARS WERE SHED. Parting from the two women Naomi loved like her own children made her experience even a deeper sorrow. Orpah reluctantly kissed her mother-in-law good-bye...but Ruth chose to remain with Naomi.

It may well have been that Ruth stayed because Naomi loved both women so much. Tears of sorrow soon turned to joy when Ruth told Naomi, "Intreat me not to leave thee, or to return from following after thee: for whither thou goest, I will go; and where thou lodgest, I will lodge: thy people shall be my people, and thy God my God" (Ruth 1:16 KJV).

God occasionally asks us to sacrifice our own comforts in order to follow Him. Sometimes, in doing so, we must give up things that we hold dear or move away from people that we love. We may feel torn and experience deep sorrow. During these times, we can be comforted to know that God's gracious mercy surrounds us. He understands how we feel. And when we obey, He blesses. He brings about good and replaces our sadness with tears of joy.

GIVE YOUR SORROWS TO JESUS
Do sadness and despair steal joy from your life?
    Give your sorrows to Jesus.
Does your heart grow weary? Are you laden with grief?
    Give your sorrows to Jesus.
He'll give you comfort. He'll shed light on your way.
    Give your sorrows to Jesus.
He'll pick up your burden. He'll take it away.
    Give your sorrows to Jesus.
Give all your sorrows to Jesus. Keep not even a one.
Lay them all at the Master's feet.
    He will take care of each one.
The night is gone. There's light in the day.
    You've given your sorrows to Jesus.
The time of singing has returned to stay.
    You've given your sorrows to Him.

Offer your bodies as living sacrifices, holy and pleasing to God—this is your spiritual act of worship. Do not conform any longer to the pattern of this world, but be transformed by the renewing of your mind. Then you will be able to test and approve what God's will is. ROMANS 12:1–2 NIV

HAVE YOU EVER experienced God's tug at your heart to help someone in need? This doesn't seem difficult unless we too are suffering. Yet along with His tug, God provides strength so we can give of ourselves. Afterward, we may look back and see His hand in it all.

We read in the Bible how Ruth pledged her loyalty to her mother-in-law, Naomi. Because of the love Ruth felt for Naomi, she was willing to give of herself. Little did she realize that her lifelong promise to Naomi would go down in history: "Whither thou goest, I will go; and where thou lodgest, I will lodge" (Ruth 1:16 KJV).

Like Naomi and Orpah, Ruth grieved for the loss of her husband. How could she find the strength to leave Moab, her family, and all that she held dear? It's doubtful that she thought about her own needs or future. She just acted out of love.

When Naomi and Ruth arrived in Bethlehem, it was during the barley harvest. Ruth went into the fields to glean barley behind the pickers so she and Naomi could have food. It happened that the field Ruth gleaned in belonged to Boaz, a relative of Naomi's deceased husband. Before long, Boaz noticed how hard Ruth was working, and he showed kindness to her. He made sure she had water and food for herself and plenty of barley to take home to Naomi.

Was it any wonder that Naomi and Ruth arrived during harvesttime and God led them to such a kind man as Boaz? God's marvelous plan for Naomi and Ruth was already starting to unfold. What good things would lie ahead?

When we choose to follow God, He always goes before us.

O Lord my God, many and many a time you have done great miracles for us, and we are ever in your thoughts. Who else can do such glorious things? No one else can be compared with you. There isn't time to tell of all your wonderful deeds. PSALM 40:5 TLB

CAN WE FOR a moment imagine the impact our words or actions could have on other people—possibly through generations or into eternity? One Sunday while Bob and I were still in college, our pastor told us that studies had showed the average person leaving a profound impression on at least one hundred people during his or her lifetime. My jaw dropped. I couldn't understand such magnitude.

Think of those we brush shoulders with every day and what kind of effect we have on their lives. Multiply how many years we live times the people whom we're able to encourage and share God's love with.

Ruth had no idea that what she did would be so important. Her main concern was to care for her mother-in-law, Naomi. Her kind attitude toward Naomi caused her to find favor with Boaz. He instructed his laborers to leave extra barley stalks for her to pick up. He began to share bread and wine vinegar with her during their meals. After working until evening fell, Ruth would take the barley, thresh it, and bring it home to Naomi.

Boaz recognized the kind and noble person Ruth was, and Boaz and Ruth fell in love. Certainly God brought them together as husband and wife. Ruth gave birth to their son and called him Obed. What immense joy she must have felt when she placed her baby in Naomi's lap.

What blessings could have been greater because of Ruth's selfless love? God used Boaz and Ruth to bring forth their son Obed, who became the father of Jesse—and Jesse, the father of David. So went their descendants through time where they traced to Joseph, the husband of Mary, the mother of Jesus, our Lord and Savior!

Jesus replied,...." 'The Lord our God is the one and only God. And you must love him with all your heart and soul and mind and strength.... You must love others as much as yourself.' No other commandments are greater than these." MARK 12:29–31 TLB

HOW CAN WE possibly love God more than our sweethearts or spouses, our children or parents? These people are more precious to us than priceless jewels. Still, this is what God calls us to do as Christians. Does loving God more than anyone else mean we cherish our dear ones less?

Obviously, our love for one another is incredibly strong. Many a story is told about boundless acts of sacrifice shown to loved ones and even to strangers.

This love, no matter how strong, is human and sometimes fragile. Even in the best of circumstances, human love errs. Unkind words may be spoken. Thoughtless actions can cut to the heart. Through the tests of life we may look at someone and wonder if we really love them anymore. The fire of human love may become vulnerable enough to flicker, fade, or even die. We have heard many times of strong affection turning to intense bitterness. But God understands and helps us when we pray.

How does God's love differ? It is unselfish, perfect, and pure. It doesn't manipulate or expect a payback. We can thank Him over and over that we are able to count on His care every day, in every circumstance. *God's* merciful compassion cleanses us from selfishness and wrong. When we put Him first, the Lord teaches us to cherish one another *more* with a deep, unselfish, measureless love.

God cherishes us in spite of our failures and appreciates our efforts to serve and obey Him. How gracious and farseeing our Lord is! His example of pure, merciful love helps us to look beyond the imperfections in others, to appreciate and give them the gracious, enduring love that God places in our hearts.

Be kind to one another, tenderhearted, forgiving one another, as God in Christ forgave you.
EPHESIANS 4:32 RSV

THERE ARE TIMES when showing kindness to others requires our going the extra mile or trying harder to help. Perhaps personally making more of an effort in what we're doing doesn't seem nearly as significant as when someone else does it for us.

Following God's leading in writing a book often includes deadlines for the book's completion. The further I get into writing, the more the momentum (and sometimes the stress) picks up. It's really true that many things we do for the Lord may be accompanied by blood, sweat, and tears.

This routine doesn't only affect my lifestyle, but that of my loving husband Bob. The extra-mile kindnesses he shows to me go far beyond what I can count. Along with his own responsibilities as pastor of our church, he cooks at least half our meals (even if some include going to local restaurants). He does housework and laundry and patiently takes my telephone messages while I'm working. All of these things have caused him to sacrifice and go the second and even third mile.

This year, a case of pneumonia caused me to struggle with illness for several months while I still attempted to write. I wasn't always pleasant to be around during my recovery time. Yet Bob took time to bring me tea, rub my neck and shoulders, and tell me that he was proud of me and loved me.

While we or our family members labor to fulfill God's callings, let's remember the source of patience and kindness that strengthen us to go that extra mile. They spring up from the selfless sacrifice of Jesus, who gave His all.

A good deed is never lost.... He who plants kindness gathers love.
—ST. BASIL THE GREAT

The LORD will keep you from all harm—He will watch over your life. PSALM 121:7 NIV

HOW MANY TIMES have you barely escaped being in an accident? When that happens, it's easy to recognize God's gracious arms of protection surrounding you.

Many of us pray for God's protection before we go anywhere. We have little knowledge about the countless times He intervenes, interrupting dangers that cross our paths. How grateful we feel when we find that He has done so.

Not long ago, an experience like this occurred when Jeanne and Lawrence left their home to go shopping in a nearby town. They had just left the store parking lot when a car darted out in front of them, cutting across three lanes of traffic. Jeanne managed to stop in time to avoid the crazy driver.

A few minutes later, when they were entering the turn lane to get on the freeway, another car that had barely exited the freeway zoomed past the vehicles in the through lanes, turned too quickly, and ended up facing Jeanne and Lawrence's car. Again, Jeanne slammed on her brakes, feeling as though their car was on its nose while the other driver slid into the correct lane and squeaked past them. They wondered at this point if their car had a "hit me" sign tacked to its bumper!

Even though Jeanne is a careful driver, both encounters were so sudden that she and Lawrence could only credit their avoidance of what might have been a tragic accident to the protecting grace of God.

What a comfort it is to know from the timeless promise in Psalm 46:1–2 that God is our protection and strength. He's with us, helping in the face of trouble and danger. We can trust in Him and not be afraid.

It is a mighty thing for a Christian to pray…not because we are mighty, but because He is mighty.
—AUTHOR UNKNOWN

Those who sow in tears shall reap in joy. PSALM 126:5 NKJV

AMONG ALL THE debilitating struggles we may be forced to face, one of the most paralyzing is depression, which enshrouds us in an emotional fog.

Focusing on the littlest tasks can be exhausting. It's difficult to sleep—and when sleep does come, dark shadows or earth-shattering nightmares can cause us to bolt up from bed in terror. Lethargy robs our strength. Enthusiasm for life begins to ebb away.

Depression is a formidable challenge. Yet nothing we go through is too great for God to overcome. Here are a few ideas that may help if you're struggling:

🙢 Give your cares completely to God, and don't take them back. No matter how paralyzed or discouraged we feel, we must obey the Lord with every fiber of our being. Then He can work without our hindrance.

🙢 Search the Scriptures and claim God's promises as your own: We can do whatever is needed through Jesus Christ who gives us strength (Philippians 4:13). God gives us direction when we acknowledge Him (Proverbs 3:5–6 NKJV). He gives us perfect peace when we keep our minds on Him and trust in Him (Isaiah 26:3). He dries our tears (Psalm 126:5). His truth sets us free (John 8:32 NKJV).

🙢 See a doctor. Some causes of depression are physical. God helps us, but He also gives us doctors who serve on His behalf.

🙢 Get plenty of vigorous exercise. This releases endorphins into the brain, which help us to think more clearly and develop positive attitudes.

🙢 Focus on things that are good. Push the bad thoughts out and bring the good thoughts in. Philippians 4:8 RSV tells us: "Whatever is true, whatever is honorable, whatever is just, whatever is pure, whatever is lovely, whatever is gracious, if there is any excellence, if there is anything worthy of praise, think about these things."

We need not ever give up. God is near. He can faithfully lift the fog and lead us into His glorious sunshine. When He does, give Him all the glory and praise.

I have inherited Your testimonies forever, for they are the joy of my heart. I have inclined my heart to perform Your statutes forever, even to the end. PSALM 119:111–112 NASB

WHAT IS A legacy? Is it something lofty and noble people of high regard pass down to those who revere them? Is it the dynamic influence of a great evangelist? Could it be the well-laid ten- or twenty-year plan of a church congregation?

A legacy can be any of the things mentioned above. However, it can also come from ordinary people like us who love the Lord and enjoy an everyday experience with Him. As we plod along doing our best, we may think our lives go unnoticed. Yet the Lord often places His hand on us in the most unexpected ways and gives us a legacy that can be passed down to those in our neighborhood, in our work, or others who are watching us. Perhaps it's a legacy being built by God to pass down to our children or our children's children, on through the generations.

When I was a teenager, I looked upon a person's legacy as something that just happened out of the blue. But as I grow in the Lord and experience the good and bad in life, I've begun to realize that legacies are often born in the most difficult of times. God does some of His greatest work through our suffering and struggles.

When times are tough, I may be tempted to sit on my legacy and do nothing. If I make poor choices, I can take them to the Lord and ask for His forgiveness. Each time I do, God tugs me to my feet and firmly urges me to start over and renew the legacy He wants me to build.

So be of good courage. Keep putting one foot in front of the other and look for the legacy the Lord is helping you to build. You just never know what lives you are touching.

LORD, You have assigned me my portion and my cup; you have made my lot secure. The boundary lines have fallen for me in pleasant places; surely I have a delightful inheritance. PSALM 16:5–6 NIV

THERE ARE SOME people who were raised in homes where Christian legacies vibrantly surrounded them through family members of all ages. This is a remarkable heritage and one to be treasured. Others grew up in families where their parents had little or no interest in the Lord. In spite of this, some, in time, accepted the Lord Jesus as their Savior.

Donna was one who didn't have the privilege of living in a Christian home. As a teenager, she really loved the Lord but felt saddened that she didn't have a legacy like her Christian friends.

The time came when she went to a church camp meeting with her youth group. Her missing Christian family heritage gnawed painfully at her heart. Why hadn't God blessed her like the others? Shortly before an evening service, a girl in the youth group named Marsha called all the teens together to meet around an outdoor fire pit. She challenged them to sincerely pray that lives would be changed in the evening service. As Donna joined the circle of clasped hands in prayer, the Holy Spirit helped her to realize that, like Marsha, she too had been given a legacy. Hers came directly from her heavenly Father. The Lord revealed to her that He doesn't have any grandchildren. She was His child, adopted by Him. Her legacy wasn't missing. God had placed it directly in her heart.

Through the years, Donna came to understand that the heritage God had given her was more important than life itself. Now that she's grown, she's a pastor's wife. She often speaks to various congregations and women's groups, telling them how we are offered a legacy through Him and can use that to honor the Lord.

[Love] bears all things, believes all things, hopes all things, endures all things. Love never fails.
1 CORINTHIANS 13:7–8 NKJV

WHEN UNCERTAINTIES AND difficulties invade out loved ones' lives, they may be tempted to lose hope. Many often long to hear words of support and belief from family and friends.

With the Lord's help, we can better express to our loved ones the confidence and hope we have in them. When someone hears a few positive words, they are often more inspired to meet the challenges placed before them.

Andrew and Stephanie experienced this when their daughter Micah was in college. Micah loved the Lord, yet temptations were strong. Some students in Micah's dorm were taking pills for energy in order to study all night and make it to class the next day.

Fortunately, Micah talked with her parents about the problem. Whenever she called or came home, Andrew and Stephanie shared their trust and pride in her. They also faithfully held her up in prayer.

One evening Micah phoned her parents. A girl in her dorm had been rushed to the hospital because of a drug overdose. Through sobbing breaths, Micah asked her parents to pray. As the three united in prayer, God's presence filled them with peace.

During summer break, Micah told her parents that what helped her most was their belief and pride in her—and their faith that she wouldn't let them down.

God loves us and sees our potential to live victorious lives through Him. He faithfully surrounds us with His presence. He puts hope and confidence in our lives, even during the most difficult times. The more we stay near to Him and feed on His Scripture, the more we'll be able to follow Him.

All we like sheep have gone astray; we have turned, every one, to his own way; and the LORD has laid on Him the iniquity of us all. ISAIAH 53:6 NKJV

MAKING A START as a young adult can be exciting and mind boggling at the same time. Yet it's good to know that the Lord's always near, helping His children and putting the right people in their paths.

Terry completed her education in bookkeeping and landed a job in a town twenty miles from where she grew up. Although she believed she was a Christian, she didn't always put God first. It wasn't long before she began seeing the wrong kind of friends and adopting their careless lifestyle. Before she knew it, she had to deal with more stress and uncertainties than she'd bargained for.

A coworker named Jim who worked four desks away from Terry started joining her during lunch breaks. Terry noticed something different about him. Their friendship grew, and Jim told her that he was a Christian.

Each time they talked, Jim reminded Terry of God's love and grace. She listened intently as he described Jesus, the good Shepherd, as told in Psalm 23. She realized she was like a lost sheep and knew she must make a decision. One night, alone at her bedside, she slipped to her knees and gave the Lord every part of her life. She vowed to Him that she would never allow anyone to come between her and God again.

Now Terry tells how the Lord gave her a new life, that He is her Shepherd and her dearest Friend. To top it all off, she and Jim became more than friends. They became husband and wife.

I'm overwhelmed when I think of how much the Lord loves me. When I lost my way, He didn't give up until He brought me back into His fold. I thank Him for His loving-kindness and grace...and for being my Shepherd.

Restore to me the joy of Your salvation, and uphold me by Your generous Spirit. PSALM 51:12 NKJV

DID YOU KNOW that God not only wants to use our lives to bless Him, but He wants to provide getaways as a blessing for us? If you could drop everything to go to your favorite place and enjoy His presence, where would it be? The mountains? High in the sky? Deep beneath the water? The Grand Canyon? A riverside or lake? Your own backyard? With family or friends?

I enjoy all of these, yet my favorite place to go is to the coast. We are only a two-hour drive from the Pacific Ocean. When I get involved in a long-term writing project, I occasionally pack my laptop and a few necessary things into my little car, give my husband a kiss good-bye, and head for a remote area called Ocean City. While there for a few days, I rent an old cabin that's so simple it doesn't even have a phone.

Before long, through inspiration from the Holy Spirit, creativity kicks in and my fingers fly. When I get tired and my brain begins to falter, I know I need to stop and break away with Him. I often like to go to the waterfront during dinnertime. Most people have left to settle in for the evening, and things have quieted down.

I drive to a secluded spot, park my car, and step out onto the sand. Paper, pen, and Bible in hand, I'm ready for my Father to minister to my soul.

There's a saying that the ocean has a direct telephone line and calls us to run away. What's even better is when God taps us on our spiritual shoulder and calls us to get away—no matter where or when—with Him. So pack your bags, dear friend, and get ready for when He calls.

You will show me the path of life; in Your presence is fullness of joy; at Your right hand are pleasure forevermore. PSALM 16:11 NKJV

OFTEN WE APPRECIATE the things our friends and family enjoy because we care about our loved ones. After having been married for so long, I've grown to like and often get excited about the things that Bob enjoys. Even when I'm alone, I like picking up a unique guitar pick for him while wandering through a music store. (It must be a thin one, I'm told.)

Since Bob drove eighteen-wheeler trucks for awhile, I've learned to be considerate of truckers on the road. Seeing old cars makes Bob dream of restoring one "some day." I like spotting "a cute one," even when I don't have a clue what the year or model is. He loves his black Suzuki motorcycle. So when I notice a bike, I think of the ones he likes the most.

I adore these things about my husband. Yet I enjoy the things of the Lord even more. He's my Savior and my Confidant, my dearest Friend.

As we walk and talk with the Lord each day, we get to know Him more and more. While we read His Word, we learn what He enjoys and appreciates in our lives and what matters most to Him. Our spirits intertwine. At times we may almost know His thoughts toward us. We appreciate His hopes and dreams for our futures. It must give Him joy when we follow His direction wherever He leads.

When His Spirit dwells within us, we enjoy things that please Him: the sunrise and sunset; the vast ocean; the tiniest bird in its nest; a newborn baby taking his or her first breath.

Perhaps what He loves most is someone accepting Him as Lord and Savior. When a new Christian enters the family of God, we rejoice along with the Lord and the angels!

Who shall separate us from the love of Christ? Shall tribulation, or distress, or persecution, or famine, or nakedness, or peril, or sword? Yet in all these things we are more than conquerors through Him who loved us. ROMANS 8:35, 37 NKJV

DO YOU KNOW that God loves you unconditionally? His love for you and me goes way beyond what our limited minds can comprehend. More than the love of family and friends, His kindness is steadfast and resilient whether we are on top of the world or in despair.

No sin is too great for God to forgive when we turn to Him. It doesn't matter whether we feel worthy of His love. To God, we are priceless. He loves us so much that He adopted us as His sons and daughters and claimed us as His own.

No problem is too great for Him to solve. No decision-making is too complex for Him to counsel. He showers his mercy on us and lifts our spirits. He calms our emotions when we have trouble with change and insecurities. He rejoices with us when we are happy. He grieves with us when we suffer loss. He holds us close to His heart when our hearts are breaking.

There's no place in heaven or on earth where we can be separated from His love. He is closer than the air we breathe. God really loves you and me. We are the apples of His eye.

God is love; His mercy brightens all the path in which we rove;
Bliss He wakes and woe He lightens: God is wisdom, God is love.
Chance and change are busy ever; man decays and ages move;
His mercy waneth never: God is wisdom, God is love.
E'en the hour that darkest seemeth will His changeless goodness prove;
From the mist His brightness streameth: God is wisdom, God is love.
He with earthly cares entwineth hope and comfort from above;
Everywhere His glory shineth: God is wisdom, God is love.

—JOHN BOWRING

Give your bodies to God. Let them be a living sacrifice, holy—the kind he can accept. When you think of what he has done for you, is this too much to ask? ...Be a new and different person with a fresh newness in all you do and think. Then you will learn from your own experience how his ways will really satisfy you. ROMANS 12:1−2 TLB

ALONG LIFE'S JOURNEYS, we experience health and illness. We rejoice during the mountaintop healthy years when we feel like we're able to see everything clearly for miles, yet we bemoan the discouraging, painful ones when we go through the dark, narrow valleys. It's often during illness and pain that we are unable to gain the answers we need regarding our suffering. Occasionally we might not be able to feel God's presence. Still, He faithfully walks with us each step of our way.

Although suffering is part of life, a positive outlook and trusting in God makes a huge difference in how we make it through. Some suffering is brought on by circumstances. Some, however, is due to our mistreating our bodies or minds. When we neglect ourselves physically, mentally, or spiritually, we ultimately suffer.

I have a close friend who had a drinking problem and chain-smoked for years. Another friend ate everything in sight and never exercised. Both knew that their health would fail unless they made drastic changes.

The first friend changed his diet and quit smoking and drinking. Now he's happier, looks younger, and has traded his vices for a treadmill and weights. He also walks almost everywhere. My other friend started the "push exercise." She pushes herself away from the table. She's also walking regularly. Both friends experienced pain while making changes, but now they're reaping the rewards of health and energy.

The Lord helps us to discipline ourselves to live rightly for Him. At first, we may experience discomfort, yet ultimately we are rewarded. God helps our minds and bodies restore themselves, and He compassionately restores our souls.

[Jesus said,...] "Remain in my love...so that my joy may be in you and that your joy may be complete." JOHN 15:10—11 NIV

WHAT IS THIS joy so many Christians talk about? Is it something we feel when everything is going great in our lives? Does it depend on how we feel? What's the difference between joy and happiness?

I believe happiness is conditional. We feel happiness when get to go to a ball game or enjoy spending time with someone we care about. It might even come from receiving an inheritance from a rich uncle! Happiness can be a good thing...yet joy surpasses all of this.

I know a lady who radiates with the joy of the Lord. When I'm around her, I recognize the Holy Spirit working in her life. Good and bad things happen to her like anyone else. But she doesn't dwell on the negative. Instead, she commits everything to the Lord and is mindful of God's goodness. She constantly encourages those around her. She doesn't consider herself better than others. She truly is my sunshine on a rainy *or* sunny day.

Where can we find joy? Joy is a fruit of the Holy Spirit. When we ask His Holy Spirit to come into our lives, He plants that little seed of joy in our souls. He nurtures it and helps it to grow. He draws us closer to Him, shows us how to obey His will in our daily lives, and teaches us to recognize the blessings that He showers upon us each day.

No matter what happens, this deep-down unconditional joy can never be snuffed out because it comes from the Lord. And as we spread around this joy, we will discover that we have plenty left over for ourselves. Better than anything, we can enjoy seeking Him first and sharing His genuine joy with others. Then we can hang onto our hats and see what happens.

Then I heard the voice of the Lord saying, "Whom shall I send? And who will go for us?" And I said, "Here am I. Send me!" ISAIAH 6:8 NIV

ARE YOU SEEKING God's call on your life? His call may be dramatic or as quiet as a whisper. No matter how He calls, God will keep speaking to your heart until you understand what He's trying to tell you. His voice rings out over the mountains and through the valleys of our lives until we hear Him inviting us to follow Him.

When God calls, we may be fearful of what is ahead or how He'll lead us. Does He have a plan for us in this uncertain, crazy world? Are we really worthy of His calling?

Because we're His children, we can believe He's already begun a good work in us.

He helps prepare us for the days ahead, whether they be stormy or as clear as glass. The best part of God's calling is how He walks ahead of us. We can simply reach out and cling to His garment and follow.

When God calls, He doesn't want us to run ahead of Him or drag our feet. He wants us to be alert to His leading so we don't miss our opportunities to serve. All we need to do is acknowledge His direction as He guides us along the way.

God sometimes gives us a dream that He wants us to acknowledge. When we do, He will move that dream forward until it becomes a vision. Don't be afraid. As you seek God's calling, He will lead you on an exciting journey and teach you great things. He will guide your feet. He will remove barriers you encounter. He will faithfully surround you with His merciful, protective presence and graciously give you His strength and power to serve. All you need to do is say, "Here am I, Lord. Send me."

Do your best to [study and] present yourself to God as one approved, a workman who does not need to be ashamed and who correctly handles the word of truth. 2 TIMOTHY 2:15 NIV

THE GOSPELS MATTHEW, Mark, Luke, and John teach us how to accept Jesus as our Savior. "Gospel" means "good news." Jesus tells us in Mark 16:15 to " 'Go into all the world and preach the gospel to every creature' " (NKJV). When we accept Jesus, we want to tell someone our good news. However, knowing how to lead someone to the Lord is often difficult.

Let me tell you what happened with my elementary Sunday school students. They had just memorized "way of salvation" Scriptures. Through this, many became Christians. Next, we talked about leading others to the Lord.

We decided to call this "The Good News Walking Fingers." We grabbed our Bibles, turned to the first page, and wrote "Way of Salvation" and "Romans 3:23" at the top of the page. Then we turned to Romans 3:23 and underlined the Scripture. In the margin, we wrote, "All of us have sinned," then adding "Romans 6:23" at the top of the page. We turned to Romans 6:23 and wrote, "God's gift is everlasting life" in the margin and "John 3:16–17" at the top of the page.

On we went, underlining the Scriptures and writing the new Scripture reference at the top of the page. With John 3:16–17, we wrote, "God loved us and sacrificed His Son for us. Jesus came to save us from sin." After 1 Corinthians 15:3, we wrote, "Jesus died for us." After Acts 16:31, "When we believe in Jesus, He saves us from sin." After John 1:12, "When we accept Jesus, we become God's very own sons and daughters." After 1 John 1:9, we wrote, "When we tell God we are sorry for our sins, He will cleanse us from what we have done wrong."

The kids were excited that they could tell their friends about Jesus' love. One girl and her friend sat side by side and "finger-walked" through the salvation Scriptures. Miraculously, her friend accepted Jesus.

Isn't it wonderful how God uses us to tell of His good news no matter what our age?

The greatest experience in life is to lead a soul to the Lord.

[The Lord said,] "I have loved you, O my people, with an everlasting love; with lovingkindness I have drawn you to me." JEREMIAH 31:3 TLB

NO MATTER WHAT our situation in life, God can use us to be a blessing to those around us and bring honor to Him. In His eyes, it doesn't matter whether we are beautiful, what color our skin is, or what language we speak. We can still be used by God. He made us. He loves us more than we can imagine.

Many people aren't accepted because they are considered "different." The story of one little girl's love and determination still softens hearts today.

She was ridiculed and treated badly because of her race when she became one of the first African American children to integrate into an all-white New Orleans school. One day in front of her scoffers, she stopped and asked God to forgive the ones who mistreated her. Even when they spoke badly about her, she said they didn't realize what they were doing. Then Ruby prayed for God to forgive them like He forgave cruel people years before who said terrible things about His Son.

Ruby Bridges Hall currently lives in New Orleans. In 1999, she formed the Ruby Bridges Foundation to promote respect and appreciation of others. She and her childhood teacher, Mrs. Henry, visit schools to share their experiences.

God is gracious, empathetic, and merciful. We are all important to Him. He looks beyond our outer shells and abilities and sees what is in our hearts. What means most to Him is that we love Him. What makes the difference in our lives is the love and compassion God has for us, no matter how varied we are—and the love, compassion, and acceptance we have for each other.

God uses gracious people to reflect His graciousness.

Surely he hath borne our griefs, and carried our sorrows... He was wounded for our transgressions, he was bruised for our iniquities: the chastisement of our peace was upon him; and with his stripes we are healed. ISAIAH 53:4–5 KJV

AT TIMES WE reach a crossroads in our lives where we know we need to let go of sorrows gone by. Maybe we are haunted by memories we want to forget but they keep coming to the surface like oil on water. Rather than being forced to relive such heartbreak, some are so painful that we might not even be able to talk about them.

Perhaps we keep praying to be freed from such grief. But healing never seems to come. There's more than praying for God's healing. There's a matter of releasing terrible memories. There's a matter of forgiving everyone involved who caused the hurts.

Sometimes we're unable to find a way to make things right. Sin is sin, and the past cannot be changed. I believe we don't have to forgive what happened—but somehow God helps us to forgive those who did wrong. If they have never said they were sorry, we can simply trust God to take care of the rest and bring those who have sinned to a point of changing their hearts.

Don't despair, dear one. God loves us. When we hurt, He hurts with us. He can help us untie the restraining knots of our heartstrings and let Him know how we feel. He wants us to allow Him to skim off our layers of sorrow. When we do, He'll gather them in His capable hands and take them away.

The Bible tells us that when we ask, Jesus bears our griefs and carries our sorrows. Through the scars He once endured, we can be healed. He can show us how to open wide our heart's door so He can cover our scars with the balm of His compassionate healing.

God is always near. Whenever our hurts start to return, God can help us to let them go again. Then we can thank Him for His empathy and love.

Thus says God the LORD, Who created the heavens and stretched them out, who spread forth the earth and that which comes from it.... "I, the LORD, have called You in righteousness, and will hold Your hand...." ISAIAH 42:5–6 NKJV

LORD, WHEN I think of Your immeasurable wisdom and the wonders You perform, I'm unable to understand it all. How is it that I barely grasp a smidgen of Your immensity, yet I personally experience Your holy presence ministering to my soul?

Who can explain the vast knowledge You possess? How did You arrange the foundations of this earth? Our world seems minute compared to the enormity of outer space. Still, You planned every tiny detail. How did You determine the world's shape and size? Certainly You didn't stretch a measuring tape from side to side. Did You speak everything into existence in a fraction of a second? Was its development quiet and serene... or was it fierce and dramatic? When You formed the earth's core and fashioned the mountains and valleys, did everything violently rumble? Did hot lava cover the ground without restrain?

Did You cause the stars to twinkle in harmony as though they were singing a silent song? Did You form the clouds and will them to scatter across the heavens or cluster like a thick blanket? When all this happened, did even the angels shout for joy?

How did You orchestrate days and nights and months and years to synchronize with the tides of the sea? How did You set up boundaries between the crashing waves and dry land? At Your command, did their depths and widths come into being and the tides advance and recede?

You, dear Lord, are the eternal Designer. In wisdom and power, You made it all. And after all this, You carefully designed me. I'm overwhelmed at how You showered Your grace and mercy on me and claimed me as Your own.

The rolling sun, the changing light,
And nights and days, Thy power confess;
But the blest volume Thou has writ,
Reveals Thy justice and Thy grace.
—ISAAC WATTS

Therefore, if anyone is in Christ, he [or she] is a new creation; old things have passed away; behold, all things have become new. 2 CORINTHIANS 5:17 NKJV

GOD IS A gracious, loving God. No matter what wrongs we've committed in the past, He's here to forgive us. All we need to do is invite Him into our hearts as our Savior. He's ready to remove the old things and replace them with a wonderful new life in Him. Kathleen had plenty of problems and regrets. Yet none of them were too big for God to handle.

Eighteen-year-old Kathleen held a cup of coffee in one hand. With the other hand, she pushed open the curtain of her luxurious third-floor apartment window in Seattle. Sharp winds pushed white powdery blankets across the sidewalks and streets below, carelessly tossing them toward Lake Union.

Kathleen shuddered when she recalled that a year before, she'd been homeless. Some nights, if she had gotten to the shelter after it closed, she'd had to sleep out on the streets downtown. Then came Bruce. When she first met him, Kathleen thought Bruce was her friend—but he'd just used her to make money.

Kathleen crumpled into a chair near the window and set her cup down. She covered her face with her hands and began to sob. She'd allowed her body to be violated more times than she could remember, but she knew it was her own doing. Prostitution brought in plenty of money and provided her with this place to live.

Kathleen pulled her small Bible from her purse. Her tears dripped onto its cover. Again she read the verses she'd recently discovered in John 3:16–17.

She leaned back and thought about how much God must love her. "God," she whispered, "I'm ready to live for you." Somehow Kathleen knew that God would bring her out of this terrible life she was trapped in.

Nothing is so great that God isn't greater!

One thing I do, forgetting those things which are behind and reaching forward to those things which are ahead, I press toward the goal for the prize of the upward call of God in Christ Jesus.
PHILIPPIANS 3:13–14 NKJV

GOD DOES MARVELOUS things in our lives after we give our hearts to Him. He changes our outlook on life. He gives us hope. Through Him, we renew our dreams for our present and future. Kathleen faced insurmountable odds in turning from her old life and following the one God had planned for her—but He was with her.

Kathleen knew that God was making a way for her to have not only everlasting life but a *new life* with Him as her Guide. She was thankful for Susan, a recent friend from the mission. Susan had helped her just two days before to ask Jesus into her heart. It was Susan who had given her the Bible. Kathleen was grateful that God forgave her sins—but could she learn to forgive herself?

She peered around the curtain again. Somewhere above the lake, the snow flurries, and the clouded morning sky was the sun. Better yet was the assurance of how the *Son of God* was helping her out of her dismal life.

Kathleen glanced at her watch and the boxes stacked around her. Susan would be arriving soon. If they hurried, she and Susan could have everything loaded in Susan's van and be out of town before Bruce called. Since she'd had the last two nights off, Kathleen was certain he would have a list of customers and instructions ready for her. She shuddered, thinking of his abusive ways, especially when he became angry.

"God, help me. Don't let him find me," she frantically whispered.

She scribbled a note. It was good-bye forever.

Whether or not our circumstances are like Kathleen's, if we want to make a change, God graciously helps us to begin again and leads us to a better future.

When God the Father, with glorious power, brought [Jesus] back to life again, you were given his wonderful new life to enjoy. ROMANS 6:4 TLB

WE MAY FEEL like walking miracles as we look back on our past and recall all God has done for us. God gave Kathleen a new start, too—one where He led the way.

It had been six months since Kathleen's move from Seattle to a small town. Susan's parents welcomed her into their home, where she paid room and board. Susan's church accepted and loved Kathleen and helped her find a job. And soon she would move into her own place.

Still, Kathleen felt lonely. Many of her new friends were married or engaged. She felt out of place, like a fifth wheel. Kathleen prayed about her need, and one day her pastor asked her to help start a Christian singles' group.

Three months later she was in her new apartment. Step-by-step, God helped her to not only accept His forgiveness but to forgive herself for her past. She was able to put everything behind her—forever. Kathleen realized she wasn't a fifth wheel; she'd become a part of the body of Christ.

She couldn't believe how He was using her to bless others. She was even scheduled to give her testimony to a church group in a neighboring town, and God would be with her as she spoke to the group.

Over the next several years, Kathleen played a major part in organizing several Christian singles' groups throughout the surrounding areas. She never stopped thanking God for Susan, who had introduced her to the Lord and showed her what it meant to be loved by God and His family.

It's never too late to start anew.

God's wonderful plans are meant for you.

He Teaches Me

I guide you in the way of wisdom and lead you along straight paths. When you walk, your steps will not be hampered; when you run, you will not stumble. Hold on to instruction, do not let it go; guard it well, for it is your life. PROVERBS 4:11–13 NIV

MY GROUP OF elementary Title I Reading students slumped in their chairs while we wrestled with a new concept. It appeared to be an impossible lesson for them to learn. The experience took me back to some struggles I once had in learning different school subjects.

Their asking why they had to learn it immediately spelled "defeat." They needed a vision of how the procedure could be useful to their daily lives—not later, but now!

I set aside the teacher's manual and invited them to brainstorm on the white board. Kids took turns writing different situations and challenges. After a few minutes, they were willing to give the reading book lessons a try.

We practiced. We drilled. I praised them a lot. We read, listened, repeated, and played plenty of learning games. Little successes meant a lot to them.

After a few days, the light of understanding came on, and they got the concept. Next, I challenged them to apply what they were learning to different situations during their day—and it really worked!

Sometimes I don't understand what my Lord is trying to teach me. How do some of His challenging lessons apply to me? Why do I have to learn them? Yet patiently and firmly He shows me how to use what He teaches me during each day. After plenty of practice, I begin to realize why it's important for me.

How grateful I am for His being the greatest teacher ever and constantly blessing me with His lessons. He is always patient, even when I struggle and complain and learn reluctantly. Through His help and His grace, I can see how to apply what I learn from Him.

"But when you are praying, first forgive anyone you are holding a grudge against, so that your Father in heaven will forgive you your sins too." MARK 11:25 TLB

WE ALL FACE disagreements. Sadly, sometimes unkind words are said and feelings get hurt. If not dealt with through prayer and concern for the other person's needs, hurt feelings can fester into a grudge-bearing, deadly cancer to the soul.

Conflict isn't always bad. To be productive, it requires a balance of honesty, love, and acceptance. It also takes a triple dose of forgiveness, no matter who is right. As if we were riding river rapids, we may feel pretty battered in the process. But if we obey our Guide, the Lord Jesus, we'll make it through intact.

Often the roughest part of conflict is being flexible to God's will. We don't *always* have to be right. We don't need to be afraid to admit when we're wrong. Knowing who's right or wrong is less important than caring and trying to comprehend how the other person feels. We must yield to the Lord as He guides us. Through it all, He cleanses our hearts and changes our stubborn wills to comply with His own. After we submit to Him and let our pride go, God makes our lives as sweet and pure as sparkling water.

No one comes out the winner in conflict unless the winner is God working in our hearts. He soothes and heals. He calms our anxieties. He helps us to forgive, look beyond the faults, and care about each other. Even if we don't agree in the end, God wants us to be gracious enough to accept the outcome.

We finally cross the line from conflict to peace, rounding the bend to the quiet waters of resolution we've sought. Our Lord and Counselor restores and heals us. And as we look back, we can thank God for His forgiveness, mercy, and peace.

If you want favor with both God and man, and a reputation for good judgment and common sense, then trust the Lord completely; don't ever trust yourself. In everything you do, put God first, and he will direct you and crown your efforts with success. PROVERBS 3:4–6 TLB

WHAT MATTERS MORE to you than anything else in this world? Certainly, a relationship with God should come first. What comes next? Your family? Your friends? Your church? Perhaps it's your job, your home, or your car.

Let's ponder the priorities in our hearts. Consider writing them down. You may discover that some of your priorities have become "a little out of whack" for one reason or another. Be watchful and pray about what God wants to see as the most important priorities.

One of my greatest faults is to work too hard. Even though my work involves good things, I occasionally discover that I allow that work to take over too much of my life. Then when I become exhausted and begin to shut down, my Lord steps in and reasons with me regarding what matters more to me than anything else. Mine is my family. It's more precious to me than life itself. When the Lord gets me to slow down a bit, I remember to appreciate the other things I enjoy in life as well.

These words of Ralph Waldo Emerson help me to recognize what is most valuable to me: "To laugh often and much; to win the respect of intelligent people and the affection of children; to earn the appreciation of honest critics and endure the betrayal of false friends; to appreciate beauty; to find the best in others; to leave the world a bit better, whether by a healthy child, a garden patch or a redeemed social condition; to know even one life has breathed easier because you have lived. This is to have succeeded."

How thankful we can be that we are a priority to the Lord. In turn, let's ask Him to show us what He wants in our lives to matter the most.

"God was with [Joseph] and delivered him out of all his troubles, and gave him favor and wisdom...."
ACTS 7:9–10 NKJV

ONE OF THE dearest stories in the Bible tells about the trials, pain, pardon, and blessings of Joseph (Genesis 37, 39–48). Terrible things happened to Joseph, but God worked it all together for good, though it was not the life Joseph probably expected. He was instead sent to a foreign land to help numerous people, including his own family, and his faithfulness was rewarded with God's grace and numerous blessings.

Like Joseph, we also face times of persecution. When they are present, let us take our focus off self-pity, anger, and bitterness. Let us instead trust and honor God in all situations. He understands it all and can use us to work things together for good and glorification of Him.

Whatever your circumstances are, dear reader, remain faithful to the Lord. Remember that God is always near, giving comfort and strength. When we're faithful, He provides grace, inner joy, and an abundant life in Him.

O Jesus, I have promised to serve Thee to the end;
Be Thou forever near me, my Master and my Friend;
I shall not fear the battle, if Thou art by my side,
Nor wander from the pathway if Thou wilt be my Guide.

O let me feel Thee near me, the world is ever near;
I see the sights that dazzle, the tempting sounds I hear;
My foes are ever near me, around me and within;
But Jesus, draw Thou nearer and shield my soul from sin.

O Jesus, Thou hast promised to all who follow Thee
That where Thou art in glory there shall Thy servant be;
And, Jesus, I have promised to serve Thee to the end;
O give me grace to follow my Master and my Friend.

—JOHN E. BODE

[Jesus said,] "Behold, I stand at the door and knock; if anyone hears My voice and opens the door, I will come in to him, and will dine with him, and he with Me." REVELATION 3:20 NASB

I WONDER HOW Moses felt when he saw the burning bush while watching his sheep on Mount Horeb. I wonder how we would have felt had we heard God firmly say, "Do not draw near this place. Take your sandals off your feet, for the place where you stand is holy ground" (Exodus 3:5 NKJV). Moses was so frightened that he hid his face. He was too terrified to look at God.

Jesus changed all this when He died for our sins on the cross. In John 6:37, He promises that when we come to Him, He will never turn us away.

Charlotte Elliott lived a happy life as a gifted artist and poet during her early years. But when Charlotte turned thirteen, her health began to fail. Family members and doctors couldn't make her better. Charlotte sunk into despair. Her family invited Dr. Malan, an evangelist, to talk with Charlotte.

Charlotte told Dr. Malan that she didn't know how to find Christ. Dr. Malan's answer was, "Come to Him just as you are." It changed Charlotte's life. Her emotional well-being dramatically improved, although she never regained her physical health.

Several years later, Charlotte's brother was raising money to build a school for needy children. Alone in her room, Charlotte thought of the words in John 6:37: "All that the Father giveth me shall come to me; and him that cometh to me I will in no wise cast out" (KJV). And she wrote the lyrics to the hymn we know today called "Just As I Am" and gave it to be sold at her brother's fund-raiser. Since then, the words to "Just As I Am" have helped countless people find God's saving mercy and grace.

"Come, all you who are thirsty, come to the waters...." ISAIAH 55:1 NIV

DO YOU WONDER if you are worthy to come before the presence of God? Perhaps you have never been brave enough to offer a prayer to the Lord. All you need to do is tell God how you feel. Our prayers don't have to be polished or formal. God loves a simple, honest prayer from the heart.

One of my cousins thought the way to get near God was to do good works. He discovered that the way is through Jesus, just as we are, as we ask Him to forgive our wrongs and receive us as His own. God's love and mercy is worth far more than any deed we can perform. We should do good things but they will always fall short when compared with God's purity. Jesus will always graciously welcome us with arms wide open, ready to give us a brand-new life in Him.

Just as I am, without one plea, but that Thy blood was shed for me,
And that Thou bidd'st me come to Thee, O Lamb of God, I come. I come.
Just as I am and waiting not to rid my soul of one dark blot,
To Thee whose blood can cleanse each spot, O Lamb of God, I come.
   I come.

Just as I am, though tossed about with many a conflict, many a doubt,
Fightings and fears within, without, O Lamb of God, I come! I come!
Just as I am, Thy love unknown hath broken every barrier down;
Now, to be Thine, yea, Thine alone, O Lamb of God, I come. I come.
—CHARLOTTE ELLIOTT

Jesus said to them again, "Peace be with you. As the Father has sent me, even so I send you."
JOHN 20:21 RSV

DOES GOD OCCASIONALLY speak to your heart about something He wants you to do? Does His calling ever seem to require far more talent than you possess? At times we may struggle with this unexpected call. Perhaps we wonder if it's really a call from the Lord—or if it's just our imagination. The very idea might be downright scary! When we reach this fork in our road, we can take our concerns to the Lord and seek His guidance. Through reading the Scriptures and seeking His presence, we can find the answer.

The thought of other people being more talented may cause our self-esteem to take a serious plunge. But when God calls and we answer, His Holy Spirit provides the skills we need for the task. He sees value in us that we may not recognize.

Even though our abilities seem small, God is big. If other people disregard what He wants us to do, we need to keep our focus on Him. He can accomplish amazing things through everyday people like you and me. Like tossing a pebble into a pond, the calling He gives us may very well cause spiritual ripples and change more lives than we can imagine. And, oh, the blessings He gives in the process. We may not see the full effect until we reach the doors of heaven.

If you hear the Lord speaking to you about a task for Him, don't question your ability. He is aware of your talents, and if you are willing to be used for Him, He will open the doors for you in the way He wants you to step through them, with His timing. He only requires your willingness, acceptance, and trust in Him.

So husbands ought to love their own wives as their own bodies; he who loves his wife loves himself....
An excellent wife is the crown of her husband. EPHESIANS 5:28; PROVERBS 12:4 NKJV

IS IT POSSIBLE for the love between a husband and wife to last forever? It's a unique challenge in this day and age. Yet adults young and old who put God first and unselfishly love each other are living proofs that it can.

Our son Jonathan and his wife Cynthia have an abiding devotion for each other. It gives Bob and me warm feelings when we hear them talk about one another. One evening Jonathan called us and told how when Cynthia curled up near him, he discovered a gray hair on her head. They were so excited that they jerked it out and held it up to the light, marveling over its silvery sheen. They carefully placed the silvery strand in a plastic baggie for safekeeping.

Bob and I chuckled. He warned them not to jerk out too many or she might grow bald! Jonathan continued with a timeless story I shall never forget. He visualized how beautiful his wife would be years from now with a head adorned in silvery gray. He pictured how they'd take walks in the moonlight, the same as they do now. In his vision his wife's silvery hair reflected the light of the moon, their love being as strong as ever. (I believe it will be even stronger.)

Isn't it incredible that God's faithful love will never leave us? The love He passed on to husbands and wives is also meant to last forever.

Grow old along with me! The best is yet to be;
The last of life, for which the first was made:
Our times are in His hand,
Who saith "A whole I planned,
Youth shows but half; trust God; see all, nor be afraid!"
—ROBERT BROWNING

Unexpected Prayer

The prayer of a righteous man is powerful and effective. JAMES 5:16 NIV

MANY OF US find it natural to join in with prayers of thanksgiving and requests when we meet for meals, share concerns with friends, or prepare to leave each other's homes after a good visit. What we seldom expect is that someone would be brave enough to offer a prayer for us in a public place because they felt led to do so.

For over a month, I had been suffering with what the doctor called "cluster headaches." I'm normally not a person who has many headaches, so these took me by surprise. There was no relief from the debilitating pain.

Because of the illness, I had missed one of my favorite things to do—working out in water aerobics. Finally, I decided I could wait no longer to go and hoped that the music and glare from the water wouldn't make me hurt even more.

While working out that night, I noticed a lady whom I knew to be a Christian watching me from across the pool. She looked concerned about my well-being. I forced a smile toward her and kept on exercising.

Afterward, while a few of us gathered in the hot tub for a short time of relaxation, the lady found out what was wrong with me. She paused for a moment and then asked if she could pray for the Lord to heal me. I gratefully accepted. Everything around us seemed to stop as she took my hands in hers and offered a quiet prayer. A week later, the doctor found a solution to my headaches and they gradually disappeared.

I'll never forget the unexpected prayer offered for me by this brave, compassionate lady standing in the middle of a hot tub filled with people.

Tribulation brings about perseverance; and perseverance, proven character; and proven character, hope; and hope does not disappoint, because the love of God has been poured out within our hearts through the Holy Spirit who was given to us. ROMANS 5:3–5 NASB

NO MATTER WHAT our past or present regrets and hurts, we can bring them to the Lord and ask for His help. Some might be from rebellious teenage years. Some could come from abusive marriages. Others may be caused by negligent or abusive parents. It's never too late to start over. All we need to do is ask God to turn our lives around and help us make a brand-new start with Him.

God's love is greater than all our regrets and troubles. He holds the key to solving our problems, but we have to trust and obey Him. His love and forgiveness go beyond all our hopes and dreams. When we ask for His direction, miracles happen. He shows us how to take the first, second, and more steps in the right direction that will bring us a deep, inner joy.

God's love can transform our lives, free us from past bondages to sin, and give us an amazing new hope in Him! Christian boundaries can be set. Old habits can be broken and new habits formed. Scars can be healed. Our lives can become brand-new.

The past can't be changed. But God can change our future for good as we follow the paths He places before us.

The biblical figure David made some dreadful choices and suffered because of them. But David asked God to forgive him. Amazingly, the Lord filled David with His love and hope, helped him start over, and pointed him in a different direction—a new direction where countless lives were blessed. He can also forgive our poor choices and point our feet in His direction so we can live new lives filled with His hope and joy.

For he guards the course of the just and protects the way of his faithful ones. PROVERBS 2:8 NIV

DO YOU GET frustrated when you are slowed down by senseless interruptions and inconveniences? Some may just happen, but occasionally God brings about delays to protect us.

The clock wearily ticked down the minutes to 3:30 a.m. Another nine-hour shift at the restaurant mercifully ended the second of my two jobs for the day. I could only think of sleep.

My coworker Tammy and I trudged across the parking lot to our cars. We always left together, for safety's sake. I climbed into my car, turned the key—and heard nothing but an irritating grind. It took fifteen minutes of shuffling jumper cables and recharging the battery before we could leave.

"Lord, this is frustrating," I muttered. "I'm so tired."

Tammy and I were going the same direction. I followed her zippy red car, and we reached the stoplight at a major intersection. Tammy made it through; I was caught on the red.

Right after Tammy went through the light, a swarm of police cars surrounded her and forced her off the street. When they saw who she was, they let her go. I decided to take a different route and was relieved to reach my safe, warm home.

The next day we discovered that there had been a double homicide in an apartment near the restaurant at the same time Tammy and I normally approached the intersection. The fugitive had escaped on foot and ran through the area where we had planned to drive. My car's stalling had kept us out of danger.

I apologized to God for my impatient muttering and thanked Him for His mercy and protection.

I lie awake at night thinking of you—of how much you have helped me—and how I rejoice through the night beneath the protecting shadow of your wings. PSALM 63:6–7 TLB

WE'VE ALL SUFFERED from heartaches, yet God often intertwines these heartaches with other happenings and causes amazing wonders. Perhaps you have occasionally felt as if you were wrapped in God's loving arms—beneath the shadow of His wings (see Psalm 63:7).

Heidi's mother passed away when she was only sixteen. How Heidi missed her. Still, Heidi grew up and became happily married. For several years, she and her husband wanted a baby, and at last, baby Tanner arrived. Though Heidi felt blessed, she wished her mother could have been with her.

One day Heidi's mother's best friend, Marcia, came to visit. Marcia gave Heidi a package containing a hand-knitted yellow-and-white baby blanket. Delicately spaced threads had been uniformly pulled through to make it more beautiful. Heidi immediately recognized the blanket as one her mother had once made for Marcia's daughter when she was born. With the blanket was a note:

Dear Tanner,

This blanket was made by your grandma for our child, Jennifer, twenty-one years ago. It is given to you with our special thoughts and love. When your mom and dad wrap you in this blanket, remember that Grandma's love from heaven is wrapped around you too.

Love, Pat, Marcia, and Jennifer

Heidi's eyes filled with tears of gratitude as she wrapped Tanner in the blanket made by her mother's hands. Added to her blessings was Heidi's getting to experience how God had miraculously woven the whole plan together. Tanner also was securely wrapped in God's protection and love—in the wings of his heavenly Father.

We aren't always spared heartache and loss. But when we trust God, He works things together for good from the past to the present to the future.

Blessings to Come

"I will pour my Spirit upon your descendants, and my blessing on your offspring." ISAIAH 44:3 RSV

THANK YOU FOR blessing me all the days of my life, dear Lord. Thank You for Your unlimited love and care. Teach me to trust through my tomorrows that You will watch over and keep me close.

I praise You for the strengthening touch of Your almighty hand in my life whenever I've been sick. How I treasure Your promise in the Bible, "Daughter, be of good cheer; your faith has made you well" (Luke 8:48 NKJV). The words have rung true more times than I can count.

Thank You for filling my life with Your powerful Holy Spirit. When challenges beyond my ability crush my spirit, I once again experience a promise fulfilled that Your grace is more than enough. When I buckle beneath burdens I'm forced to endure, I soon find that Your strength is made perfect in my weakness.

Thank You for Your clear wisdom and direction— for Your presence so sure and true. Thank You for never leaving me. You, Lord, are my dearest Friend.

Do you often marvel at the blessings God gives?
Keep trusting and loving.
God shows no limit of His kindness and grace.
He still has blessings to come!

Do you ever wonder if they're too good to be true?
Keep trusting and loving.
God shows His love in infinite ways.
He still has blessings to come!

Do you often feel the touch of His hand?
Keep trusting and loving.
He holds on tight and never lets go.
He still has blessings to come!

Do you ever feel the power of His Spirit?
Keep trusting and loving.
His strength and wisdom are great.
He still has blessings to come!

Do you know for sure He'll always be close?
Keep trusting and loving.
He'll never leave us alone.
He always has blessings to come!

I will lift up mine eyes unto the hills, from whence cometh my help. My help cometh from the LORD, *which made heaven and earth.* PSALM 121:1–2 KJV

PERHAPS YOU BEGIN your morning with prayer, asking the Lord to grant you physical and mental energy to make it through the day. You may pray for spiritual strength to overcome challenges and temptations. From time to time, you (like me) might ask the Lord to send a word or action of encouragement your way. God can answer in some unexpected moments and circumstances! One answer happened to me last week.

I began my day by bringing my adoration, gratefulness, and the needs of others and myself to the Lord in prayer. I prayed for His wisdom and strength. Then I asked Him to send an encouraging, unexpected blessing my way.

Later on, while driving toward home, I had a Christian radio station playing inspiring songs on my car radio. I stopped at a local store, and while hurrying away from the store, I encountered a rain shower. Frankly, I love the rain and consider it a blessing in itself. I smiled and thanked the Lord for it.

As I was heading across the parking lot to my car, a lady drove past me with her driver's window rolled down—rain and all. She was singing out as though no one could hear her: "I will lift up my eyes." My head spun in her direction. Could it be? I hurriedly climbed into my car and turned on the radio to hear the tail end of the song I loved. It was indeed a confirmation of God's little unexpected blessing, my energy booster, bestowed upon me. Before I pulled out of my parking space, I had one more thing to thank Him for.

Would you like for the Lord to give you some kind of unexpected "energy booster" blessing? Just ask Him and see what happens.

Do not be dismayed. I am your God. I will strengthen you; I will help you... ISAIAH 41:10 TLB

SOMETIMES GOD GIVES us goals and dreams that we know we must fulfill. Many may be easy to achieve. But others might be so challenging that we wonder if we'll ever be able to complete what He's assigned us to do.

God has given you something special to accomplish. When your task gets difficult and discouraging, don't lose heart. All things are possible when God is involved.

Let me tell you about a man who felt God leading him to invent something no one else believed would work. After much labor and many failures, he put his invention to the test, running an announcement in the New York paper. He and his partners hand-wrapped two miles of wire in cotton, tar, and rubber and rowed across New York harbor to lay the wire. Operators stood on opposite banks. Everything tested perfectly.

Early the next morning, fishermen accidentally cut the wire—and he was labeled a failure and a fraud. But at age fifty-one, he received money to test his invention again. He and his partners had two months to lay a line between Baltimore, Maryland, and Washington, D.C.

Sitting in a room of the U.S. Supreme Court building, surrounded by dignitaries and reporters, he began the coded message: "What hath God wrought!" Later, his inventions—the Morse code and Morse telegraph—were used around the world. Samuel Morse himself said that many could have invented those things, but God saw fit to use him in the right place at the right time.

When God gives you a dream that becomes extremely difficult to accomplish, remember that He also gives hope. Keep trusting. In His timing, He will bring to pass what He has planned.

Therefore we do not lose heart. 2 CORINTHIANS 4:16 NKJV

HAVE YOU EVER tried to succeed at something but only experienced defeat? Perhaps no matter how you attempted it you just couldn't find the right answers. Be assured that even though we can't guarantee success, God can. He wants to help.

We can take our defeats to Him and allow Him to teach us through each failure we experience. Rather than measuring success by accomplishment, we can measure it by how fully we trust and obey His will. When we're discouraged, He is near. He surrounds us with His merciful love and grace, takes our hands, and gently lifts us to our feet—then helps us to try again.

END OF THE ROPE

Are you at the end of your rope, struggling with strife and pain?
Do you feel you can't hang on? For whatever you might gain?
Do your sufferings overshadow everything that is good?
You'll find that at the end of the rope God provides all that's good.

Are you at the end of your rope with a load you cannot bear?
No matter how hard you struggle or try, does no one seem to care?
Do you beg for strength to hold on, when your being aches with pain?
You'll find that at the end of the rope God is waiting, once again.

There at the end of your rope, You'll see God's work is best.
There you can learn His answers for life, while letting Him work
*   out the rest.*
If your goals and dreams are maturing, your heart and mind renewed,
You've found that at the end of the rope God lovingly cares for you.

Now this is the confidence that we have in Him, that if we ask anything according to His will, He hears us. 1 JOHN 5:14 NKJV

WE READ IN the Bible about times Jesus put others before Himself. He must have often been tired from the demands pressing in from every side. Even so, He never stopped caring and loving.

Recently, I suffered from a bad case of pneumonia. Even after I recovered, I felt weakened. To add to this, my husband was sick as well. I longed for a blessing of encouragement and brought my need to the Lord in prayer.

The following Sunday morning, my Sunday school students were gathered around me, finishing up a project. A young mother named Kristi slipped up behind me and told me she loved and appreciated me. Then she handed me a gift box of beautiful lavender soap.

I was overwhelmed. She had no idea that it was the scent I loved the most or that lavender helps me to relax after a long day. It was a gift that came from her heart. Kristi has four children; her plate is full with activities. She passed a gift on to me that she could have used for herself.

When I returned home to my sick husband and had a chance to ponder my day, I thanked the Lord for the priceless gift He had led Kristi to give to me. He already knew what I needed most and answered my prayer with a sweet gift of love.

Isn't it wonderful how, when we take our needs to the Lord, He answers them in the most unexpected ways?

God has a way of knowing the longings of our hearts better than we do ourselves.

He who has mercy on the poor, happy is he. PROVERBS 14:21 NKJV

ACTS OF MERCY may not seem that important, but we never know how much they can mean.

Wendy, a teacher and a mom, had just finished a busy day at school, and she was eager to get home to her family. But a quick trip to the grocery store for an easy meal came first.

She steered into the parking lot in time to see a man who appeared to be homeless asking for help from passing shoppers. Some people glanced away. Others shook their heads. A few gave some change. Was he really destitute, or did he need a quick fix or a drink?

Wendy noticed an old car parked near him with a woman and small children inside, and she knew she had to help. While buying her groceries, she purchased some nonperishable items including bread, peanut butter, jelly, and some other practical things. When she left the store, Wendy drove over to where the man stood and handed him a bag of groceries.

"Here, sir. Maybe this will help," she said with a smile. Wendy pulled away and glanced in her rearview mirror. The woman was spreading peanut butter sandwiches as fast as she could, while the children excitedly bounced up and down on the seat.

Tears came to Wendy's eyes. How surprising, that God would help her to see to their needs. "Father, I promise to always be willing to show mercy to others in any way You direct," Wendy whispered. "Take care of this family, I pray. Help the dad to find work and a home. Thank You for the warm feeling this gave me."

Now Wendy carries a few nonperishable things in her car, ready to help someone else. She receives a big blessing in return for each small act of mercy.

We are the ones who strayed away like sheep! We, who left God's paths to follow our own. Yet God laid on him the guilt and sins of every one of us! ISAIAH 53:6 TLB

ISN'T IT AMAZING how Jesus cares for each of us? He assures us that He is our good Shepherd. He is the entrance, or the gate, to our salvation. He calls us to follow Him so we won't be scattered like lost sheep. When we do, He draws us safely into His fold, where we can find secure pasture. He mercifully changes our lives from sin and chaos to joy and peace.

Some say shepherds gathered their sheep into the fold for the night and then lay by the gate to protect them throughout the night. Being a shepherd like David during Bible times must have taken great strength. The shepherds would travel steep mountains and hot, dry valleys and would have fought off wild animals.

A few years ago, I had the privilege of flying by helicopter over alp-like country in Montana. I saw herds of sheep grazing throughout the area with dedicated dogs standing guard on high vantage points or herding sheep together.

Jesus tells of a good shepherd who had one hundred sheep in his care. The shepherd discovered one missing. He left the other ninety-nine in a safe place and went in search of the one that was lost. Over craggy mountains he climbed. Down the steep banks into hot, dry valleys he went. Searching. Calling. With perseverance, the shepherd found his sheep and lovingly carried it home on his shoulders, rejoicing with each step.

Think of how much more Jesus loves and cares for you and me. He will never abandon us. Like the shepherd in His story, Jesus faithfully watches over us, night and day. When we tend to stray, He calls and reaches out to us until we answer. He loves us enough to never give up until we're safely in His fold.

"Suppose one of you has a hundred sheep and loses one of them. Does he not...go after the lost sheep until he finds it? And when he finds it, he joyfully puts it on his shoulders and goes home."
LUKE 15:4–6 NIV

DO YOU EVER feel like you are getting helplessly lost in a maze of daily living? Does life sometimes feel too overwhelming to handle? Do you wonder if anyone even cares? Our Savior understands and cares.

No matter how lost we may be in the turmoil of trials and struggles, God is able to find us. When He does, He mercifully reaches out to us in the confusing shuffle of our lives, grasps our trembling hands, and draws us to His heart.

No matter how dark and foreboding the narrow valleys we may be forced to walk, the Shepherd never ever abandons us. He is as close to us as the air we breathe.

Fear not, dear reader. Take the Savior's steady hand. Hold on tight, and stay close by His side. He knows the way.

There were ninety and nine that safely lay
in the shelter of the fold.
But one was out on the hills away,
far off from the gates of gold.
Away on the mountains wild and bare,
away from the tender Shepherd's care.

"Lord, Thou hast here Thy ninety and nine;
are they not enough for Thee?"
But the Shepherd made answer:
"This of Mine has wandered away from Me;
And although the road be rough and steep,
I go to the desert to find My sheep."

And all through the mountains, thunder-riven
and up from the rocky steep,

There arose a glad cry to the gate of heaven,
"Rejoice! I have found My sheep!"
And the angels echoed around the throne,
"Rejoice, for the Lord brings back His own!"
—ELIZABETH CECELIA DOUGLAS CLEPHANE

For God has not given us a spirit of fear, but of power and of love and of a sound mind.
2 TIMOTHY 1:7 NKJV

WHAT MAKES LIFE worth living? Certainly, our families and friends bring numerous blessings to us. Perhaps our lives are enriched because of our work, hobbies, traveling, or our simply enjoying some downtime.

All of these things are good within themselves, yet they are conditional or temporary. We have no control over what happens to us outwardly because of different circumstances that come our way. But there is something we can personally do in order to obtain abundant lives that are definitely worth living. I believe the key exists in making our lives count.

I read a newspaper article about a delightful woman who said that her secret to having a long, happy life was to thank the good Lord each morning for another day. She stayed active, spreading rays of sunshine to family, friends, and complete strangers. Through the years she's learned (and is still learning) about as many different things as possible. She attributes her longevity to her faith in the Lord—and also to her enthusiasm for life and her working to make it count for something good. She just celebrated her 102nd birthday!

Along with the benefits of making our lives count by spreading sunshine and encouragement to those around us comes the enjoyment of our own lives being rich and full of gratitude. Jesus reminds us in John 15 that when we love each other, our own lives will also be filled with joy.

How can we make our lives count? As we bring this question to the Lord, asking for His guidance, the possibilities of what He has graciously planned for us are limitless. This might possibly be one of the best adventures we will ever take.

Be satisfied with nothing but your best.
—EDWARD ROWLAND SILL

Dear friends, let us practice loving each other, for love comes from God and those who are loving and kind show that they are the children of God, and that they are getting to know him better.
1 JOHN 4:7 TLB

WHEN GOD MADE each of us, He broke the mold! We are unique. Whether we're young or old, rich or poor, able-bodied or healthy, learning-impaired or intelligent, white-collar workers or blue-collar workers, government leaders or unemployed...God gave us our individual personalities and abilities. He loves us as His own. Whatever our race, whatever our home, neighborhood or country, we are equal in God's sight. What matters most is that we have invited Jesus to become our Lord and Savior and are living a life in Him.

In the same way, God wants our church congregations to welcome people from different "molds" to be a part of our fellowship. God doesn't judge us because of our individuality. Neither should we judge each other. Instead, He looks into our hearts. We aren't meant to size up another. We're meant to lift others in prayer and win new souls for Him. The family of God means we're brothers and sisters in the Lord—His family, His children.

How grateful we can be that God's grace and love is passed on to each of us and that we can simply be ourselves. Because He loves us, we can be free to love one another and to bless the Lord in any way we can. Because we're precious to God, we should to be precious to each other as well.

From the moment we come kicking and screaming into this world, we already belong to Him. Although we're unique, He takes pride in our being made in His image. At the moment we ask Him into our hearts, His mercy surrounds us and we become part of the family of God. And when we take our last breath, we will still belong to Him. He's already looking forward to taking us home to be with Him forever!

Purify My Heart

Don't copy the behavior and customs of this world, but be a new and different person with a fresh newness in all you do and think. Then you will learn from your own experience how his ways will really satisfy you. ROMANS 12:2 TLB

PURIFY MY HEART, O Father. Test me and try me. Probe my mind and soul. Reach in and sweep away my cobwebs of anger. Clear my heart of jealousy, I pray. Remove all thoughts of malice from my injured, weary soul. Let not my mouth speak slander. Guard me against all wrong thoughts and actions. Replace them with Your pure fragrance of compassion, empathy, and love. Cleanse me and fill me with Your Holy Spirit. I long to walk continually in Your sure way. I pray that you would grant me Your strength so all I think, say, and do are pleasing to You.

I know that whatever I think, *so am I*. Help me to focus only on the things that are true and gracious, pure and lovely, admirable and praiseworthy. After these good things are planted in my mind, let me practice them in my everyday life. I pray for You to also instill them in my heart for now and eternity.

The next time the world crushes in on me, help me to think of You and Your gracious, forgiving love. When I'm tempted to get angry, please grant me Your patience. When I become frustrated, help me to pause and pray. Dear Father, dim my vision of the difficulties and temptations constantly trying to invade my life. Bring to light Your unfailing counsel and guidance. Thank You for providing Your mighty power and victory over trouble and turmoil. Thank You for showing me how to be more than a conqueror through You.

You, O Lord, are all that is good. You are holy. You are kind and merciful. Because of Your forgiveness, I am made clean—worthy of being Your child. Everything that I am, everything that I shall be, I wholeheartedly give it all to You.

[Jesus said,] "I have called you friends.... You did not choose Me but I chose you...."
JOHN 15:15–16 NASB

DO YOU HAVE a friend who is so dear to you that whenever you are around him or her, everything seems to be okay no matter what's happening? That kind of friend is a fair-weather, cloudy weather, and even a scary stormy-weather friend—someone you can always count on.

Most of us have many friends, yet often there are only a few who are emotionally or physically close enough to be there when times get tough. Perhaps one provides an open door and a listening ear. Another may show up at our door with a casserole or a big hug. Perhaps you have a friend like mine who snatches you up and runs away with you for a drive in the country or a fun lunch date. These kinds of friends offer reassurance and hope for our tomorrows.

My neighbor Linda is this type of friend. When I lost a family member, she was at my door with a plate of cookies. She sat with me for a couple of hours, comforting and caring. We just talked about whatever came to our minds. When Linda had surgery and I went to see her in the hospital, she introduced me as her best friend. Nothing could have mattered more to me at that moment. When we squeezed each other's hands, we knew everything would be all right.

Recently, Bob and I were visiting with a delightful lady named Clem. He asked her how she was. She smiled and said, "I'm okay, because God takes care of me." I decided to plant her words deeply into my memory bank. Because God is our dearest friend and takes care of us, we can just know everything's going to be okay.

You have preserved me because I was honest; you have admitted me forever to your presence.
PSALM 41:12 TLB

THERE ARE MANY things our friends do and say that we thoroughly enjoy. Perhaps one of our most treasured is when we receive their heartfelt approval. Our best friends often know us so well that they are clearly aware of our daily challenges. They hope with us. They believe in us. And they rejoice with us over a job well done. When our friends tell us how proud they are of our determination and efforts, their gifts of approval are worth far more than anything else.

My closest friends are like that. After spending months working on a book, I can hardly wait to share it with them. A smile comes to my face when their reply is, "Nice job, Anita. I'm proud of you!"

When we think of the dearest Friend in our lives, our heavenly Father, we usually ponder the countless things He does for us and for those we love and care about. Each time we notice the blessings He bestows, we offer our praise, gratitude, and approval.

As we keep putting one foot before the other during each day, wholeheartedly committing our motives and actions to Him, we may frequently turn to Him to see if we are on the right track. But we may never whisper the words, "Are You proud of me, Lord?"

When the battles in life are thick and the challenges almost more than we can bear, we have the privilege of going to our Father in prayer and seeking His approval. When our hearts are in tune with His, we can sense the warm presence of the Holy Spirit saying to our hearts, "Well done, good and faithful servant."

When our hearts are wholly in tune with His, God must look upon us and smile.

As it is written, "How beautiful are the feet of those who bring good news!" ROMANS 10:15 NIV

FATHER, I AM so grateful for Your faithfulness through these difficult challenges I have been facing. During this time, I've felt as though one thing after another bombarded me. All the while, I kept my focus on You for Your direction and strength. Each time something went wrong, I put my trust in You. I was determined to not allow anything to trip me up, preventing me from doing what I was supposed to do.

Even if things were to become tougher, still I would be faithful to live a holy life, acceptable and pleasing to You. Each time I've reconfirmed my decision to do so, I was amazed at how You lifted me spiritually and physically and You worked out the circumstances around me to bring good. Thank You, Father. I couldn't have done this except through Your powerful Holy Spirit working in my life.

Are You proud of me, Father? I tried my best to be faithful and do the right thing. I wish I could hear You say those words like an earthly father. But even though I may not hear You audibly, I sense You speaking words of approval to my heart:

"My dear child, I see your feet moving forward, faithfully bringing good news and proclaiming peace. How beautiful your feet are! I am proud of you and love you dearly. As much as My Father loves Me, so have I loved you. Now remain and continue in My love."

How I love You, dear Father. You have done so many marvelous things for me. Again and again will I give my heart to You. In You, I live and move and have my being. Because of Your love for me, I will follow You all the days of my life.

They shall obtain joy and gladness, and sorrow and sighing shall flee away. ISAIAH 35:10 KJV

WHAT IS THE greatest reward we can receive in heaven? The absence of sickness, sorrow, and sin? Complete and uninhibited joy? Will the ultimate reward go to those who gave their lives for their Savior? What about the great leaders, missionaries, and evangelists who gave their all? Or the faithful Christians who taught children to love and serve God? Will there be a reward for those who accepted Christ in the ebb of their earthly lives?

To me the greatest reward will be to see our Savior face-to-face. There we will finally be in His holy presence and experience His grace for all eternity.

&

What will it be like when I get to be with You in heaven, Lord? Will there be more Christians than anyone can count from every nationality, rank, and race? What about my loved ones? I look forward to being reunited with them. Will everyone be dressed in white and sing praises to You, our God and King? I wonder if we'll get to see angels gathered around Your throne.

How unworthy I feel to enter Your glorious kingdom. Thank You for taking my sins away and making me as white as snow so I can belong to You. Whatever good I've done is nothing in light of Your grace.

I want to kneel before You and tell You how much I love You. There will be no more hunger or thirst, illness or grief. You have promised to wipe away all of my tears, which pale in the light of Your radiant glory!

My greatest reward will be when I can look into Your eyes. Perhaps You will take my hand, wrap me in Your arms and say, "My child, welcome home."

March 26 | Love Is Positive

Fix your thoughts on what is true and good and right. Think about things that are pure and lovely, and dwell on the fine, good things in others. Think about all you can praise God for and be glad about.
PHILIPPIANS 4:8 TLB

IF YOU COULD think of the most important attribute you'd like to bring into your life, what would it be? Happiness? Security? Companionship or friends? These and many more are important, yet I believe there's one more that could turn into a life-changing experience. It's that of finding a positive mind-set.

Sometimes we can become so buried under the cares of life that we occasionally aren't able see anything good. But the more we think negatively, the more we feed into the "down" attitude that plagues so many.

Jesus really loves us. He pours love and goodness into us every single day. And the Holy Spirit radiates the powerful, uplifting character of our heavenly Father. He wants us to renew our minds (Romans 12:1–2) and embrace this abundant life He offers us. It may not be a life filled with lots of money or material things, but as we seek Him first, God will bless us with a rich spirit filled with joy and peace of mind.

I decided to conduct an experiment to recharge my own positive mind-set. In doing so, I'm discovering that the most precious gift of love I can give to my family and others is to rejuvenate my attitude.

I'm already seeing the difference it's making. I decided to take this one step further: to consistently think of five things God does for me each day and then share five more good things with people around me.

Thinking positively can be contagious. Even a smile is good. Recently I shared my idea with the Sunday school students I teach. I challenged them to practice the five-positive-things idea in their lives. I look forward to hearing how it's going.

Try it and see how it works for you.

The grace of the Lord Jesus Christ be with your spirit. PHILIPPIANS 4:23 NASB

LORD, I NEED Your help and direction with my attitude. There's this lady I've been trying to relate to who's nice to me one day and giving me the cold shoulder the next. She often makes belittling remarks to me that cause me to feel put down.

It seems she's only polite and considerate when she wants me to do something for her. And when she needs my help, she usually lets me know at the last minute, expecting me to be at her beck and call. What bothers me most is that I really care about her and am praying for her almost every day. I am so frustrated, Lord. Please help me know what to do.

Teach me, I pray, how to have a right spirit around her, rather than reacting to her moodiness. Show me how to set up boundaries on how I want to be treated, yet still have the insight and compassion to love her unconditionally.

I think of how You, Lord Jesus, came to this earth and lived among both selfish and unselfish people. In all situations, You were full of mercy and truth. Throughout time, Your followers learned to be kind and gracious. Because of this, You showered them with one blessing after another.

Give me grace like Yours, dear Lord. Rather than my picking up on her turmoil, I ask You to fill me to overflowing with a gracious attitude—one filled with peace of heart and mind.

Now I bring this lady and her troubles to You. Surround her with Your love and compassion. Give her an inner joy that helps to overshadow her heartaches and troubles. And Lord, grant me Your grace so she may also see Your love through me.

Show me the path where I should go, O Lord; point out the right road for me to walk. Lead me; teach me; for you are the God who gives me salvation. PSALM 25:4–5 TLB

SOMETIMES THE PATH the Lord leads us on can be like a favorite walking trail. We might want to return to it often. It helps us relax. It becomes a good thing to do.

When we reach the decision to follow Him, our spirits usually begin to soar. We hungrily devour Scriptures from the Bible as if we're craving tasty life-giving morsels of bread. We experience His kindness and concern for us as we drink from His cleansing water. But a piece of bread, a drink of water, and rest for the body can only strengthen us for one day. In the same way, we need the Lord to fortify our souls and minds again and again. Before long, we discover that it truly is a good thing to do.

When we pray, the Holy Spirit gives energy that spiritually recharges and renews us. We can rise from our knees, grasp the hem of His robe, hold on tightly, and follow Him wherever He leads.

Every day is an adventure with our Lord. Each one begins with His starting us on His holy path as He patiently leads the way. Spending time in prayer opens new doors and gives us direction.

It's never too soon or too late to begin following the path He has for you. Get a glimpse of His awesome, merciful grace through prayer and Bible study. See what a fantastic life He has in the making for you.

After you've tried this path with Jesus for a while and made it a way of life, you will look back on your well-worn trail and see how it has been the best road you could have ever taken: a life that's free, filled with joy and victory.

"It shall come to pass that before they call, I will answer; and while they are still speaking, I will hear."
ISAIAH 65:24 NKJV

OCCASIONALLY, WHEN WE pray, we may be filled with anxiety because of the severity of our needs. At times, gigantic fear looms over us with foreboding, cruel threats. When we cringe and shy away from our problems, the giants often become bigger and cause us to feel totally helpless. We might not be able to see over, under, around, or through them because they're too overwhelming. We may get in way over our heads!

Yet in the midst of our turmoil and worry, we know we can retreat to the safety of our Father's arms and allow Him to surround us with His comfort and mercy. There, as we go to Him in prayer, we can leave our plight in the hands of the One who knows what's best.

Waiting for the Lord to answer our prayers may seem like an eternity. Although we love Him and try to do His will, we may at times wonder why it must take so long for a solution. A quiet, calming voice often whispers to our hearts as we ask Him to give us patience. His timing and wisdom are perfect. He knows our prayers before we ask. And Jesus has already brought them to His Father in heaven on our behalf.

Trust Him, dear reader. Do not fear. He wisely determines the best way to answer your prayers. Leave your request at His feet and rest in His love and care.

In His time, the Lord simultaneously directs us and performs His miraculous will like a carefully-planned symphony. How grateful we can be for His wise and perfect plans and for the miracles that He mercifully brings about.

Let's write down His answers on our hearts and praise Him for all that He's done and will do.

I will bless the LORD at all times; His praise shall continually be in my mouth. PSALM 34:1 NKJV

WHAT CAN WE give God that He hasn't already given us? He provides us with life, our souls, and bountiful blessings of living here on earth. There's only one thing we can give. With every ounce of our beings, we can give Him our praise—our wholehearted, unconditional offering of thanksgiving.

We most often call on God when things go wrong. As situations become urgent, we pray all the harder. After God graciously answers our pleas for help and works things out better than we thought possible, we sometimes forget to return to prayer and give Him the thanks He richly deserves.

But how can we thank Him during hopeless and troubled times? When Paul and Silas were in prison (Acts 16), they had no idea whether they would see the light of day again as they sat there, beaten and bound in chains. Still they prayed and sang hymns to the Lord. Our praise to God can help us to also rise above "hopeless" circumstances.

How can we praise Him when things seem so wrong? Praising Him during trials requires our sacrifice and commitment (Psalm 50:14–15). Try this: stuff a piece of paper and a writing implement in your pocket for the day and then focus on God's goodness and blessings—big and little—that He has given you. Each time you think of a blessing throughout the day, stop and write it down. It won't be long before that piece of paper is looking pretty dog-eared.

When you have quiet time, pull out your notes from several days and begin thanking God for His goodness and mercy. Bask in His holy presence and experience the marvelous victories that He has given you!

Oh, praise the Lord, for he has listened to my pleadings! He is my strength, my shield from every danger. PSALM 28:6−7 TLB

WHEN TROUBLES SURROUND us on all sides and we are paralyzed with fear, we may find that only God can give us the strength to pray. We know He cares. We know He loves us. We also know He wants our love, our confidence in Him, and our praise.

No matter how hard things are, keep praising Him all the time. Remember, praise is the only gift we can give God that He hasn't already given to us. Thank Him for being Your dearest Friend, your source of strength. Exalt His name. Tell Him again and again that you wholeheartedly believe in Him and that He is the Lord and Master of your life.

Praise is a gift to God that, in turn, amazingly drives away our fears. When we do this with a sincere heart, God will deliver us from our fears and direct us in the ways we are to go. Things may not always go our way, but we will see victory. He truly does help us through troubled times.

The more we lift God up, the more He surrounds us with His gracious love. The more we lift Him up, the more He places His angels around us and delivers us and those we pray for from evil and harm. Taste and see that God is good! Experience the blessings He has in store for you as you glorify and praise His name at all times.

A GAELIC BLESSING
May there always be work for your hands to do.
May your purse always hold a coin or two.
May the sun always shine warm on your windowpane.
May a rainbow be certain to follow each rain.
May the hand of a friend always be near you.
And may God fill your heart with blessings to cheer you.

"Forget the former things; do not dwell on the past. See, I am doing a new thing!"
ISAIAH 43:18–19 NIV

I KNOW A young man named David who is one of the most kindhearted people I've ever met. He has been hurt and betrayed many times, but each time, he is willing to forgive and offer the other person a second chance to do what's right. David has a pure heart, and he exhibits peace of mind and soul. He's this way because of his love for the Lord. He doesn't waste his energy on harboring memories filled with bitterness and anger. Instead, he demonstrates ways of releasing the hurts to the Lord and returning acts of kindness in their place.

Not long ago I talked with a woman who is bound by bitterness toward friends and family members for the big or little offenses they've committed against her. She's an unhappy person; her body language shows how trapped she is in her bitter, angry outlook on life.

When we learn to forgive those who have done wrong to us, we experience a remarkable freedom. Our emotions become lighter. Even our health improves. Instead of holding onto bad happenings from the past, we can learn to release them to the Lord. Whether the offender is sorry or not, we need not allow the hurts to burden us anymore. Instead, we can fly as eagles above any circumstances and be caught up instead with the powerful forgiving freedom provided by the Lord.

Give your hurts to the Lord, dear one. If you need to, take them to Him again and again, claiming His love and victory. His forgiveness for us and others is greater than the power of sin. He meets our needs when we ask. He is sufficient. He has broad shoulders. When we ask for help, He overcomes it all and sets us free.

Your love, O Lord, reaches to the heavens, your faithfulness to the skies. Your righteousness is like the mighty mountains, your justice like the great deep. PSALM 36:5–6 NIV

JESUS LOVES US beyond limits, beyond circumstances, beyond understanding. A sacrifice made in this true story makes me think of how much greater His love is.

A tiny spark started the fire, but it burst into a ceiling-high flame. Soon it slashed its destructive tongue through the old apartments. Occupants escaped with only the clothing on their backs.

Firemen hooked up hoses, set up extension ladders, and made sure everyone was safely out. The entire building was soon consumed by the flames.

But what was coming out of a broken basement window? A frightened cat carried something to a nearby tree. Gently lowering a kitten, she looked up pleadingly at a lady nearby and ran back to the window, darting through the damaged glass for another kitten.

Her hair grew singed, her face charred so badly that she looked like she could no longer see. Each time out with a kitten, she touched her babies with her nose, appearing to count them. Finally she collapsed from exhaustion beside her litter.

Paramedics took her and the kittens to an animal shelter, where workers nursed them back to health and managed to save part of the mother's eyesight. Hundreds of people offered to take in the cat and kittens.

The intense love of this cat compares to the love we have for those dearest to us. We'd give our lives for any one of them. But as great as this love is, God's love and mercy go way beyond.

He allowed His Son to die for us so we could be freed from sin and have eternal life. When we give Him our hearts, we experience His immeasurable love.

But seek first the kingdom of God and His righteousness, and all these things shall be added to you.
Matthew 6:33 NKJV

ISN'T IT COMFORTING to know how much God loves and treasures us? We are His children. He created us in our mothers' wombs and knew what we would look like, what our personalities would be like, and what our talents would be. He wants our lives to be full, joy-filled ones that glorify Him. We are treasured by Him.

Sadly, many of us for one reason or another feel we aren't valuable to God, ourselves, or anyone else. Suffering from abuse can make us think this way. We feel trapped, not knowing a way out. The Lord wants us to be kind and loving, but He never intended for us to be mistreated or abused. Again, it's important to remember that we are mercifully loved and treasured by God. We are priceless to Him, and we need to *view* ourselves as being priceless.

It takes strength to not allow ourselves to remain in abusive situations. Yet as we faithfully read God's Word and determine to love Him above anything or anyone else, we can be certain that God will bring us through. I love His promise regarding trials and temptation in I Corinthians 10:13 (RSV): "No temptation [or trial] has overtaken you that is not common to man [or woman]. God is faithful, and He will not let you be tempted [or tried] beyond your strength, but with the temptation will also provide the way of escape, that you may be able to endure it."

If you or someone you know is suffering from abuse, seek out a good pastor, Christian friend, or counselor for help. You need not be alone. Stay true to living your life for the Lord and put Him first above all else. He loves and treasures you.

"No longer do I call you servants, for a servant does not know what his master is doing; but I have called you friends, for all things that I heard from My Father I have made known to you. You did not choose Me, but I chose you." JOHN 15:15–16 NKJV

WHAT A TREASURE we have in the friendships God gives us. I'm glad my friends aren't like me; that would be pretty boring. I like to compare them to my flower garden. Some are flamboyant. Others are quiet and reserved. One friend can bring humor into any situation to help lighten things. They are all sizes, shapes, and colors. They are rich and poor, elderly and young.

Though we may have several friends, our closest ones are often few. Abraham Lincoln described it perfectly when he said: "The better part of one's life consists of his friendships."

Above all, our dearest friend is Jesus. He loves us no matter what's going on in our lives, or how happy or grumpy we may feel. He's always willing to listen and care. Unlike us, He never experiences overload. His understanding and forgiveness go beyond measure.

When the time drew near for Jesus to be crucified, He and His disciples met in the upper room to eat and pray. Jesus described the steadfast love He had for His Father and encouraged His disciples to love each other as much as He loved them. They might even be required to give their life for a friend. When they loved that much their joy would be made complete.

Jesus told His disciples they were no longer servants. Instead, He called them His friends. He already knew some would betray Him, but even so, He had enough love to forgive, and He encouraged them to remain true.

Every so often we might search our hearts, asking what measure of friendship we can give to the Lord. Sometimes, rather than picking up the phone to talk with our friends, we can pick up a Bible and have a nice, long conversation with our best Friend, Jesus.

April 5 ‖ Servant of Love

[Jesus said,] "This do...in remembrance of Me." 1 CORINTHIANS 11:25 NKJV

ONE OF THE greatest privileges the Lord gives us is when He welcomes us to commemorate the Last Supper by taking communion with Him and our fellow brothers and sisters in the Lord.

Confusion and anxiety filled the air of the upper guest room where Jesus and His disciples had gathered. The meal was just being served when Jesus got up from the table to wash the disciples' feet. He knew that Judas was about to betray Him. Sadly, He'd soon be deserted by most of the other disciples too. In spite of their lack of understanding and dedication, Jesus loved each one of them.

Jesus removed His outer garment and wrapped a towel around His waist. Quietly, deliberately, He poured water into a basin and began washing the disciples' feet and then drying them with the towel. He was doing the job of the lowliest of servants. Surely the disciples were too shocked to even speak.

Then Jesus came to Peter. "And Peter said to Him, 'Lord, are You washing my feet?' Jesus answered and said to him, 'What I am doing you do not understand now, but you will know after this.' Peter said to Him, 'You shall never wash my feet!' Jesus answered him, 'If I do not wash you, you have no part with Me.' Simon Peter said to Him, 'Lord, not my feet only, but also my hands and my head!' " (John 13:6–9 NKJV).

This loving act of cleansing His disciples physically and spiritually goes beyond human comprehension. The King of kings and Lord of lords knelt in love and servanthood, washing dirty, unworthy feet. This was only the beginning of the love He showed for His disciples—and us.

No service on our part can ever compare to His selfless acts of love.

Then saith he to Thomas, Reach hither thy finger, and behold my hands; and reach hither thy hand, and thrust it into my side: and be not faithless, but believing. JOHN 20:27 KJV

HOW CAN WE grasp the plans God has in store for our future? The very thought is mind-boggling. To ponder these things on a regular basis seems fruitless... but when our lives are in an upheaval and we don't know what will happen from one minute to the next, our limited understanding of how God will bring us through each day can be wearisome and frightening.

We read in John 20 that after Jesus died and rose again, the disciples hid behind locked doors for fear of being killed by the Jews. Jesus went through those doors and stood among the disciples. Everyone, except Thomas who wasn't there, believed He was the Lord.

A week later, Jesus came to His disciples again. He invited Thomas to touch the scars in His hands and His side. When Thomas did so, he believed. Jesus went on to explain, "Because you have seen me, you have believed; blessed are those who have not seen and yet have believed" (verse 29 NIV).

When we face uncertain times in our walk with the Lord, we can tap into that little seed of faith firmly buried in our souls and allow the Holy Spirit to liberally water it with His loving care. No matter how insecure we feel, God gives us the strength to look to Him in faith and behold His nail-scarred hands that reach out to us. Slowly, we manage to reach toward the Lord and place our fingers into the center of His palms. He helps us to our feet and encourages us to trust and follow Him.

Behold His hands, dear reader. I can almost see Him reaching out to us and telling us with calm assurance, "It's all right, dear child. Have faith in Me. I'm taking care of everything."

You will make known to me the path of life; in Your presence is fullness of joy; in Your right hand there are pleasures forever. PSALM 16:11 NASB

LORD, EVERYWHERE I look, I learn about tragedy, greed, crime, and violence. What concerns me most is seeing people who lose hope or suffer from depression.

It's easy to get bogged down with the bad things that are happening, Lord. Yet instead, I'm learning to do my best each day to help those around me and try to make this world a better place to live. After having done all I can, I have to leave everything to You.

No matter what my circumstances are, I choose Your joy, which is my strength. It has an amazing way of sustaining me every single day. Each time I bring my burdens to You, You fill my mouth with laughter. You put songs of gratefulness on my lips. You remind me to offer cheerful smiles and encouraging words to those around me. And You promise me that my simple actions, empowered by Your Holy Spirit, bring joy to their hearts and health to their bones.

You fill me with a greater contentment than what I can obtain from anyone or anything else. Your joy weaves itself through every fiber of my being. You bless me with Your comforting, satisfying peace.

At day's end, I release the turmoil that has been forced upon me and invite Your holy presence to fill my soul's cup to the brim. In so doing, I lie down on my bed and rest peacefully while songs of Your joy and assurance flow through my mind.

I will honor You, dear Lord, with my mind, body, and soul. How grateful I am to reap the countless blessings of the unquenchable joy and gladness You give and the way its brightness overcomes all the hopelessness in this world.

Joy is a gift from God, hidden below the surface of every situation.
—JANICE LEWIS CLARK

The Lord Jesus Christ be with your spirit. Grace be with you. Amen. 2 TIMOTHY 4:22 NKJV

CAN YOU THINK of a day when God's marvelous mercy and grace followed you all day long? During your work, did you feel Him near to you? When you had to make difficult decisions and untangle problems, did you sense His helping you to find the right answers? When heated tensions arose, did you sense a peacefulness within you that could only come from the Lord? While you were going through traffic, did the signals seem to mostly be on green? Were people surprisingly polite?

Perhaps this was a day where God not only showered you with His grace but a day when you remembered to be totally in tune to His directing your steps.

God answers our prayers for help in making decisions and solving problems: "Make me walk in the path of Your commandments, for I delight in it" (Psalm 119:35 NKJV).

When we call on Him, He gives us peace, even when turmoil surrounds us: Jesus said, "Peace I leave with you, My peace I give to you; not as the world gives do I give to you. Let not your heart be troubled, neither let it be afraid" (John 14:27–28 NKJV).

He reminds us to be polite and considerate to those around us: "Blessed are the merciful, for they shall obtain mercy" (Matthew 5:7 NKJV).

Grace given to others often reaps the blessings of grace received: "And my God shall supply all your need according to His riches in glory by Christ Jesus" (Philippians 4:19 NKJV).

Think of the ways God has blessed you this day. Praise Him for the graciousness, mercy, and peace of heart and mind that He gives. Through His loving-kindness, He is the generous Provider of all that is good.

Many, O Lord my God, are the wonders you have done. The things you planned for us no one can recount to you. PSALM 40:5 NIV

THINK OF THE goals and dreams you have for your life. Think of the ways God is calling you to do something for Him. You might able to accomplish some right now. However, others might take years of dedicated work. Either way, when God gives us goals and dreams, He does so in His own perfect way and timing.

Perhaps, like me, you want everything to fit together immediately so you can move forward as planned. The lengthy process of waiting might be excruciating. Yet trying to turn the clock forward and getting ahead of God can hinder the process of what He is doing in our lives. While we're required to wait, we may become discouraged and want to settle for second-best goals. Even worse, we may think about completely giving up. God's goals and dreams often take time, patience, and dedication.

The Reverend Dr. T. DeWitt Talmage compares this process to leaves in the springtime. He says leaves aren't created in the spring. Instead, months before, at the beginning of summer, they are being fashioned for the following year. Near the bottom of every leaf stem is a cradle. In it lies an infant germ or seed. The winds rock it and the birds sing to it through the summer. The seed in the cradle remains while the old leaf drifts away. During the next springtime, the seed opens and sprouts a new green leaf.

Like a fallen leaf, we could allow our sights to drop or we can trust God to keep them elevated according to His calling. He wants us to hold on tight and trust Him during the perfect process and development of what He has planned for us—a process often lifting us even higher than any of the sights in our goals and dreams.

[Jesus said,] *"Never will I leave you; never will I forsake you."* HEBREWS 13:5 NIV

SOME OF US experience times when we feel totally alone. Although there may be people everywhere, we might feel as though we're stranded on a desert island with no one to share our cares and concerns.

Charles Wesley, a well-loved hymn writer, experienced this feeling. He suffered from pleurisy, fever, and dysentery so badly that he wondered if he would recover.

Alone in his room, Charles lifted a feeble prayer to the One he knew would never leave him. The Lord graciously answered his prayer and gave him a vision to comfort him in one of his darkest hours. In the vision, a woman entered his room and told him he would be healed through the name of Jesus Christ.

Charles took his vision as a sign that God would heal him. He deliberately looked up Scriptures that promised him hope and courage. Immediately, the Lord honored his faith and restored his health.

Through this experience, Charles experienced a drive more than ever before to win souls. Surely God had a reason for saving his life. It was then he wrote the cherished hymn, "Jesus, Lover of My Soul." Its words reassure us that we are never alone.

God promises us in His Word that He will never leave us, no matter what the circumstances are. Our help comes from the Lord (Psalm 121:2). He is with us when we go through deep waters (Isaiah 43:2). He keeps us from harm and watches over us (Psalm 121:7). He will never, ever leave us (Hebrews 13:5).

When the struggles you're going through are too much to bear alone, thank Him for being near. Although all seems hopeless, the Bible promises that nothing is impossible when we trust in Him.

This is the day the LORD has made; we will rejoice and be glad in it. PSALM 118:24 NKJV

WHAT I LOVE about spring is Easter season. Bulbs pushing up from the ground and buds and colorful blossoms popping out on trees bring new hope. It's a reminder to praise God for His marvelous works.

When Palm Sunday arrives, we worship Him with songs of praise, commemorating the triumphant entry of Jesus into Jerusalem. Children might even wave palm branches. Again the miraculous story unfolds.

Before Jesus approached Jerusalem, He told two disciples to go to a village ahead of them, find a tied donkey and its colt, and bring them to Him. The owners allowed the disciples to take the animals to Jesus. Jesus was about to ride a colt that had never been ridden. Doing so would normally be quite a struggle. But Jesus could persuade an animal to do what He wanted.

Jesus rode down the Mount of Olives toward Jerusalem. Crowds of people laid palm branches and cloaks before Him, enthusiastically shouting praises to God for all the miracles they'd seen, saying: "Blessed is the King who comes in the name of the LORD! Peace in heaven and glory in the highest!" (Luke 19:38 NKJV). Even then, the Pharisees tried to stop the shouts of praise.

The response Jesus gave on that great day still applies: "I tell you that if these [people] should keep silent, the stones would immediately cry out" (Luke 19:40 NKJV). When Jesus saw Jerusalem, He broke down and wept: "If you had known, even you, especially in this your day, the things that make for your peace!" (Luke 19:42 NKJV).

Let us accept the peace that Jesus offers us today—a peace that comes through His saving grace. In all circumstances, let us sing: "Blessed be our King, our Lord!"

"Fear not, for I have redeemed you; I have called you by your name; you are Mine."
ISAIAH 43:1 NKJV

NOT FAR FROM where Jesus had been crucified was a garden and an unused tomb owned by Joseph from Arimathea. Joseph and Nicodemus wrapped the body of Jesus in spices and linen and laid Him in Joseph's tomb. A huge rock was rolled in front of the tomb's opening, and Pilate ordered soldiers to stand guard so no one could steal the body and claim that Jesus had risen after three days.

On the day after the Sabbath, Mary Magdalene and others discovered that the body of Jesus was gone. The tomb was open and there were only grave linens and the cloth that had been wrapped around His head.

According to the account in the Gospel of John, Mary Magdalene remained behind after the others left. Tears streamed down her cheeks as she again peered into the tomb. She saw two angels in gleaming white clothes sitting at the head and the foot of where Jesus once laid. The angels asked her why she was weeping.

Between what most likely were sobbing breaths, she told them: "Because they have taken away my Lord, and I do not know where they have laid Him" (John 20:13 NKJV). Then she turned around and saw Jesus.

The Lord asked Mary, "Woman, why are you weeping? Whom are you seeking?"

Mary didn't recognize Jesus. Mary responded: "Sir, if You have carried Him away, tell me where You have laid Him, and I will take Him away."

Then Jesus answered, "Mary!" (John 20:14–16 NKJV).

Immediately, Mary knew He was her Lord.

When life seems hopeless and you long to feel the Lord's merciful presence, seek Him with all your heart. Listen for His voice. He is only a prayer away.

[Jesus said,] "And if I go and prepare a place for you, I will come again and receive you to Myself; that where I am, there you may be also." JOHN 14:3 NKJV

WHAT WILL IT be like when we get to see our Lord Jesus face-to-face? Will that be when we die and are taken to heaven to be with Him? Or will Jesus return to us during our lifetime? Will we see Him surrounded by angels? Will we hear the trumpet sounding, proclaiming the King of kings, Lord of lords as He descends through the clouds in all His glory? No matter how it happens, we shall finally get to see His face.

After Jesus rose from the grave, He continued being with His followers. He told them He was about to go home to be with His heavenly Father. He promised that He would never leave them (or us) alone. He said He would send the Comforter, the Holy Spirit, to help them and give them the power needed to serve Him. He instructed them to wait and pray for the Comforter to come and also told them to not be troubled or afraid. He was going to heaven to prepare a beautiful place, and someday, He would bring them (and us) with Him to His heavenly home.

One day while Jesus and His followers stood together, He was taken up into the sky right in front of them. He kept ascending until a cloud hid Him from their view. His followers tried to see Him but were unable to do so. Perhaps they felt lost and deserted. But two men dressed in white appeared to the group, telling them that in the same way Jesus was taken into heaven, He would return (Acts 1:7–11).

What a wonderful promise that someday we shall get to see the magnificent face of Jesus. We will look into His gracious, forgiving eyes. Oh, at last, what a day that will be!

Oh, taste and see that the LORD *is good; blessed is the man [or woman] who trusts in Him!*
PSALM 34:8 NKJV

THERE WAS A sign I read not long ago that said, "I am satisfied with the love of Jesus." I pondered that incredible statement for quite a while. The more I thought about it, the more I came to realize that as I apply this standard to my everyday life, it proves to be absolutely true!

There is nothing false or artificial about the unlimited mercy and love of our Lord Jesus Christ. When we search the Bible for answers to what we are dealing with, the Holy Spirit has a way of giving us just the direction and encouragement that we need.

During times in our lives when our stress level is up, we may turn to things in our lives that appear to be quick fixes—like entertainment and yummy comfort foods. These things might be all right in themselves, but they only meet our hunger for peace and fulfillment for a short time and don't really fulfill the needs that God can meet.

The spiritual fruit we learn about in Galatians 5:22–23 is mentally, emotionally, and spiritually satisfying, unlike other falsely proclaimed fruits we so often have to contend with: "But the fruit of the Spirit is love, joy, peace, longsuffering, kindness, goodness, faithfulness, gentleness, self-control" (NKJV).

It's so good to know that as we apply these wise teachings to our lives, we can experience an indescribable peace and happiness with Jesus as our Guide. Similar to eating right, all we need to do is to place taking care of our spiritual welfare ahead of anything else, follow the Bible's directions, and enjoy the genuine fruit of God's Spirit.

But I trust in your unfailing love; my heart rejoices in your salvation. PSALM 13:5 NIV

LIVING FOR THE Lord is an exciting adventure. Whatever our journey involves, we can enjoy partnership with Him. Great things happen when the Lord is our central focus. He becomes our advisor and encourager.

Several years ago, I felt the Lord leading me to write a book on prayer. I was working two jobs then, so it took me four years to complete the book. It was through God's strength that I was able to do so.

One Sunday during evening service, Bob spoke about using our talents for the Lord. He took some loose change from his pocket and passed it out. When he came to me, he handed me two quarters.

Bob continued talking, and my mind began to wander. As I sat there rubbing those quarters together, I felt the Lord's encouraging love. I began to pray silently. I asked God to use the book I had written in any way He wanted. As a token of my faith, I would spend the quarters on a stamp. A couple of days later, I sent out a submission letter—and before long, the book was accepted and published.

I thought of a restaurant I'd been in where the owners had posted their first paycheck on a wall. That was nice. But what did the Lord want from me? More important than book sales or income was for God to use my writings to touch the searching hearts of those who read them and to make a difference in each life.

Now as I look at a picture frame on my office windowsill containing two other quarters, I'm reminded that great things really do happen when we trust and follow Him.

What do you think the Lord has planned for you? Trust Him...and get ready for the adventure.

Creativity is a God-given ability to take something ordinary and make it into something special.
—EMILIE BARNES

He has caused his wonderful works to be remembered; the Lord is gracious and merciful.
Psalm 111:4 RSV

FROM THE MOMENT we follow God's call, we must work with Him each step of the way. Everything may go smoothly, or it may become an emotional roller coaster. Still, He will guide us.

When I began writing, all I had was an old computer that looked as if it had been rescued from the ark—and an equally ancient printer. I was thankful for them, but since my computer wasn't compatible with much, I could only send out hard copies of the manuscript.

In spite of poor equipment, I mustered the faith and determination to keep writing. At last I completed the final draft and began printing it out. Halfway through, however, my printer's tape cartridge ran out of ink. I took the cartridge to an office supply store; unfortunately, the cartridges were no longer available.

I knew that God wanted me to send out this book, no matter what! How could this become possible? I returned home in tears and asked God for help—but when I shoved the cartridge back into the printer, a screw flew out and the cartridge wouldn't stay down! What would I do now?

I felt Him coaxing me to stop and pray. Then I realized that the tape had three colors: red, black, and blue. If I pushed the cartridge down, it would print red ink. I found some heavy-duty packaging tape and prayed feverishly before taping the cartridge into the printer.

"God, please make it work," I whispered.

The manuscript printed out in bright red. I hurried to a copy machine, made a black master, and mailed it.

Each time I think of that experience, I'm reminded of how God makes a way for us to follow His call when we combine our talents and determination with His will.

One of the secrets of life is to make stepping-stones out of stumbling blocks.
—Jack Penn

But I will always trust in you and in your mercy and shall rejoice in your salvation. I will sing to the Lord because he has blessed me so richly. PSALM 13:5–6 TLB

ISN'T IT GOOD that the Lord loves us with an understanding, merciful love! All He wants in return is for us to give Him our wholehearted love, trust, and obedience. Join with me in this next prayer as we commit to Him.

Father, during the past, present, and future of my life, I thank You for helping me to be strong and of good courage. I will not fear, for You are the Lord, my God. Thank You for always being with me.

Through the ups and downs in my life, I know You'll never fail me. Even though I might have my own ideas of how life should go, You know what is best and will always care for me.

Yesterday is past, today is fleeting, and tomorrow is around the bend. Life is too short for me to hold onto any phase of my life and miss out on the blessings You have in store for me.

Help me to forget what is behind me and to look forward without fear toward things to come. I will press toward the goals You set for me. Each time I hear You call, I will follow.

Remind me, Lord, to hold onto a positive attitude. Help me focus on whatever is just and pure. Encourage me to think about things that are lovely, honest, and encouraging. Let me look for the best in situations and people and exercise an uplifting outlook.

In all circumstances, I will trust in You. Each day as I follow Your leading, I will build from the past, take advantage of the present, and look forward to the future. Because of Your mercy and goodness, I thank You for a peace that surpasses all my comprehension. In Jesus' name, amen.

We will rejoice in your salvation, and in the name of our God we will set up our banners!
PSALM 20:5 NKJV

FATHER, I JUST finished getting ready for work. I recall glancing in the mirror to see if I looked all right. Outside the fact that I have some untamable strands of hair, I passed the test. Just before I left the mirror and entered the living room to take some time with You, I remember the last thing I did: I gave myself a big smile.

How do I look during the day, Father? As much as I try otherwise when things aren't going right, I realize I don't always reflect a good attitude. Please forgive me. I know my smiles are contagious. When I smile at others, they automatically smile back at me. However, when I frown at others, they reflect my negative attitude or give looks of concern. It's evident that the expressions on my face reflect what is in my soul.

Help me to bring some happiness to those around me today. I want the look on my face to reflect You. Please strengthen and guide me through Your Holy Spirit.

❧

My work day is almost over, Father. Nearly everyone has left. After I finish a few last-minute things, I'll be ready to call it a day. Yet in the quietness of this moment I lean back and enjoy Your holy presence. I feel Your warm approval in all that was said and done. Thank You for faithfully guiding me and filling me with Your joy and strength.

It's dark outside now, and again, I see my reflection smiling at me through the window's reflection. Then I see past my face and sense that You, too, are smiling as You peer into my soul. Thank You, Father, for helping me to reflect You during this day—especially with my smile.

He who sows righteousness reaps a sure reward. PROVERBS 11:18 NIV

AT TIMES WE wonder if our individual giving really matters. Can we meet our budgets when we give to others? Do others really benefit from our giving? What if we are the ones who are in need of help? God often answers our questions through miracles and blessings.

Let me tell you about one couple who had suffered serious health problems and struggled with bills they couldn't pay. When they went to their pastor for advice, he asked them if they were tithing. They weren't. He showed them in the Bible how giving to God what was rightfully His was most important. He encouraged them to tithe for three months and see what would happen.

A month later, the couple received a surprising letter from the hospital telling them that their medical expenses were paid. Somehow, they were able to pay the rest of their bills and had money to spare. Needless to say, the couple continued to tithe.

A small church was struggling in attendance and finances. During a board meeting, a member suggested that the congregation begin tithing their income to a mission church. Immediately, the small church started. Within a couple of months, the small church's income had increased. People from all around came to help with repair projects. Enthusiasm grew. Church attendance began to climb and the pastor and his wife from the mission church reported how other churches were also helping them. They were scheduled to break ground and start building a new church quite soon.

The Bible says that there is a gain to our giving. What we give, God gives back to us in "good measure, pressed down, shaken together and running over" (Luke 6: 38 NIV).

As we take the step of faith and begin tithing, we can also enjoy the blessings of giving and see the mighty ways God works.

"For my thoughts are not your thoughts, neither are your ways my ways," declares the LORD.
ISAIAH 55:8 NIV

HAVE YOU EVER held a job that made you wonder why you were even there? I have.

I taught special education at a local elementary school during the day and loved every minute of it, but I'd taken on a moonlighting job at a fast-food restaurant to help pay extra bills. I tried to keep a good attitude about working the latter; however, even though I'd deliberately chosen it as an opposite type of work from my day job, I hit an emotional and physical low.

Arriving at work fifteen minutes early gave me a chance to lean my head back against the seat and close my eyes before I left my car. "Lord, what am I doing here?" I whispered. "I'm doing my best—but why here? I see many employees just putting in their time. Some are tired and discouraged, barely keeping up financially and physically. Only a few have dreams and goals. How can I make a difference? Lead me to someone I can help and encourage."

I pulled my Bible from my glove box and opened it to Jeremiah 29. It was His promise that even though I felt exhausted, He had a plan for me in the workplace He had put me in. His mercy and peace filled my heart.

"Lord," I whispered, "thank You for Your answer."

I left my car, trudged across the pavement, clocked in, and counted my till. Grill and fryer smells and rhythmic beeping timers drew me into a changing-hat mode. Thoughts of my school day faded while customer service responsibilities took over.

I sent up a silent prayer, telling God I'd be the best employee possible and leave the rest to Him, whether I understood His plan or not.

But the plans of the LORD stand firm forever, the purposes of his heart through all generations.
PSALM 33:11 NIV

SOMETIMES IT'S DIFFICULT to visualize the purpose God has for us in uncomfortable work surroundings. Still, He has a plan.

Shortly after I clocked in at my fast-food job, I looked up to see my manager with a slip of a teenager in tow. The girl had green eyes, freckled cheeks, and a warm grin filled with silver braces. The manager asked me to train her for customer service.

She's just a little thing, I thought. *I hope she can make it.*

I welcomed her and began the training. I noticed Brenda's great attitude and work habits. She confided that she had a learning disability. I assured her we'd take it a little slower during her training and told her to not worry. One day, Brenda told me that before I'd arrived for my shift, she'd "lost it" during a rush. "I don't think I have what it takes," she said.

There was something special about Brenda, though. Time for my "buck-up" speech I'd recited to kids countless times before. "Brenda, don't give up. You'll have to work twice as hard as others, but be determined and hang in there." I continued while silently praying for guidance. "Albert Einstein, Benjamin Franklin, Michael Landon, Tom Cruise, Bruce Jenner, former Miss America Heather Whitestone, and many others had and do have disabilities. Some even go on to college."

Brenda's eyes brightened. "Thanks," she chirped.

Thank You, Lord. She bought my speech!

I prayed for Brenda often. She'd told me she was a Christian. I knew she'd do well with compassionate, understanding help from the Lord. She didn't give up. She became one of the most dedicated employees. I couldn't help but wonder if she was why God had put me there.

Many, O Lord my God, are the wonders you have done. The things you planned for us no one can recount to you; were I to speak and tell of them, they would be too many to declare. PSALM 40:5 NIV

AS WE LABOR for the Lord, He plants new dreams that we never thought would be possible.

One day Brenda came to work, bouncing with enthusiasm. "Guess what, Anita! I've started helping teach some little kids with learning disabilities how to swim. It's so much fun!"

Brenda's flicker of hope showed the beginning of a dream bursting into reality. After a month, she decided to take another step. "I want to go to college after I graduate," she said. "I'll study to be a teacher's assistant just like you. I want to teach special ed kids."

I felt a warm glow inside me. Not long after, Brenda's grade point soared to a 3.5. She never let anyone convince her she couldn't do it. The last time I saw Brenda, she was ready to graduate and had earned two college scholarships.

Did I have a purpose in working in fast food? Yes. God planted a dream in Brenda's heart to help other kids. Wherever Brenda is, my prayers go with her.

About five years ago, I was able to leave my employment at the restaurant. Now I'm retired from full-time teaching and am a substitute teacher's assistant.

As I continue teaching and inspiring children to follow their hopes and dreams, the promise from Jeremiah 29 that God planted in my mind that evening years ago still remains strong and true: He decisively plans and charts the courses for our lives when we trust Him. And He gives us purpose and hope for the future.

Through my uncomfortable work experience, I discovered that when God plants dreams in the hearts of those who love Him, we often stand back and marvel at His wise and gracious ways.

April 23 | Escaping to You

He will give his people strength. He will bless them with peace. PSALM 29:11 TLB

I LOVE ESCAPING to You, dear Lord. No matter where I go, whether it be miles away, in my own backyard, or in a quiet corner of our home, You are with me—listening, calming, encouraging, removing my stress and cares.

In Your holy presence, I find a pleasant resting place. As I bow before You, O Lord, I feel truly awed and humbled. Thank You for meeting with me here. The distractions around me fade into nothingness as I hear You gently whispering to my soul.

"Pause, listen, and pray, dear child. Drink in My presence. Know that I am your Counselor, your Savior, your Physician, your Confidant, and your Friend. I am your Shepherd, and you, dear child, are my sheep. I am with you, surrounding you with my love all of the time. Rest awhile. Let everything go. Drink in the presence of my Spirit. Take time to be refreshed and renewed."

Here, I feel an indescribable serenity that I know only comes from You, dear Lord. Here, You speak to my heart and help me to lay aside my burdens. Soon, I put my confidence completely in You and realize that all is well with my soul.

Thank You for this quiet time that You have prepared for me. As we commune with each other, I feel refreshed and refilled. I don't want to depart from here, but I pray that You will remain with me as I leave this place and go about my duties. Thank You for Your gracious presence. You are my dearest Love, my Lord. I know You dwell within me no matter where I must go. Still, I already look forward to the next time I can return here and meet with You. In Jesus' name, amen.

Tell me what to do, O Lord.... PSALM 27:11 TLB

DO YOU EVER "just have a feeling" that you need to pray for someone and possibly give them a phone call or a visit? This happened to me last week. Our neighbors, Dave and Linda, had done a favor for us, and in turn, I decided to make a pie for them as a token of thanks. But the day I had planned to take the pie over to their house, I wasn't able to go.

However, the next day I had a strong feeling that taking time that afternoon to visit must be my top priority. The Scripture in 1 Timothy 2:1 came to mind: "Pray much for others; plead for God's mercy upon them; give thanks for all He is going to do for them" (TLB).

Fifteen minutes after I took a pie out of the oven, I headed across the street to Dave and Linda's. Linda was in tears when she met me at the door. I placed the pie on the counter and encircled her in my arms. It turned out that she and Dave had to have Tinker, their nineteen-year-old kitty, put to sleep. At that moment, Dave was burying Tinker in the backyard.

What made things more difficult was that Tinker had been dying of cancer—the same disease Linda had been courageously fighting (and winning over) for more than a year. Linda and I grasped hands and prayed together for peace and comfort during this time of grief.

Through tear-filled eyes, Linda told me, "You came at the perfect time. I'm so glad you're here."

The next time you "have a feeling," pause and pray and find out what God is trying to tell you. You may very likely be part of someone else's answered prayer.

God whispers little thoughts to us in order to bring about big blessings.

He guides the humble in what is right and teaches them his way. PSALM 25:9 NIV

ORGANIST THOMAS GRAPE and choir member Elvina Mabel Hall of the Monument Street Methodist Church in Baltimore had served in the church for years. Thomas felt he should write a tune that would go with words written by William Bradbury in the mid-1800s. Thomas Grape's melody (called "All to Him I Owe") fell into place as though the Lord was dictating.

Thomas gave the music to his pastor, the Reverend Schrick, but the pastor didn't think it matched Bradbury's words. However, the pastor tucked the tune away in a folder—perhaps there would be a day God could use it.

One Sunday morning in 1865 after the choir had finished singing, Elvina Hall listened quietly from the choir loft while the pastor spoke about forgiveness. His sermon caused her to think about the merciful redemption of Jesus, and she became filled with gratitude toward the Lord for what He had done for her.

She felt Him leading her to write a poem as an offering of her praise. There was no paper in sight, so Elvina grabbed a hymnal. She flipped to the blank flyleaf and started writing. By the end of the service, Elvina had written four verses.

After the service, she showed the poem to her pastor. Rev. Schrick pulled Thomas Grape's music from the folder—and the music and poem matched perfectly!

God used an amateur organist and a choir member to fit together a timeless hymn. The title was changed to "Jesus Paid It All." Rev. Schrick had the hymn published in the hymnal *Sabbath Chords* in 1868. Today it continues to remind us of the merciful forgiveness of our Lord.

The next time you feel God urging you to do something, follow His leading—glorious things can happen.

Because he bends down and listens, I will pray as long as I breathe! PSALM 116:2 TLB

LORD, THANK YOU for making a difference in my life. Before I accepted You as my Savior, I felt as though I were wandering in circles. I was lost until You knocked at my heart's door and asked me to invite You in.

I can't imagine how You had the compassion and graciousness to take my sorrowful heart just as it was and simply love and forgive me. You provided me with a brand-new start in life, Lord. You picked me up and turned my life around. You gave me freedom over temptation and wrong choices.

You have filled me with Your unquenchable joy. Because Your Holy Spirit dwells within me, I have a drive to tell others of Your wonderful love and grace.

Thank You for mercifully seeing worth in me, Lord. Thank You for giving me purpose in life. Thank You for promising me that You will always be with me.

I really love You, Lord. My heart belongs to You.

JESUS PAID IT ALL

I hear the Savior say, "Thy strength indeed is small;
Child of weakness, watch and pray, find in Me thine all in all."
Lord, now indeed I find Thy Pow'r, and Thine alone,
Can change the leper's spots and melt the heart of stone.

For nothing good have I whereby Thy grace to claim—
I'll wash my garments white in the blood of Calvary's Lamb.
And when, before the throne, I stand in Him complete,
"Jesus died my soul to save," my lips shall still repeat.

Jesus paid it all, all to him I owe;
Sin had left a crimson stain, He wash'd it white as snow.
—ELVINA M. HALL AND JOHN THOMAS GRAPE

Fear not, for I am with you. Do not be dismayed. I am your God. I will strengthen you; I will help you; I will uphold you with my victorious right hand. ISAIAH 41:10 TLB

WHEN TRAGEDY STRIKES, God supplies His saving grace.

Kent and Cathy Shoop loved being church pastors and singing for the Lord. Cathy was also a school librarian. Yet soon their lives would change.

One early November morning, Cathy bundled up and drove toward her aerobics class. Suddenly, she hit black ice. The car struck the railing, went airborne, and landed upside down on the riverbank below.

Cathy lay sprawled on the ground near her crushed car, unable to move. As she drifted in and out of consciousness, God's indescribable peace surrounded her.

Screeching tires rallied Cathy. A second car had crashed against the bridge's railing, and people were talking! Cathy mustered all her strength and cried for help. They heard her and called for an ambulance.

A helicopter emergency crew kept Cathy alive while they transported her to a hospital. She had a ruptured spleen, a punctured lung, and a compressed spinal cord. For days, Cathy teetered between life and death. She was paralyzed from the chest down. Kent and their grown children hovered near, and God's presence remained.

Intense physical therapy began. Cathy's main focus became "I can do all things through Christ who strengthens me" (Philippians 4:13 NKJV). Five months later, Cathy returned to teaching and ministry. She continued thinking, "I can do all things...."

Then her energy level crashed. The words "I can" were backfiring. God was teaching Cathy that she could do all things *through Christ* as He strengthened her. After much prayer, Cathy learned to pace herself and lean more on God. Life and time to accomplish God's will grew more precious.

Today, Cathy's retired. She and Kent still pastor a church, and they have made their country home into a bed-and-breakfast. And because of God's mercy, Cathy and Kent continue to be a blessing to many.

In spite of the trials and tragedies we might face, God can still use us to help and encourage others too.

Love Grows in Grace

The LORD is gracious and compassionate, slow to anger and rich in love. The LORD is good to all; he has compassion on all he has made. PSALM 145:8−9 NIV

WHAT IS THIS grace we hear and read about? Does graciousness automatically happen? Or does it grow with the love God gives us for another person? I often admire a gracious host or hostess, a person who considers the feelings of others, or someone who is unselfish and kind.

Dr. Thomas Guthrie, a renowned minister in the 1800s, describes grace so beautifully, comparing God's grace to an arch. The more weight placed upon it, the firmer it stands. His kindness is dependable and sufficient to meet all our needs, just as He promises in 2 Corinthians 12:9: "My grace is sufficient for thee: for my strength is made perfect in weakness" (KJV).

Dr. Guthrie goes on to say that God's grace is like an overflowing well that never goes dry. Though we are undeserving, He graciously loves us and forgives us of our shortcomings.

Whatever the need in our lives—for more love, a pure heart, a tender conscience, or humility—our Lord provides it all. His grace allows us to shed our tears of gratefulness at His feet or to spill our offerings of honor and love upon His head. We can never ask too much or too little of the Lord.

The kind of grace that grows often comes from being considerate to those who are inconsiderate...or bearing up under difficulties and pressures that can only be withstood through the help of our gracious Lord. The only certainty in this uncertain world is what He gives to us. He helps us to grow in grace through new life lessons, and His portion of love and grace is always enough.

Balancing Mercy and Wisdom

For the LORD *is good; His mercy is everlasting, and His truth endures to all generations.*
PSALM 100:5 NKJV

LORD, WHEN I see the sin, sickness, and destitution around me, I'm driven to frustration. Why is this happening? What can I do to help? I'm only one person. I hurt for those who suffer. Some are victims of circumstances, but some problems are ones that others bring on themselves. It frustrates me when someone isn't willing to take hold of ambition and responsibility.

I know I'm not meant to solve all of life's problems. On what condition do I show mercy? Grant me love, discernment, and the ability to know Your will, I pray. Show me how to encourage others when they have given up. Help me to understand how they feel. Guide me to recognize when You want me to help and when You want me to gently steer them toward being able to help themselves.

Along with my trying to solve the problems, I know I must still must be willing to trust You to work things out in Your own way. Help me to not get in the way of what You are trying to accomplish. You know the big picture and what is best.

I know we aren't supposed to allow ourselves to be mistreated. Still, You tell us to forgive as You have forgiven us. Grudges and hatred can consume our lives like a deadly cancer. Such things aren't of You. No matter what the case may be, I'll keep praying for those who have done wrong, that they may turn their hearts to You.

I think of when I've been in want. I recall so many problems I created for myself and others. Thank You for Your mercy and forgiveness. Thank You for the forgiveness I've received from those whom I have wronged.

How I praise You, Lord, for Your goodness and grace.

Oh, give thanks to the LORD, for He is good! For His mercy endures forever.
1 CHRONICLES 16:34 NKJV

THERE'S NO PROBLEM so great, no wrong so catastrophic that God's mercy isn't greater. His love has no limits; it goes beyond any measure.

Whatever situation we're in, God is waiting for us to come to His throne, His mercy seat, where we can cast all our wrongs and cares at His feet and plead for His forgiveness. When we do, He's ready to wrap us in His loving arms and whisper, "I forgive you, My child."

How grateful we can be that God's mercy endures for all time. When everything seems lost and we turn to Him for help, He does mighty wonders in our lives.

He is the One who made the heavens and the galaxies—the sun to shine by day and the moon by night. He is the One who placed the earth in space and spilled the waters upon it. And He is the same God who lovingly, mercifully, cares about us and teaches us how to be merciful to others.

Let's thank and praise Him for His great love and His mercy that endures forever.

From every stormy wind that blows, from every swelling tide of woes,
There is a calm, a sure retreat; 'tis found beneath the mercy seat.
There is a place where Jesus sheds the oil of gladness on our heads;
A place than all besides more sweet; it is the blood-bought mercy seat.

There is a scene where spirits blend,
*   where friend holds fellowship with friend;*
Though sundered far, by faith they meet around one common mercy seat.
Ah! There on eagles' wings we soar, and sin and sense seem all no more;
And heav'n comes down, our souls to greet,
*   while glory crowns the mercy seat.*
    —HUGH STOWELL

Restore to me the joy of Your salvation, and uphold me by Your generous Spirit. PSALM 51:12 NKJV

LORD, IT'S THE end of a long week. I feel drained. I've been giving of myself to others and have found little time to be alone with You. It isn't by choice, Lord. It just happened. Thank You for giving me this quiet time so we can communicate—just You and me.

I feel like a hard, dried-up sponge from having to function in these dry and weary surroundings. I'm grateful that I can come to You in prayer and soak up Your holy presence. Let the light of Your face shine upon me, dear Lord. The more I talk and listen to You, the more I feel my frustrations and weariness disappearing. The more You talk and I listen, the more I feel You filling the sponge of my thirsty soul—so full that it spills over and cleanses anything in my life that isn't pleasing to You.

As I bow before You, Lord, I'm grateful to be totally immersed in Your presence. Your love overshadows the negative things I've had to endure, and You pump new vitality into me. Thank You for showering me with an enthusiasm that will spill over on the lives of those around me. Thank You for leading me on a path that is straight and sure. How blessed it is to be filled with Your unconditional joy.

It's time to rest, Lord. As I do, I lie down and sleep in comfort and safety, knowing that You are here with me, filling me with a peace only You can give. Whispers of love and gratitude rest on my lips while Your words of comfort fill my dreams. There in my mind's eye, I see Your face smiling down on me.

When morning comes, I will be refreshed and satisfied, my soul revitalized by Your loving presence.

Now faith is the substance of things hoped for, the evidence of things not seen. HEBREWS 11:1 NKJV

HOW OFTEN HAVE you longed for a one- or two-week getaway with God during your most busy or stressful times? Unfortunately, these escapes are few and far between. Recently I experienced a different getaway with God that only lasted a few seconds, yet the brief lessons of faith and hope He taught will remain with me for a lifetime.

I was driving south on the I-5 freeway. While going that way, I usually enjoy glancing at magnificent Mt. Rainier. Viewing its dips and curves causes me to want to be hiking the trails as I've done in times past.

On this particular day, I had a lot on my mind and was praying for God to answer my prayers or give me some kind of assurance that He was already taking care of my concerns. Instead of a hike, He gave me the most amazing view of the mountain that I've ever seen. It was completely covered by what appeared to be a canopy of white. I only had a few seconds to get a good look and drive on while thanking Him for this special scene.

For the next hour or two, He brought to my mind the words from Isaiah 40:22, when He firmly told His people to trust Him with their needs: "He stretches out the heavens like a canopy, and spreads them out like a tent to live in" (NIV).

It was as though He were teaching me that in the same way He cared for thousands of people back then, He certainly had enough mercy to help with the simple requests that I'd brought before Him.

Has God blessed you with a few-second getaway that has increased your faith and hope in him? If so, perhaps He's also given you a memory that will last a lifetime.

Let Your hand become my help, for I have chosen Your precepts. Psalm 119:173 NKJV

WHAT CAN BE more challenging than raising children? The Lord's help makes a world of difference as we struggle daily to do the right things.

Susanna was a remarkable mother who lived many years ago. Times were tough in her day. She had nineteen children, but only nine lived beyond infancy. She taught them basic education, including Greek and Latin. She made music come alive. Her children learned to read poetry and music, play musical instruments, and write and compose their own music.

Some people said she was too strict, yet her immense love helped temper the times when she had to be firm with discipline. She taught her children the value of natural consequences and made them work hard to solve their problems. And although she was busy with family and household responsibilities, she spent fifteen minutes a day with each child and faithfully held each one up in prayer. Susanna retained love and respect from her family, and she expected the best from them, even into adulthood. She encouraged them to make serving God the center of their lives—their very purpose for being.

I wonder if Susanna Wesley knew that God was helping her mold the lives of her sons John and Charles and her grandson Samuel S. Wesley into great Christian leaders. The wisdom and love she gave multiplied through her offspring's outstanding sermons, poetry, and hymns that still inspire us today.

Susanna Wesley may inspire us to set new goals, but we don't need to "measure up" to her. We can simply be ourselves and know that God graciously understands and helps. He knows our strengths and weakness and stays close to us, helping every day.

My help comes from the LORD, who made heaven and earth. PSALM 121:2 RSV

IT WOULD BE easy to think of Susanna Wesley as someone who must have been constantly inspired and driven by God—a mother who held all the wisdom from the Bible in her mind, heart, and soul. More than likely, however, she suffered the same insecurities and struggles as all of us. I wonder how many times she poured out her mixed feelings, concerns, and burdens to her heavenly Father in the same way we do today.

It's a comfort to me that Susanna wasn't perfect. When she wasn't at her best, God was there with her—graciously, patiently correcting her errors and helping to make things right.

There's something more valuable than being the "perfect mother." It is constantly asking our merciful Lord to create and recreate a pure heart within us so we can pass a sincere, unselfish love on to our priceless kids. When we fall short, His grace helps bridge our gaps. Praise be to Him for doing so.

Thank You for my children, Lord. They are my most precious gifts from You. I look at them and see how they reflect different family members with their hair, eyes, dimples, and smiles. I pray they will have Your eyes and learn the miraculous wonders of Your ways.

Help me teach my children the lessons in Your Word. Remind me to talk about Your Scriptures in our home. May this become a way of life for them. Throughout their days, I pray that my children and grandchildren will apply your lessons to decisions they make.

Thank You, Lord, for Your grace and forgiveness. Thank You for Your love and Your guidance. Use our family, I pray, to bring honor to You.

Not unto us, O LORD, not unto us, but to Your name give glory, because of Your mercy, because of Your truth. PSALM 115:1 NKJV

ONE OF THE most rewarding experiences in our lives might be when we give up something we want for ourselves in order to help someone else.

Today, I flip through a worn devotional Bible I received from my secret pal, Marvelene. She must have overheard my putting it on my "wish list." Although it cost more than the limit suggested for secret-pal gifts, Marvelene decided to fulfill my wish. It's still my favorite Bible. Its margins are filled with my dated prayer requests, promises, and answers to prayer. Through the years, I've written thoughts to remember in the front and back flyleafs. I still use these reminders during speaking engagements and in the books I write. I'll never forget the kindness of this sister's heart.

In Luke 21, there is a poor widow who gave from the depths of her soul. Maybe she hoped the rich people around her wouldn't notice how she put two very small copper coins into the temple treasury. The offering wasn't much, but it was all she had. And she wanted to give it to God.

Apparently no one paid attention to her. If they had, she may have been looked down upon. But Jesus diverted His attention from the rich people parading their extravagant gifts and saw the woman's unselfish act.

Everyone around Jesus must have heard Him honor the widow when He said, "This poor widow has put in more than all the others. All these people gave their gifts out of their wealth; but she out of her poverty put in all she had to live on" (Luke 21:3–4 NIV).

At times we may feel badly because we have little to give. But when we do our best, our meager offering often becomes much when God blesses it.

As the purse is emptied, the heart is filled. —VICTOR HUGO

Be beautiful inside, in your hearts, with the lasting charm of a gentle and quiet spirit which is so precious to God. I PETER 3:4 TLB

HOW DO YOU feel about growing older? Some people are concerned when another "zero" in their ages turns up. Others even become depressed as though life is passing them by. However, it doesn't have to be that way.

Let's consider being less interested regarding our age in life and being more interested about our outlook toward life. I love what Proverbs says about growing older:

❧ "She is a woman of strength and dignity, and has no fear of old age" (Proverbs 31:25 TLB). Proverbs 31:25 NIV says it this way: "She is clothed with strength and dignity; she can laugh at the days to come."

❧ "Charm is deceitful and beauty is passing, but a woman who fears the LORD, she shall be praised" (Proverbs 31:30 NKJV).

❧ "A cheerful look brings joy to the heart, and good news gives health to the bones" (Proverbs 15:30 NIV).

❧ "The silver-haired head is a crown of glory, if it is found in the way of righteousness (Proverbs 16:31 NKJV).

As we turn the next corner in celebration of our birth, we may begin to see signs of age. But God is in no way finished with us yet as long as we're here on this earth.

I have a treasured friend named Jeanne. She's about to turn eighty-eight years old. She teaches a senior Sunday school class and still does some guest speaking at different churches. I'm amazed at how her enthusiasm for life is absolutely contagious. I laughingly tell her that I want to be like her when I grow up.

No matter our abilities or ages, let's keep on being a blessing for the Lord, making our days count for Him!

Two Mothers, One Prayer

[Jesus said,] "For where two or three are gathered in my name, there am I in the midst of them."
MATTHEW 18:20 RSV

DURING THE PRECARIOUS years of raising teenagers, many parents discover that their greatest help is prayer. More powerful is uniting in prayer with a friend and confidante. Laverne, her husband John, and her friend Jennifer did this and saw miracles happen.

Laverne and John's fifteen-year-old daughter Chelsie had disappeared. Laverne and John tapped every resource they could think of to locate Chelsie. Friends and family prayed, especially her friend Jennifer.

Exhausted, Laverne prayed fervently. "Father," she sobbed, "I've pleaded constantly for help. I still haven't received an answer. *Please* hear our prayers."

More tears spilled. She remembered her recent talk with Jennifer. Jennifer's son Adam had disappeared four years earlier at age eighteen. Jennifer had said: "A prayer pact is formed between us, Laverne, so don't fear. God knows the needs of both of our kids. Let's trust and thank Him daily for answers and help to come."

Then Laverne began praising God for listening to her prayers and Jennifer's. Peace filled Laverne's heart, and her faith grew stronger.

Whenever Laverne felt anxious, she gave her daughter to God. She quoted promises from the Bible of God's care, and she praised Him for His gracious love.

One evening the phone rang. A timid voice came over the line. Chelsie wanted to come home. Laverne and John's friends and family were thankful for her safe return—she'd been missing for several months. Next Laverne and Jennifer trusted God in finding Adam.

When life seems out of control and we feel helpless about our problems, we can remember that God is greater than whatever we're going through. There's no limit to where He goes and what He accomplishes. What we *can* do is wait and pray and trust.

The beginning of anxiety is the end of faith, and the beginning of true faith is the end of anxiety.
—GEORGE MÜLLER

The earnest prayer of a righteous man has great power and wonderful results. JAMES 5:16 TLB

WAITING FOR ANSWERS to prayer is difficult. Uncertainties can be excruciating. But when our hearts are filled with anguish and we can't see God's hand at work, we can still be confident in His gracious care. The more we must wait, the more we need to trust Him.

Adam had been a model child. But in his senior year, he began drinking, slipped into alcoholism, and disappeared. After four years, Adam ended up on the streets of Los Angeles. Alcohol and drugs had consumed him. His six-foot-three frame had dwindled to skin draped over bones. Each day he became weaker, sleeping wherever he could. People stepped around him, fearful of getting involved. In time, Adam could barely move or breathe.

Far away, Adam's mother, Jennifer, and Chelsie's mother, Laverne, prayed more than ever. One day, Mark, a dedicated street minister, spotted Adam huddled and shaking in an unused doorway. God spoke to Mark's heart. The minister gathered the foul-smelling, dying young man in his strong arms and carried him to a nearby mission.

The identification Adam carried provided Jennifer's phone number. She was called immediately, informed of her son's location, and told he might be dying. Mother and son were reunited in a Los Angeles hospital.

Eventually, Adam successfully completed a drug and alcohol treatment program with much prayer backing him up, and he returned home. He's employed at a part-time job and helps his mother with expenses and home maintenance.

God goes where we can't go. He speaks to hearts when our voices can't be heard. Keep believing! He sees the whole picture, and His grace never fails.

Prayer moves the hand that moves the world.
—E. M. BOUNDS

He who has mercy on the poor, happy is he. PROVERBS 14:21 NKJV

SOME OF US spent childhood without our natural parents. Some were adopted; others were shuffled from place to place. Others lost parents early to death. Can good things come from these childhood experiences? Yes. Many times blessings come from the gracious, loving hand of God.

Life wasn't always easy when Virginia was a little girl. For unknown reasons, her parents were unable to care for her. Fortunately, her aunt and uncle adopted Virginia and her brother. The Christian couple watched over the kids and loved them like their own. They took them to church regularly and taught them about the love of God.

When Virginia grew up and married, *she* passed on the mercy and graciousness shown to her by taking in children and loving them like her own. She also took in the disabled and bedridden elderly. Her door was always open. Extra plates were often set at her welcoming table. For years, she passed on the blessings she'd received during her own childhood. Through her words and actions, Virginia shared the love and mercy of God.

Through His all-knowing, precise purpose, God weaves His mercies through generations like colorful threads in a tapestry. He places the well-planned strands in the hands of another person and weaves His endless threads in and out of the lives of someone new. He uses many of us to pass on His kindness and care.

Through the methodical motions of His Holy Spirit, we can look for His kindheartedness to carry on this beautiful tapestry of love through future generations. Someday in heaven, the embroidery of God's loving mercies that have interlaced our lives will come to full view. How big and magnificent they will be!

He is the Head of the body made up of his people—that is, his church—which He began; and he is the Leader.... COLOSSIANS 1:18 TLB

THE BEST THING that happens in our lives is when we invite Jesus to become our Savior. When we ask Him to forgive our wrongs and come into our hearts, He removes each sin—no matter how large or small. We become one of His children. We become part of His family—the kingdom of God.

When I was eighteen, someone showed me how to give Jesus first place in my life. After I invited Him into my heart, I was awestruck at how He lifted the burdens of sin and confusion. In their place, He gave me joy, freedom of heart, and enthusiasm for life.

Becoming a Christian was only the beginning. My friend introduced me to other Christian friends. They showed me how to read my Bible, starting with the book of John. They were there to help and encourage me. I discovered a partnership with Jesus, my best Friend. He began revealing the plans He had in store for me.

God's love and mercy toward us are everlasting. He wants us to open our hearts and invite Him in.

YOUR KINGDOM
How dear Your kingdom, Father, that dwells within my heart.
Your love and grace go with me; each morning's a new start.
How dear Your family, Father, who love and care and give.
They pray for me and help. We laugh and love and live.
My smiles and tears You welcome, You take each as Your own.
And lift them up to heaven, to God's eternal throne.

...For I know whom I have believed and am persuaded that He is able to keep what [and whom] I have committed to Him until that Day. 2 TIMOTHY 1:12 NKJV

IF YOU ARE praying for a loved one who is battling against the things of the Lord, take heart. The Lord can go places that you cannot. His Spirit can speak directly to the heart, where your voice can't be heard. While drawing from the chambers of life lessons learned, the Lord keeps whispering into the depths of your loved one's soul. He places angels of protection around him or her. He promises to watch over your dear one by day and nestle him or her close at night.

Believe in the one you care about. Trust the One who surrounds and loves and keeps us in His loving arms. He will never, ever let go. No matter how far or how long this loved one strays, you can be sure of God's faithful hand being there, gently, firmly drawing the lost back to a marvelous reunion with Him.

When your dear one turns to the Lord, remember to forgive and love and rejoice.

SHEPHERD MY LOVED ONE

Shepherd my loved one with faithfulness, Lord, while the apron strings
    are breaking.
Stay close to my loved one with enduring love when life's teachings are
    cast aside.
Be near to my loved one and grant comfort while life is lonely and lost.
Protect my loved one with Your mighty power when sin and dangers lurk.
Hold onto my loved one with perseverance while we watch and wait.
Bring back my loved one with Your mercy from temptation's
    regret and blame.
Rejoice with my loved one and give grace as he enters Your sure, strong fold.
Let me embrace my loved one with forgiveness and whisper,
    "Welcome home."

And the LORD will guide you continually, and satisfy your desire with good things, and make your bones strong; and you shall be like a watered garden, like a spring of water, whose waters fail not.
ISAIAH 58:11 RSV

TO ME, THERE'S nothing more discouraging than comparing myself to someone else. Do you ever feel that way? If you're a mother, do you sometimes shake your head in despair while watching the "perfect mothers" juggle households, jobs, and church responsibilities?

My friend Diane seemed like one of those perfect moms. I often wondered how she mastered this remarkable art of motherhood—until she invited me over for tea.

The day was nice, so the kids could play outside. I could barely blink back the tears when she asked me how I was able to do such a great job as a mom.

We shared our needs and prayed together, forming a pact to remain close and keep each other in prayer.

God answered one of my prayers that day. He taught me that all I had to do was to be myself.

🐌

Father, no matter how hard I try to meet the needs of our busy family, I'm rarely able to get everything done. When I see the bumper stickers on cars that say "SuperMom," I cringe. How can I ever measure up to these daily challenges and expectations?

Show me mercy, Lord. Please bridge my gaps. When things get frustrating, keep my attitude in check and my motives pure. And help me to always maintain my sense of humor!

Give me the wisdom to do only the things You want me to do and to never be afraid to say no. Remind me to ask for help and to be quick to express my appreciation.

Help me take a deep breath and relax during the chaos. Thank You for understanding. Thank You for replacing my stress with confidence and a joyful heart.

It is good to be near God. I have made the Sovereign LORD my refuge. PSALM 73:28 NIV

WHEN WE WERE children, we very likely had a place where we could curl up and find tranquility and comfort when we needed it. It may have been in our mothers' arms, our own beds, or a private nook—or it may have come in a form of a hug, our "blankies," pacifiers, fingers, or thumbs.

These were all comforting. Yet we can find a solace in the presence of God that's far more calming and secure than anything or anyone else. It's under the wings of Jesus, close to His tender, loving heart, that nothing and no one can come between the never-failing refuge we get to enjoy through Him.

The Bible says we are the apples of His eye. What a privilege it is to offer the prayer in Psalm 17:8: "Keep me as the apple of your eye; hide me under the shadow of your wings" (NIV).

He loves us with an everlasting love; He has hopes and dreams for us. At times, He shares with us His dreams, preparing us for what He has available in our futures. In turn, we can share our hopes with Him and appreciate His guiding us through the years. "He fulfills the desires of those who fear him" (Psalm 145:19 NIV).

Isn't it encouraging to know that we can draw near to the heart of God any time, day or night? During those sacred moments we're together, we may think of His faithful promise in Psalm 145:18: "The LORD is near to all who call on him" (NIV).

Oh, turn to me, and have mercy on me! Give Your strength to Your servant.... Show me a sign for good.... You, LORD, have helped me and comforted me. PSALM 86:16–17 NKJV

THERE'S AN OLD Christian song that says, "Precious memories, how they linger. How they ever flood my soul." I never thought much about this song until after I grew up. Some of our memories are precious and flood our souls with warmth and joy. Yet others that are unpleasant, heartbreaking, and possibly terrifying can flood our beings like raging, engulfing rivers.

What can we possibly do with these memories? We can hold onto the good ones, but unfortunately we aren't able to block the bad ones from our minds. We can't go back and change things. The best choice is to keep bringing them to the feet of Jesus and ask for understanding, comfort, and healing.

Our friend, Goldie, was very dear to us while she was here on this earth. Goldie was a good listener and a wonderful prayer warrior. As a young mother, I seldom had time to mend things. Goldie graciously helped me, often doing it for me. She made beautiful quilts for everyone in our family. All but one has been worn to threads. I keep the final one tucked away for special occasions.

I wondered why Goldie mixed the dark and light pieces together in her quilts. She said they were part of the memories taken from old family members' and friends' clothing. She sewed the pieces together with bright embroidery thread. I imagine there were a lot of prayers mixed in with the thread that represented the love of the Lord.

God wants to stitch our good and bad memories together with His blessings of forgiveness, comfort, and healing. Don't be afraid to hand Him the thread and listen to Him lovingly say, "I'll mend this for you."

"In repentance and rest is your salvation, in quietness and trust is your strength...."
ISAIAH 30:15 NIV

BEING ABLE TO feel self-confident is important to most of us. We usually experience our share of mistakes and learn to take them in stride; some bungles can be uproariously funny. Yet when we or someone else commits a series of blunders, humor may turn to frustration, pain, and possibly insecurity.

Lack of confidence is no respecter of persons. It can strike because of how we perceive our appearance, go through illness, experience grief, or feel debilitating failure. Even the talented and successful suffer. Some feel discouraged when returning from college or the armed forces. I struggled with insecurity after quitting a second job of over ten years.

Instead of peace and contentment, insecurity can turn our lives topsy-turvy. We wonder how we fit in with others. The more we're pressed to measure up to expectations, the more our frustrations grow. We feel less productive. We might become clumsy, dropping things, or stammering for words in public. Perhaps we even avoid people who are dear to us. We might think that if we can't be at our best then we don't want to be around anyone. The more we suffer, the worse it gets. Yet our Lord and our loved ones can help us experience victory.

When we can't get past our lack of confidence, God understands what we're going through. He loves us right where we are. In the midst of our struggles, let's remember this: we aren't failing God when we're doing our best. He loves us. He is constantly near, encouraging and comforting us during these difficult times. No matter how great our problems are, our caring, merciful Lord is greater. As we turn to Him for help, He will guide us, and His victorious power and love can bring us through.

In him and through faith in him we may approach God with freedom and confidence.
EPHESIANS 3:12 NIV

WHEN WE'RE SUCCESSFUL with our endeavors, our confidence builds; yet when challenges overwhelm us, we can trust in God for His strength and direction. He's always greater than the mountainous insecurities we face. With His help, we can learn to confront a giant lack of self-esteem head-on. Trying to bolster ourselves and use the "thumbs-up" philosophy might not be enough. Often, change has to come from within.

God doesn't want us to suffer. Instead, let's pray for His help and for encouraging words from those whom we trust and love; search the Scriptures; and glean advice from uplifting Christian books.

When we feel fragile, let's shove negative thoughts from our minds and replace them with positive promises from God's Word (see Psalm 139:14).

During my struggles with insecurity, God answered my prayers in astounding ways. Those who understood eased up on pushing me so hard. Encouraging words bolstered my spirits. Best of all, I felt God's assurance.

The more we accept His love, the more we'll feel we can be a blessing for Him. He mends our frayed emotions and renews our way of thinking to an "I can" attitude. Whenever an inkling of insecurity strikes, let's pull up a Scripture from our mental log. We can tell ourselves we know we're not perfect, but with God's help we can do what He wants us to do through Him. He graciously gives us the courage and strength we need.

No matter what's going on in our lives, we need not be afraid of bungling. If we try and fail, at least we've done something. To keep on trying is to succeed.

God helps us say, "I can!" He fits us in His plan.

A soft answer turns away wrath, but a harsh word stirs up anger. PROVERBS 15:1 NKJV

LORD, I BLEW it—again. A person I care about made an insensitive remark toward me and before I knew it, I shot back an unkind comment. Soon we both spoke harshly and began yelling at each other.

I feel sick at heart, Lord. I don't know what to do. Now this person is upset and doesn't want to talk. Surely I should have been able to state my point of view...but that wasn't happening. In frustration, I stomped off.

Now that we've made a mess of things and have hurt each other, the best thing I can think of is to come to You in earnest prayer. Please help us, Lord. Perhaps I need to respect this person's feelings in wanting some space. Now we can take some time to think—and pray. I seek Your direction, Lord.

"If you are angry, don't sin by nursing your grudge. Don't let the sun go down with you still angry—get over it quickly; for when you are angry, you give a mighty foothold to the devil" (Ephesians 4:26–27 TLB). "Pray without ceasing" (1 Thessalonians 5:17 KJV).

Lord, help me to not hold a grudge. Instead, I will keep praying until a solution comes.

"The LORD is gracious and compassionate, slow to anger and rich in love...good to all; he has compassion on all he has made" (Psalm 145:8–9 NIV).

Help me to shed this defensive attitude of mine and to be willing to understand how this other person feels.

"Love...will hardly even notice when others do it wrong" (1 Corinthians 13:5 TLB).

As we have done before, help us to pray together before we talk. Thank You already for helping us to forgive and keep on loving.

Be kind to one another, tenderhearted, forgiving one another, as God in Christ forgave you.
Ephesians 4:32 RSV

GOD HELPS US to forgive others for what they have done to us. But it's often more difficult to accept forgiveness from someone we've hurt—or to forgive ourselves.

A story in *Gems of Truth and Beauty* tells about Dwight Moody and his family—and the miracle of forgiveness. His oldest brother rebelled and left home, with their mother longing for her son's return. The mother watched and prayed each night for months but never heard a word.

Dwight's brother finally made his way home. He was afraid of facing his mother after being gone so long, with his long, unkempt hair and dirty clothes. He climbed up a hillside and saw his mother through the window. She looked so sad. How could she forgive him?

Tears flowed down his cheeks when his mother noticed him through the window. At once she hurried to the door. The son ran to the house and stopped. He hung his head, barely meeting his mother's gaze.

The son stammered as he apologized for the way he left. He said he would never enter the house until she forgave him. Arms flew around him and mother and son wept on each other's shoulders.

What if the son hadn't accepted forgiveness that day? It took courage to confess his wrong actions and beg for mercy. Instead, a family was united through humility, forgiveness, and love.

God wants to forgive us of our wrongdoings. Without hesitation, He loves us even when we're worn to nothing and our hearts are torn from needless, wasted inroads of time. But when we acknowledge to Him that we've done wrong and then ask for and accept His forgiveness, we are united with the wondrous family of God.

May your unfailing love rest upon us, O LORD, even as we put our hope in you. PSALM 33:22 NIV

PERHAPS YOU'RE FAMILIAR with the poem by Myra Welch called "The Touch of the Master's Hand." It describes a battered violin up for auction. No one wanted it until a gray-haired man stepped forward. He picked it up, dusted it off, tightened its strings, and played a melody sweet and clear. The difference was the master's touch—much like the Master's touch in our lives.

Similar to that violin, a girl named Carolyn was beaten and neglected as a child. She had been told she was worthless. One day a Sunday school teacher led Carolyn to accept Jesus as her Savior, and from then on, she felt Him near all the time.

As an adult, she learned through Scriptures and prayer how to let go of her past and accept His healing. She soon realized she was a priceless treasure to Him. In time, Carolyn learned to forgive and move forward.

Still, she wondered what good could come from her tragic childhood until she taught a group of Sunday school children who really needed her help. Every child faced brokenness in one form or another. Some suffered abuse and neglect no one could prevent.

Carolyn could empathize. The Lord gave her the courage to tell them how she had experienced similar circumstances. They started sharing their problems and praying together for help and protection. Each Sunday, she taught them Scriptures of hope and assured them that they would make it through. God answered their prayers and continues to provide faith and direction each day.

What good came from such tragedy in Carolyn's life? The Lord took her heartache and gave hope to children who desperately needed to know that they were treasured by Him.

But those who hope in the LORD will renew their strength. They will soar on wings like eagles; they will run and not grow weary, they will walk and not be faint. ISAIAH 40:31 NIV

FATHER, AGAIN I come to You asking for comfort and hope for the future. Memories of my tortured past flood my mind and cause me to think I must not be good enough to have ever deserved better. Please help me to change my focus, Lord. I had been convinced for so long that I was of little worth to anyone. I know this isn't the right way to feel, but all the past experiences of horrible heartache and failure are difficult to shake.

Receive my feelings of anguish and despair, dear Father, and change them to a complete hope and trust in You. Lift this burden I bear and replace it with a newly found freedom that can only come from You. Release me from my childhood terrors. Nestle me in Your wings.

Help me to forgive and to let go of the past. I place it all in Your capable hands. Thank You for Your comfort and love and for showing me how much You really treasure me. For in You alone can I find Your consolation and indescribable peace.

What good can come from a past such as mine, Father? Is there a way You can use it to help others and glorify You? Take my life. Direct my path as I place my future in Your hands. I give You all the praise.

BRING HIM EVERY HEARTACHE
If you have ever suffered, just listen to His voice.
Bring Him every heartache. You need to make this choice.
O think of how He's with you. Just trust His love and care.
O see how He will help you. He always answers prayer.
Bring Him every heartache, and you will surely see,
Each one of them He'll take—and set your spirit free!

I guide you in the way of wisdom and lead you along straight paths. PROVERBS 4:11 NIV

WHATEVER OUR SITUATION in life, we may feel as if we're following a map in order to stay on the path God has set before us.

Being a single parent of three sons, Ann's life was usually hectic. Her oldest son, Jeff, was a Boy Scout patrol leader and had a part-time job. After work one weekend, Jeff was to join the scouts for a camping trip in the woods. Ann agreed to drive him to the unfamiliar campsite. Jeff gave good directions, but Ann still had to find her way home. Jeff led the way up a dark, narrow trail to the scouts' campsite. Along the way, Ann tried to memorize every turn so she could return safely to her car with her flashlight.

When they arrived at Jeff's patrol tent, everyone else was asleep. Ann hugged her son good-bye, prayed for guidance, then backtracked to the exact spot that led to the trail. While firmly gripping her flashlight, Ann thanked God for getting her that far. Down the dark, steep trail she fearfully walked, hoping she wouldn't misstep and fall. Suddenly, the moonlight broke through the clouds. It was so bright that Ann no longer needed her flashlight. The thought struck her that she was "walking in the light." Its meaning soon grew deeper than walking in the moonlight. She felt as if she were wrapped in a warm, fuzzy blanket of God's grace and protection as she practically floated down the hill and back to her car. From there, she easily found her way back home.

Whether you are a young adult finding your way, a parent searching for wisdom, a senior adult asking to be used for God, or an elderly person experiencing the power of prayer, He faithfully makes clear the way.

Walk in the light! Thy path shall be a path, though thorny, bright! For God, by grace, shall dwell in thee, and God Himself is light. Amen.
—BERNARD BARTON

God's Perfect Gifts

Every good and perfect gift is from above, coming down from the Father of the heavenly lights, who does not change like shifting shadows. JAMES 1:17 NIV

THINK OF THE most treasured gift you have ever received. Was it a new car? A precious heirloom? A valuable piece of jewelry?

A friend of mine received a beautiful ruby-filled fortieth wedding anniversary ring from her husband. She loved it and wore it all the time. One day, she slipped on her gardening gloves and did a little work in her backyard. But at the end of the day, she was saddened to discover that a center prong on her ring was bent—and one lovely ruby was missing. No amount of searching found the valuable stone. It was a priceless gift but an imperfect one.

Even more precious than the lost ruby and the love it represents are the priceless gifts of eternal love and grace that God showers upon each of us every day. They are perfect and certain. His gracious blessings neither change nor shift. They are forever and sure from the One who loves us most.

God also blesses us with "everyday" gifts, like a rainstorm after a long dry spell or a gorgeous rainbow filling the sky, reminding us of His merciful, unfailing love.

Other gifts come in the form of His help for each day and the hope He gives for tomorrow. During the hurry-scurry, turmoil and chaos, and stressful situations we're often forced to face, He quietly speaks to our hearts and showers us with peace—similar to the rainstorm that comes after a dry spell.

All we need to do each day is purposely look for the gifts He freely sends our way. We can thank and praise Him for all His wonderful acts and, in return, bring glory and honor to His Name. We can be grateful for the daily strength He gives us as we seek His face and direction.

May the love and favor of the Lord Jesus Christ rest upon you. I CORINTHIANS 16:23 TLB

GOD GRACIOUSLY SHOWERS our families with love and causes them to grow in most unusual ways. Love in our family grew stronger when a tiny kitten named Orange entered our lives.

One afternoon, two of our sons, David and Jonathan, had just arrived home from school. David quickly completed his chores and went outside to play. I started dinner while Jonathan finished his homework at the table.

Suddenly, David burst through the door. "Mom, I really need your help out front." I turned off the stove and followed him outside, with Jonathan on my heels.

Neighborhood kids clustered on the grass around the tiniest orange kitten I'd ever seen away from its mother. Its miniature face was covered with blood, and the poor kitten shivered uncontrollably.

David explained. "Some big black cat beat it up."

"Does it belong to anyone?" I asked. Of course, the answer was, "No."

We gathered up the kitten and took it inside. First, we prayed. Then Jonathan wrapped the shivering ball of fur in a towel and settled into our rocking chair. David knelt beside him, offering warm milk from his fingertip. The kitten kept trembling and didn't respond. What if he didn't accept our love?

As I cooked dinner, my heart was warmed from the kindhearted efforts put forth by our sons. Jonathan snuggled it close to his chest, rocking and singing softly. Finally, after two hours of continuous TLC, the kitten stopped shivering and gingerly lapped milk from David's finger.

Little did we know what lessons God was going to teach us about love through that kitten.

Even the smallest act of love expands to fill the heart and open new doors.

Be completely humble and gentle; be patient, bearing with one another in love. EPHESIANS 4:32 NIV

I NEVER STOPPED to think about what God was trying to teach us while we were opening our hearts and home to the little kitten we had rescued.

Finally, the kitten was out of mortal danger and healing was beginning. Pleas to keep him were met with the words, "Only until we can find another home."

It took a lot of love from the whole family and plenty of care to nurse the little orange fluffball back to health, but we succeeded. None of us was able, of course, to find it another home. Orange, the kitten would be called. That's how big it was—the size of a fluffy little orange. It gradually won the affection of everyone in our family, including my husband, Bob.

Orange taught our family what compassion and tireless devotion were all about. We were beginning to realize that love came in two parts: to graciously give love, and to graciously receive love. The only way that kitten could have survived was by recognizing the help being given by two caring boys—and being willing to accept and trust their love. Best of all was the pleasure Orange gave us as a part of our family.

God has far more love for you and me than what we were capable of giving Orange. Isn't it great how the Lord cares about us as He offers His merciful love and protection! The only way we can benefit, though, is to recognize and accept His love personally.

God's love is faithful. He remains with us day and night. Through good times and bad, He never leaves us. No matter where we are, we can turn to Him with our concerns and care. His love has no limit—a love we only need to receive.

Jesus answered, "I am the way and the truth and the life. No one comes to the Father except through me." JOHN 14:6 NIV

WHAT WILL IT be like when we get to enter the gates of heaven? Will going to heaven be a simple thing?

My friend LeeAnn thought that going to heaven would be as automatic as entering this world as a newborn baby. She was a good person. She believed that God was someone she could pray to occasionally. Certainly He was kind and loving enough to allow her to enter heaven's gates.

Then LeeAnn started attending a church that told her about Jesus. She learned through the Bible that it was necessary for her to confess her sins to Jesus, ask for His forgiveness, invite Him into her heart, and give Him first place in her life.

LeeAnn knew that neither sin nor anyone living a sinful life would be allowed to enter heaven. She was grateful that Jesus helped her accept Him as her Savior.

Sometime later, LeeAnn's mother, Ruby, became gravely ill. Ruby also felt she would automatically go to heaven. The thought of her mother possibly spending eternity separated from the Lord grieved LeeAnn.

One day while visiting Ruby in the hospital, LeeAnn explained to her mother how to ask Jesus into her heart. How the angels must have rejoiced along with LeeAnn when Ruby prayed and became a Christian. Now LeeAnn and her mother knew Ruby's final home would be in heaven with Him. Soon after, Ruby left this earthly home and joined her Father in heaven.

Do you know Jesus as your Savior? If you aren't sure, ask Him to enter your heart. If you do know Him, encourage others to accept Him. The Savior is waiting. He's already preparing a home in heaven for those who belong to Him.

You Matter Most

"Then you will call upon Me and come and pray to Me, and I will listen to you. You will seek Me and find Me when you search for Me with all your heart." JEREMIAH 29:12–13 NASB

LORD, I COME to You seeking Your presence. Right now my mind is racing in all directions. The concerns I'm dealing with heap around me like a gigantic mountain. Details and what-ifs press in on every side to the point where I can't even focus. Everything seems to be out of control. I'm hurt and frustrated because of stress and the ill treatment of others. All my efforts are futile.

Little things have become major, Lord. Petty remarks and attitudes circulate like irritating insects. They drive me to complete distraction! When I try to pray, I can't feel Your presence. It's almost like my prayers aren't going any higher than the ceiling.

How I miss Your nearness, Lord. I long for our time together. How long must I have to wrestle with my thoughts? I know it isn't Your will for it to get the better of me. I need You.

What matters most is You, dear Lord. Though I can't feel Your presence, I trust that You are near. Rather than focusing on my problems, I will center my thoughts on You. I am so grateful that You love me all of the time. I praise You for Your marvelous deeds and the purposeful work of Your hands. How profound are Your all-encompassing thoughts. You help me put things into perspective.

The things bothering me are starting to fade. Please forgive my shortsighted attitude, and help me to forgive others who are involved. Instead, I will think about You. Thank You for Your presence, and for giving me peace of mind. Thank You for helping me to see things from Your point of view.

I really love You, Lord. Remind me to stay near to You throughout this day so I can bring glory and honor to You.

Let us run with perseverance, [patience, and endurance] the race marked out for us. Let us fix our eyes on Jesus, the author and perfecter of our faith.... HEBREWS 12:1–2 NIV

ISN'T IT EXCITING how the Lord puts us in positions to make differences in the lives of those around us? It's like running a race. As we prepare, He teaches us through His Word how to hold onto things that are beneficial and helpful to us and others and get rid of unnecessary ones that can entangle or bog us down. The Lord knows what's best for us. As He patiently leads, we learn to put His lessons into practice. Before long, we're amazed at how much better we're doing. Soon we step up to the starting line. We concentrate completely on Him and are now ready ourselves to run the race He sets before us.

Sometimes it's scary, and we pray for faith. Other times we grow weary and begin to lose heart. In the midst of it all, we must not lose sight of our first love, Jesus Christ. He sees the whole picture and guides us through. No matter the challenges, we need to keep looking to Jesus, who is running right alongside us, every step of the way. When the race gets rough, He's still there. When we feel weak, He provides us with the strength we need for that moment.

We can read in Romans 5:3–5 that when we face hardships, our sufferings generate patience, endurance, and perseverance. Then perseverance produces character and hope. In turn, hope won't disappoint us, because the Holy Spirit places love and hope within us in order for us to keep running the race for Him. The more we persevere in the calling He gives us, the more we amazingly mature and become complete in Him.

Keep holding the hand of Jesus, dear one. Keep focusing on Him. Keep on running the race! And make a difference for others each day.

Listen, my son [and daughter], and be wise, and keep your heart on the right path.
PROVERBS 23:19 NIV

LORD, RIGHT NOW I'm going through difficult times. I feel completely pressed down from stress and concerns. It seems as though I'm handling each problem as it comes along, but months of dealing with these trials are taxing my strength. Nothing in life appears to be going right. Please lift me out of the pit of despair that I'm slipping into. Pull me from this emotional bog.

Steady my feet, Lord. Plant them on Your sure, solid path. Help me to take life one step at a time. Watch over my heart, I pray. Keep my mind fixed on Your loving compassion. Help my eyes to look straight ahead. Watch over my pathway in order that all my behavior will be sound and upright. Grant Your wisdom to enter my heart. Teach me how to use discretion and understanding. Replace my anxiety and depression with Your advice and knowledge. May a peace that comes from You fill my soul.

I place my confidence in You, Lord, and trust You to buffer and handle each challenge that arises. You are my Rescuer. You are my Advisor. You, Lord, are my Strength. Your Word promises me that as I trust You to watch over my heart, You will bring forth energizing springs of life. Thank You, Lord, for the glorious things You do for me. In my distress I called upon You, and You heard my voice. Thank You for how I can rely on Your help and direction rather than negative circumstances around me. In You I put my trust. I stand before You in amazement of Your wonderful ways. You have put a song of victory and adoration in my heart, Lord, because of all You do for me. Thank You for steadying my feet and placing them upon Your path.

If you do these things, God will shed his own glorious light upon you. He will heal you; your godliness will lead you forward, and goodness will be a shield before you, and the glory of the Lord will protect you from behind. ISAIAH 58:8 TLB

FATHER, I'M AMAZED at how You work in such strange ways. Here I was, going full-steam ahead with my busy schedule and all my responsibilities. Everything was going great, and I was making good progress. Then this happened.

I glanced up from my paperwork and noticed my coworker standing near my desk just looking at me, nervously shuffling from one foot to the other. He completely rattled my train of thought, Lord! I recalled the cruel things he's often said about me behind my back. And I cringed and wanted to glare at him or hint that I was busy and didn't have time to talk.

Somehow You managed to penetrate the hurt and anger within me and helped me to see his needs. As You always remind me, I flipped on the switch and tuned in to Your Holy Spirit. Thank You for urging me to offer him a cold soda and a chair. Thank You for graciously guiding and directing me to set my mixed feelings aside, to put my mountain of work on hold, and to just listen to him. I hope he saw You in my life in spite of my faults.

Although I've been praying for him for a long time, I was surprised that he came to me. Forgive me, I pray, for when I've reacted badly. No matter if he doesn't say he's sorry or if he still goes away and talks ill of me, help me to be gracious enough to reflect You in my life. Let Your light shine through me. Help my coworker to want to ask about You. Help me to not get in the way of Your persistently speaking to his heart. In Jesus' name, amen.

And my God shall supply all your need according to His riches in glory by Christ Jesus.
PHILIPPIANS 4:19 NKJV

OFTEN, WE DON'T think much about our showing acts of kindness to others. Yet when one is shown to us, we realize how special it is to be on the receiving end. It could be thoughtful deeds we know will happen or some that unexpectedly come our way. Some kindnesses are surprisingly given by strangers; several may take place by circumstance. However, others are direct answers to our prayers.

Sylvia lived in her trailer-park home at the edge of town for many years. When something needed to be fixed, she usually solved the problem herself—but one day her phone went dead. Obviously, she couldn't fix it.

She contacted the phone company, asking for help. When a repairman checked her phone, he discovered that the lines running under the trailer were rusting out. Regrettably, the repairman's boss wouldn't allow him to crawl under the trailer.

When Sylvia heard the news, she was very gracious and thanked the repairman for his time. Still, she knew this was a serious matter. She lived alone, had health problems, and needed her phone. Since Sylvia is a Christian, she brought her need to the Lord in prayer and had complete faith in Him to provide.

To Sylvia's surprise, the repairman showed up on her doorstep early the next morning. After talking with his boss, the repairman had received permission to do the job on his own time, and he solved the problem. Sylvia was overwhelmed with gratitude that a stranger would go to so much trouble to help her. Certainly, God used this kind man as an answer to her faith-filled prayer.

You hear, O LORD, the desire of the afflicted; you encourage them, and you listen to their cry.
PSALM 10:17 NIV

MANY OF US have gone through times of loneliness for one reason or another. In spite of her loneliness, the widowed mother of a friend of mine did something special that changed her life and the lives of others.

After Shirley's husband died, she felt crushed. Shirley loved her grown children, but she needed friends too. Now that she was retired from teaching, what would she do? She asked God to give her direction and fill the gap.

One afternoon, Shirley checked her mail. Along with the bills and junk mail, in the stack was a letter from Miami. It was from a student she'd once had in third grade.

Dear Mrs. Green,

I've been thinking about you. I hope this letter reaches you. You were my favorite teacher. I want to thank you for showing me through your life what it means to be a Christian. Please write back when you can.

Sincerely, Jennifer

Shirley felt as if electricity went through the letter. She wrote immediately and renewed their friendship. When Shirley added Jennifer's new address to her little book, she noticed lots of friends she could write to. Soon she had pen pals from all over. Shirley's list grew to over fifty correspondents, and her loneliness disappeared. She enjoys traveling and visiting friends, including Jennifer, and welcoming friends in return at home. And the best part of God's answer to prayer is how Shirley helps to encourage other people.

The Lord will help you to overcome your loneliness too. Trust Him to lead the way.

The LORD is my light and my salvation; whom shall I fear? The LORD is the strength of my life; of whom shall I be afraid? PSALM 27:1 NKJV

HAVE YOU EVER stepped outside after a hot summer day when the sky was clear and the stars lit up the night? Perhaps the cool night air made you want to remain there for hours. That's what happened to me the night I wrote the following praise to the Lord.

❧

Father, I step out to our backyard and breathe in the cool night air. I stretch out on a lawn chaise and gaze up at the countless stars You have spilled across the endless sky and arranged into a magnificent canopy. I wonder what it would be like if they weren't there. Their twinkling presence gives me a sense of security and peace because You are in it all.

Here in this nighttime cathedral I offer You my praise. I rest in Your holy presence and enjoy Your boundless love. You are my Light and my Salvation. You are my Stronghold, O Lord. I shall not be afraid. You, Father, are the constant life-giving fountain of my life. In You I have no need to walk in darkness.

You send forth the light of Your truth to illuminate my path. In all my ways, Your hand, Your arm, and the light of Your countenance guide me to decisions right and true. As You go before me, I praise You for keeping my feet sure and firmly planted on solid ground.

Shine Your light on me, Father, that I may be empowered to glorify You, giving You all praise and honor. Let the reflected light of Your love radiate from me to everyone I meet.

Hours have passed like minutes, Father. Though it's late, I feel refreshed in You. Remain with me through the night, I pray, so my thoughts will be of You when I awake.

Lord, teach us to pray. LUKE 11:1 NASB

ONE OF MY favorite things to do is walk in the early mornings down a park trail a short distance from our home. What makes this walk special is the way it stretches out for about a mile alongside the soothing Green River. Others who stroll or run on the trail appear to enjoy the solitude and beauty in nature as much as I do.

Even more special is the absolute joy and fulfillment I gain from whispering prayers to my beloved Savior while I walk. I take pleasure in telling Him how much I love Him and appreciate His nearness. What better company can I have than to walk and talk with my Lord? He is my dearest Friend. Even though He knows everything that's going on in my life, I gain comfort in sharing detail by detail with Him the daily joys and disappointments I experience. When I near the end of the trail and head toward my car, I know I must face whatever lies ahead for me that day.

This is when I whisper one more prayer: "Lord, I want to walk with You all through my day. If I become distracted and forget about Your constant presence, give my spirit a little nudge and remind me that You are near."

I value the passage in the Bible that tells how Noah walked with God. God and Noah must have known each other well and regularly walked and talked together. This may well have been the reason Noah understood God's warnings of an approaching deadly flood and His detailed instructions on how to build an ark.

I wonder what would have happened if Noah had not listened to God. I wonder what good can come about in my life as I learn to continually commune with Him.

And I—in righteousness I will see your face; when I awake, I will be satisfied with seeing your likeness. PSALM 17:15 NIV

LIFE CAN OFTEN get a little crazy, can't it? Like me, you might feel like stepping off the world for a brief period of time and making a date with God to "just talk." Try doing that some time.

Several years ago our son and daughter-in-love, Dan and Stayci, lived in a quiet area. Their home was surrounded by trees, a Christian camp made for retreats, a bird sanctuary, and a pond. A pasture corralling their horse and goat spread from the foot of their back upper deck. Even as their children played, the surroundings sent out messages of tranquility.

Dan's a morning person like me. He'd often told me the most beautiful time of day at their home was at sunrise. It was peaceful. Birds were everywhere. I found myself longing to witness it and "just talk" with the Lord.

I finally did something about my wish. I asked Dan and Stayci if I could spend the night with them and enjoy the quiet time. The answer, of course, was yes. The time finally arrived. I came home from teaching, gave my husband a good-bye kiss, and headed for my date with the Lord.

After a terrific evening together and a quick night's sleep, I awakened at four thirty. I was ready to enjoy my time with God. I shuffled into the kitchen, trying not to make a sound. My nose immediately picked up the warm aroma of freshly brewed coffee. Stayci had thoughtfully set the timer the previous night. I filled my cup and slipped out to the deck with my Bible, notebook, and a paper towel for the dew-dampened table. My time with my gracious Lord was about to begin.

Sometimes it takes real effort to set a date with the Lord, but the fantastic outcome is worth it.

You have filled my heart with greater joy.... PSALM 4:7 NIV

HOW GRATEFUL I am whenever I can have a date with the Lord—a chance to "just talk." It doesn't have to be in a certain place. Wherever I can do it, God has a marvelous way of making His incredible blessings unfold before me.

When I stepped out onto Dan and Stayci's deck at four thirty in the morning, I could see the full moon casting a silvery sheen, making the night almost as light as day. I spread out my materials and took a deep breath. Stars hung in the sky like sparkly diamonds. Nothing stirred except the horse and goat.

I prayed, thought, and prayed some more. Sweet-smelling dew settled around me. My mind began to focus on why I was there. The moon bid its adieu and faded. The sun silently crested and painted the horizon behind me with graduated shades of purple, blue, silver, and brilliant yellow. Its rays slivered through the trees of the bird sanctuary across the road, playing with the shadows.

I took more of my thoughts to God. This time I was willing to open my heart and listen to what He might be trying to teach me. "How I long for You to create a clean heart in me, Lord," I whispered. "Teach me from Your Word, I pray. Help me draw from Your wisdom."

I opened my Bible and began reading: "Blessed are those who hunger and thirst for righteousness" (Matthew 5:6 NIV). I turned to a story in my Bible. I read about a sensitive eight-year-old boy named Josiah who became king of the Israelites and did what was right in God's sight. His life inspired me.

I could already sense God graciously ministering to my heart.

Let the light of your face shine upon us, O Lord. PSALM 4:6 NIV

THE DATES WE make with the Lord need to allow us as much time as possible to be alone with Him. It takes time to settle in and focus on God. For a while we tell Him everything that's going on in our lives. But then we're able to listen to what He's trying to teach us.

During my early-morning date on the deck with God, I felt the rising sun wrap around my shoulders like a warm blanket. It caressed the back of my neck. In a similar way I sensed God's warm presence wrapping around my heart with His comfort and peace.

The trees exploded with birds. They soared and dipped in perfect aerodynamic fashion as if they were performing daily drills—propelling, floating, gliding to trees and rooftops. Eventually they settled, finding their morning meals, gently chirruping to their young and giving them breakfast. Barn swallows zoomed in and out of open stable windows like skilled pilots.

How did they become so accomplished? Was it from hours of practice? Did they learn from those with experience? Or both?

This is the answer You're trying to show me, Lord.

I realized I must search and listen with an open heart. I must follow God's lead and hear the words of wise people. I must apply what I learn to my life and put to practice God's priceless lessons.

I bowed my head, acknowledging the Author of the beauty that surrounded me. My decision making, goals, and wants were coming into focus, in accordance with His will. I could feel His Spirit tenderly filling and nurturing my thirsty soul.

Each time we go to God, we get to enjoy fresh, new fellowship with Him and be truly blessed.

Love Listens to Wisdom

For wisdom will enter your heart, and knowledge will be pleasant to your soul. Discretion will protect you, and understanding will guard you. PROVERBS 2:10−11 NIV

LORD, I ALMOST made some very poor choices the other day that would have hurt several people and created chaos and discord. If it hadn't been for a wise friend, I don't know what would have happened.

At first I was offended by my friend's advice until I stepped away from the situation and thought and prayed about it. You sent this brave person to me for a reason. I realized I wasn't acting with the unselfish love that comes from You. I felt I knew what was best and was refusing to surrender my opinions. I am so sorry for being stubborn and wanting to demand my own way. Thank You for urging my friend to step forward and talk with me.

As Your Word says, wisdom brings understanding; its lessons are far more valuable than the finest of jewels. Had I not listened to Your wisdom given by my friend, I would have experienced discord, bewilderment, heartbreak, and guilt. Instead, after I came to You in prayer and relinquished my own way, You gave me peace of heart and mind.

Your wisdom is like a tree of life I can hold onto. That same wisdom that established the earth and created the heavens provides me with humility, discernment, and help to make wise choices. No matter my years, I will seek Your wisdom, Lord, and tuck it in my mind and heart. Let me always be willing to turn to wise Christians and heed their advice. Grant me Your wisdom so I can bring honor and glory to You.

Thank You for intervening during my time of confusion and stubbornness. Thank You for Your forgiveness. I praise You, too, for the gracious love my friend showed to me.

Blessed is the man [or woman] who trusts in the LORD. JEREMIAH 17:7 NASB

HAVE YOU EVER faced a problem so complex that you couldn't find a solution no matter how much you dwelled on the circumstance and searched for answers?

God has some keys to unlock the impossible doors. Matthew 11:28 says to come to Jesus and He will give us rest. He will shoulder our heavy load.

Workers throughout history carried heavy loads by placing wooden yokes over their shoulders, like those used for draft animals, in order to help lighten their burdens. Even then, some were extremely difficult to lift. Eventually, the worker would buckle from weariness unless a kind person came along and helped with the load.

In the same way, our loads of worry and difficulty can become far too heavy for us to bear. When this happens, our Savior is near, offering to help us. All we need to do is release our burden to Him and allow Him to carry it—then listen, and trust Him to lead us.

We may think we have the right answers. At times our stubborn mind-set might cause us to insist on how we want things done. Yet our ways are not always Jesus' ways. When we give Him our problems, we can trust that He sees the whole picture and will bring us through in His time and by His means. Before long our heavy, stress-filled burden becomes much lighter.

In 2 Corinthians 12:9 we read that Jesus said: "My grace is sufficient for you, for My strength is made perfect in weakness" (NIV). Whether it's family struggles, difficulties at work, lack of income, or other situations, we can trust Jesus to bridge the gaps we are unable to fill. He can work in the most amazing ways to bring about His perfect will. The results will be far better than what we could imagine.

The more we see our sinfulness, the more we see God's abounding grace forgiving us.
ROMANS 5:20 TLB

ALL OF US have done wrong things. Yet among all the sins we've committed, all the thoughtless actions we've taken, all the irresponsible judgment calls we've made, all the regrets we possess, are there any that outweigh the gracious, forgiving love of God? Of course not.

God's grace is far greater than any of our wrongs. He is all-compassionate. He is all-powerful. He wholly forgives our contrite, repentant hearts. It is never too late to turn our hearts over to Him and make a U-turn.

Almighty Father, thank You for Your unconditional kindness, love, and forgiveness and for descending from Your heavenly kingdom to live among us here on earth.

When I think of the way You viewed my sins and showed Your mercy and grace by dying for me, I am overwhelmed with gratitude. Thank You, Father, for Your immeasurable love. Thank You for the merciful way You took all the sins from my repentant heart and cast them completely away as far as the east is from the west. How I praise You for cleansing my heart and making me as white as snow.

Father, I give my love to You in return. No amount of good that I may do can ever make up for all You have done for me. How thankful I am that I belong to You because of Your gracious love and forgiveness.

Marvelous grace of our loving Lord,
Grace that exceeds our sin and our guilt!
Yonder on Calvary's mount outpoured,
There where the blood of the Lamb was spilt.
—JULIA H. JOHNSTON

Well then, shall we keep on sinning so that God can keep on showing us more and more kindness and forgiveness? Of course not! ...For sin's power over us was broken when we became Christians.
ROMANS 6:1–2 TLB

HAVE YOU EVER felt like you were drowning in the consequences of your own wrongdoing? Many of us have. We try and try to undo past wrongs without success. Then out of sheer desperation, we call out to God to rescue us from our circumstances.

That is when Jesus begins helping us. In the same way He stilled the storms while He was with His disciples on the Sea of Galilee, Jesus grasps our hands, forgives our sins, calms our storms, and tells us to "sin no more." He patiently yet firmly points us toward the refuge of the cross that He died on for every one of us, and guides us to a joy-filled life in Him.

Lord, thank You for the way You rescued me from the self-destructive life I was living and set my feet on the Rock of Your foundation. No longer will I build my life on wrong choices. Instead, I will live for You.

Though things of the past may haunt me, I know You are more powerful. You are with me, helping me work through the problems to make a life that's full and rich and free from temptation and sin.

I'm excited as I move forward. I'm already seeing a wonderful new beginning with You as my Guide. I look back and marvel at all You are doing in my life.

Sin and despair, like the sea waves cold,
Threaten the soul with infinite loss;
Grace that is greater, yes, grace untold,
Points to the Refuge, the Mighty Cross.
—JULIA H. JOHNSTON

"Come, let's talk this over!" says the Lord; "no matter how deep the stain of your sins, I can take it out and make you as clean as freshly fallen snow. Even if you are stained as red as crimson, I can make you white as wool!" ISAIAH 1:18 TLB

A FRIEND OF mine who teaches elementary school wore a beautiful pearl-white top to school one day. As she was working on a project with her students, a child accidentally swiped a red marker along the shirt, leaving an eight-inch mark. My friend tried all sorts of stain removers on it, but nothing worked. She managed to make it lighter but could still see a faint stain when she looked at it from a certain angle.

Perhaps that's why the Lord describes our sins as being like scarlet. Without the shedding of Jesus' blood our stains would never fade from view.

When I was twelve years old, I got a bad cut on my hand and the blood frightened me. As my mother tended it, she told me to not be afraid of blood; it has a way of naturally cleansing a wound.

In Moses' time the shedding of an unblemished animal's blood was the only thing that symbolized people being pure before the Lord. Moses took the blood of calves, water, scarlet wool, and branches of hyssop and sprinkled the blood on the tabernacle and everything used in the holy ceremonies. The Bible tells us that when Jesus died on the cross, He didn't sprinkle His blood in a man-made sanctuary. Instead, "He entered heaven itself, now to appear for us in God's presence" (Hebrews 9:24 NIV). So when we accept Him, we can have victory over sin once and for all.

Dark is the stain that we cannot hide.
What can avail to wash it away?
Look! There is flowing a crimson tide,
Brighter than snow you may be today.
—JULIA H. JOHNSTON

We can see and understand only a little about God now, as if we were peering at his reflection in a poor mirror; but someday we are going to see him in his completeness, face to face.... Then I will see everything clearly, just as clearly as God sees into my heart right now. 1 Corinthians 13:12 TLB

DO YOU EVER wonder how you will feel when you one day see your Savior face-to-face? Some friends of mine and I discussed what we will do when we meet Him in heaven. A few said they will stand up and rejoice. Others said they thought they would be so overcome with gratitude and humility that they would drop prostrate on their faces before Him. I'm still not sure what I will do. I guess I'll have to wait and see.

After Moses received the tablets of the Ten Commandments and other instructions, he returned to the Israelites waiting in the valley. His face was so radiant because he had been with God that he had to cover his face when he talked to the people.

Just think. That's only a sample of how radiant the face of Jesus must be. I wonder if we will bask in His brilliance and be filled with everlasting joy. Although I feel unworthy to come before Him in heaven someday, I realize that through His forgiving grace I will be able to do so. He is my Savior. When that time comes, I want to bow before Him and then run into His arms as He welcomes me home.

Marvelous, infinite, matchless grace,
Freely bestowed on all who believe!
You that are longing to see His face,
Will you this moment His grace receive?

Grace, grace, God's grace,
Grace that will pardon and cleanse within;
Grace, grace, God's grace,
Grace that is greater than all our sin!
　　—JULIA H. JOHNSTON

For His merciful kindness is great toward us, and the truth of the LORD endures forever. Praise the LORD! PSALM 117:2 NKJV

A LOVING TOUCH given by a family member or friend can soothe our tense muscles and calm our frazzled emotions. Often, the kind action makes us feel loved.

It was the end of a long night on my second job in a fast-food restaurant. Standing on concrete night after night had taken its toll. I was getting painful bone spurs in the bottom of each foot.

When I arrived home around one a.m., I was surprised to see that a light was still on inside. Our oldest son, Bob Jr., was visiting from out of town. The moment I unlocked the door and saw Bob sitting on the living-room couch with a smile on his face, I realized he had waited up for me. I stepped through the door, sank to the couch, and kicked off my work shoes.

Bob and I began visiting about the events of our day. He took my feet in his hands, and ever so gently, he began massaging them. I recoiled at the mere thought of my son touching my sweaty feet. He never paused but kept rubbing and listening to me tell about my night's work. I think that was one of the greatest acts of love I have ever experienced, one I will treasure and never forget.

How good it is that we can also enjoy the tender, loving touch of our heavenly Father just when we need Him the most. He has a way of wrapping His spiritual blanket of comfort around us and showing us how much He cares. Our bodies soon relax while we tell Him about our difficulties and dilemmas of the day. He graciously listens, loves, and understands.

"Whatever you did for one of the least of these brothers [and sisters] of mine, you did for me."
MATTHEW 25:40 NIV

WHAT IF A stranger approached you to tell you about a friend or acquaintance who needs help? The stranger might be ill-kempt or covered with tattoos or have strange hair. You might be tempted to distrust him and disregard what he's saying. You might even feel concerned about your own safety.

When Linda was growing up, an unlikely stranger showed up at her home when she was playing in her backyard. The stranger happened to be a burly tomcat. The cat was meowing persistently. He would walk away a short distance, stop, look back at her, and keep meowing as though he wanted her to follow him. Finally, Linda followed the cat into a nearby field. There among the bushes, huddled together, was a litter of newborn kittens in poor shape.

Linda gathered up the kittens and carried them back to her house with the tomcat following closely behind. She and her family managed to nurse all but one kitten back to health. She later found out the mother cat was hit by a car two days before. Had she waited to follow the tomcat, the kittens would have died.

Tomcats don't normally like kittens, and they often destroy them. But God cares for animals, and amazingly He had a different plan for this litter.

No matter what the unlikely rescuer looks like, God understands. He unconditionally loves the rescuer and the ones needing help. We never know when the one being rescued may be you or me or someone we love.

Let your eyes look straight ahead, fix your gaze directly before you. Make level paths for your feet and take only ways that are firm. Do not swerve to the right or the left; keep your foot from evil.
PROVERBS 4:25–27 NIV

OVERCOMING TEMPTATION IS often our greatest struggle in living a life pleasing to God. Whether the temptations are obvious or subtle, we must flee from them as fast as we can.

The devil often tempts us in our weakest areas. He's no gentleman. But we can refuse to dwell on the temptation and give our problems to the Lord. As we trust and obey Him and claim His promises in the Bible, He mercifully delivers us from each one we encounter. (See 1 Corinthians 10:13.)

It isn't a sin to be tempted. Jesus was tempted, and He used the Scriptures to overcome. (See Matthew 4:1–11.) We can look directly ahead and focus on the Lord to help us keep our way straight, level, and true, our faith firmly planted in His mighty power and strength.

My husband, Bob, recently took up walking several miles every few days in order to lose some weight and shape up. One day I joined him on his walk through town. As we trekked down Main Street, Bob shared a valuable lesson with me. He said that walking was not the hard part. The challenge was passing the pizza shop, a hot dog stand, the doughnut store, two deli shops, and an ice cream parlor without stopping for a bite.

Bob's story makes me think about our walk with God. It isn't our walk with Him that's difficult, it's walking (or running) past the temptations. We can do so only by focusing on Him. When we do, we can thank Him for His mercy and grace as He leads and helps us every step of the way.

But when the kindness and love of God our Savior appeared, he saved us, not because of righteous things we had done, but because of his mercy. TITUS 3:4–5 NIV

HOW CAN WE ever be holy in God's sight? No matter how much we try to do everything right, some things still go wrong. We live in a sin-sick world that is constantly trying to pull us away from the holy things of God. Others' actions and poor judgment cause us to suffer. How we long to live a life pure and pleasing to God.

To whom does a holy life belong? Holy living and wisdom are often gained by years of experience in the school of hard knocks, but primarily they are found by hungering and thirsting for the unfailing lessons of God found in His Word.

Are right living and wisdom reserved only for the elderly? Most of us would probably say yes; however, this isn't always the case. We see older people who make wise choices, and we don't fear following their examples. Unfortunately, there are others who no longer seek wise advice or think discerningly within God's will. Sometimes they suffer sad consequences.

What about the young? How many times have you seen or heard the pure and perceptive words of children, teenagers, or young adults who truly love the Lord with all their hearts? I have, more times than I can count.

Josiah became king of the Israelites when he was only eight. How was he, at such a young age, able to make the important decisions required of a king? The Bible says that even then, Josiah listened to the advice given by those who loved God. And at age sixteen he sincerely sought the will of the God of his ancestor, David.

Holy living belongs to those who turn to God for His forgiveness, wisdom, and grace.

"So do not fear, for I am with you; do not be dismayed, for I am your God. I will strengthen you and help you; I will uphold you with my righteous right hand." ISAIAH 41:10 NIV.

THERE ARE TIMES in our Christian walk that the Lord calls us to do something for Him that we may be afraid to try. He might be inviting us to teach a Sunday school class, sing a song, or greet people when they enter the church. Perhaps He wants us to tell our friends about His wonderful love.

New things can be pretty frightening. Still, in order to say "yes" to the Lord's call, we simply need to take that first step. It only needs to be a baby step, but it's a step of faith in following His lead.

When our children began pulling themselves to their feet, holding onto furniture and trying to steady their wobbly legs, their eyes were filled with excitement. Then the day came when their daddy and I coaxed them into taking their first steps. They began by grasping our fingers. Then we taught them to hold onto the end of the broomstick so they weren't as close to us. Next, we encouraged them to let go and take one step after another. When they fell, we were there to gently help them to their feet so they could try again.

Let's not be afraid to take that first step. When we do, we can ask our Christian friends to lend a hand and take these steps with us. Best of all, Jesus is always near and catches us when we fall. Believe it or not, even the most accomplished people make mistakes. And when they do, He is there to help them back to their feet so they can "keep on keeping on" for Him.

So let's put one foot in front of the other, dear friend, and see what exciting things the Lord has in store for us.

A man must leave his father and mother when he marries so that he can be perfectly joined to his wife, and the two shall be one. EPHESIANS 5:31 TLB

THE CHURCH WAS packed as the ceremony began. Bob and I stepped forward and faced Pastor Jerry Phillips. My father stood by my other side, and we were flanked by four young men. Our friend Phil sang, then Bob and I sang to one another. We gazed into each other's love-struck eyes as Pastor Jerry read our vows. Two of the young men presented our rings, and we exchanged our tokens of love.

Pastor Jerry reminded us of the sanctity of marriage. Then came the part, "Who gives this woman to be married to this man?" A deep, reverent "We do" chorused from my father and our four grown sons. We paused and prayed, thanking God for the marriage and family He gave us. Bob and I hugged and kissed at the end of renewing our vows in celebration of our fortieth wedding anniversary.

Forty years plus. We love each other more than ever. He still looks at me with a sparkle in his eyes. He opens doors for me, rubs my back, and buys me flowers. My heart still goes pitter-patter when he enters a room. When we go somewhere, I still dress to look my best for my sweetheart and friend.

Our anniversary was a celebration of life with the ones we love most: each other, our sons, daughters-in-love, grandchildren, parents, and our family of God. Most of all, we celebrated our love for the Lord, the Author and Finisher of it all.

Good marriages don't just happen. They require love, graciousness, forgiveness, and commitment that we receive from God and give to each other. As we change, grow, and mature, we can enjoy falling in love with each other over and over again.

Those who sow in tears will reap with songs of joy. PSALM 126:5 NIV

HOW CAN WE find comfort when a loved one dies? The pain is beyond description. Death is so final.

Horatio Gates Spafford and his wife, Anna, planned a trip by sea with their four young daughters to visit relatives and friends in Europe. Unfortunately, Horatio had to remain behind because of business responsibilities.

While on their trans-Atlantic voyage, the ship in which Anna and the girls traveled struck an English vessel. Damage to the ship's hull was so great that their ship sank within twenty minutes. Anna vividly remembered pulling her daughters near and praying for them. Icy water swept the three older girls away. Then Anna's youngest child was torn from her arms. Anna was rescued and brought aboard a lifeboat. The words she telegraphed to her husband sadly declared, "Saved alone."

The couple reunited ten days later. Although they suffered tremendous grief, the two attested, "It is well." Horatio Spafford later felt inspired to write a poem that became a beloved hymn, "It Is Well with My Soul." Its words continue to comfort and encourage people to this day.

ૠ

Father, when memories of losing my loved one return, I feel them sear my soul like a hot iron. The pain feels almost as fierce now as it was back then. Again You remind me that I'm not grieving for my loved one, but for myself. Take my grief, Father, and replace it with the joy of Your salvation. Once I sowed with tears, but now I reap with songs of joy. Thank You, Father, for Your comfort. It truly is well with my soul.

It will be well with those who fear God. ECCLESIASTES 8:12 NKJV

WHATEVER THE TRIALS and sorrows we face, our heavenly Father welcomes us to bring them to Him in prayer. We can lay every burden before Him and not pick it up again. When we release our burdens to God, He consoles our hearts. He comforts our emotions and helps dry our tears. He cheers us with words of promise from the Bible that give us hope for days to come.

Henry Ward Beecher describes God's consolation as a singular sweetness of words sent down from heaven to men and women struggling through life's problems. He said they are like open glades in a dark forest, where the sun lies on warm banks. How comforting to know that God is our consolation. He's the Source of our peace of mind. As we turn to Him, He provides all the strength we need. It is then we can victoriously say, "It is well with my soul!"

When peace, like a river, attendeth my way,
When sorrows like sea billows roll;
Whatever my lot, Thou hast taught me to say,
It is well, it is well with my soul.

Though Satan should buffet, though trials should come,
Let this blest assurance control,
That Christ has regarded my helpless estate,
And hath shed His own blood for my soul.

My sin, oh, the bliss of this glorious thought!
My sin not in part, but the whole
Is nailed to the cross and I bear it no more,
Praise the Lord, praise the Lord, O my soul!
        —HORATIO G. SPAFFORD

For He shall give His angels charge over you, to keep you in all your ways. In their hands they shall bear you up, lest you dash your foot against a stone. PSALM 91:11–12 NKJV

WHETHER THE STORMS of life we face are mild or terrifyingly severe, our strength to get through them can reach a low ebb. In our most discouraging moments, we may cry out to the Lord for assurance that He's watching out not only for us but for the ones we love, as well. God has a way of helping us through present trials by reminding us of Scriptures or memories of the past.

Sam and Cindy were experiencing their twenty-year-old daughter Jennifer's breaking-away years. Not only had she moved out of state, but she seldom contacted her parents. Even though Sam and Cindy continually prayed for their daughter, Cindy's anxiousness sometimes outweighed her faith. Jennifer loved the Lord, but she was making unwise choices.

One afternoon while praying for Jennifer, Cindy felt the Lord bring a memory to mind of when Jennifer was a child and had a bike accident. A lady whom no one else could see or hear helped Jennifer safely home. Jennifer and her parents believed the lady was a guardian angel.

With that memory God assured Cindy that He was still with her daughter and would continue to be all through her life. Cindy knew she could rest in God's care and could trust Jennifer to mature as an adult and draw closer to the Lord.

Years later, Sam and Cindy still rely on in the Lord for His gracious help and direction. Best of all, Jennifer's relationship with the Lord is causing her to grow closer to Him every day.

When you or someone you know is going through life's storms, don't be afraid to ask the Lord for His assurance of His unlimited love and care. When you ask Him, the Lord will be with you and your family all the time.

Because you are my help, I sing in the shadow of your wings. PSALM 63:7 NIV

LORD, WHEN THE storms of life surround me and stress crowds in on every side, I'm thankful that I can flee to Your bosom for protection and grace. When all else fails, I'm grateful that You never leave me alone. You, Lord, are my strength and my shield. In You I find the help I so desperately need. I place all my trust in You.

You are my all in all, Lord. You heal the sick. You encourage the discouraged. You comfort me when I grieve. When I'm searching, You lead the way. When I'm struggling, You pick up my heavy load. When I'm weary, You grant me rest and peace. You, dear Lord, I love above all else. You are the answer to all my needs. How I adore You. You are holy. You are life.

How plenteous is Your grace! How forgiving, Your unconditional love! Even though I'm undeserving, You gave Your life so I can be free from sin, and will someday be in heaven with You.

May my praise to You go beyond the confines of this world I live in—above the clouds, above the stars, clear to Your heavens above. In Jesus' name, amen.

Jesus, Lover of my soul, let me to Thy bosom fly,
While the nearer waters roll, while the tempest still is high.
Hide me, O my Savior, hide, till the storm of life is past;
Safe into the haven guide; O receive my soul at last.

Plenteous grace with Thee is found, grace to cover all my sin;
Let the healing streams abound; make and keep me pure within.
Thou of life the Fountain art; freely let me take of Thee;
Spring Thou up within my heart; rise to all eternity.

—CHARLES WESLEY

Your lovingkindness, O LORD, extends to the heavens, Your faithfulness reaches to the skies.
PSALM 36:5 NASB

SOMETIMES WE ARE thrust into uncomfortable situations, whether they are brought on by our own actions, the poor decisions of family or friends, or unkind coworkers. These challenges have a way of bringing out either the worst or the best in us.

Joseph experienced an especially challenging situation. He was his father's favorite child. The colorful coat his father made for him didn't go over well with his brothers. Jealousy set in. At age seventeen, he enjoyed tattling about his brothers to his father. To make matters worse, he told his brothers that he dreamed they would one day bow down to him. Their anger grew.

One day Joseph's father sent him to the fields to check on his brothers. They threw him into a pit, intending to leave him to die, and they stole his coat, covered it with animal's blood, and planned to convince their father that Joseph had been killed by a wild animal. They changed their minds, though, and sold Joseph as a slave to a caravan of Ishmaelites. The caravan took him to Egypt and sold him to Potiphar, an army leader.

Joseph worked conscientiously for his master. Even though God didn't immediately bring Joseph out of his circumstances, He rewarded him for his unwavering faithfulness. Potiphar was so pleased that he put Joseph in charge of his entire household.

No matter our circumstances, God remains near. We can be thankful for how God rewards us when we are faithful to Him.

Life's challenges are not supposed to paralyze you; they're supposed to help you discover who you are.
—LEWIS DUNCOMBE

Help me to do your will, for you are my God. Lead me in good paths, for your Spirit is good.
PSALM 143:10 TLB

THE THEORY OF taking the lemons in our lives and making them into lemonade may pay off in some situations, yet even when we are striving to obey God and follow His lead, we can face setbacks and discouragement. Our best intentions may be misunderstood so that once again we are forced to suffer. But God is still with us. He brings us through each struggle and helps us to stand true to Him.

During his years in slavery, Joseph drew close to God. He began to gain wisdom from the Lord, and his attitude tremendously improved. Joseph was loyal to Potiphar, the Egyptian officer, but when Potiphar's wife wrongfully accused him, Joseph was thrown into prison. There God gave him the ability to interpret the dreams of other prisoners. Eventually word reached Pharaoh, who thought that Joseph could interpret a disturbing dream he had had.

Joseph was finally released from prison. Before long Pharaoh grew to realize Joseph was blessed with the spirit of the Lord. It may have been Joseph's loyalty and his selfless ways that led Pharaoh to give his own ring to Joseph and put a chain around his neck. He even provided Joseph with a chariot of his own. Everywhere Joseph went, people respected him. God certainly had honored him for his unwavering faithfulness.

During our trying times, God watches over us as well. When we allow Him, He brings out the best in us and helps us to gain wisdom and understanding. We may often think back in amazement at how He brings victory through nearly impossible times.

Best of all is, God is with us.
—JOHN WESLEY

Blessed are the merciful, for they shall obtain mercy. Blessed are the pure in heart, for they shall see God. Blessed are the peacemakers, for they shall be called sons [and daughters] of God.
MATTHEW 5:7–9 NKJV

A TIME MAY come when we must face the hurts in our past. As we call on God, He helps us to search our hearts and find the capacity to forgive others—and sometimes even ourselves.

Joseph came to this place of forgiveness years after being sold into slavery. Now thirty years old and married with two sons, the next time he saw his brothers he no longer felt anger towards them. Instead, he was able to say: "God has made me forget all my toil and all my father's house."

During that time, God led Joseph to store away crops while harvests were plentiful. Then a seven-year famine struck the land. No one in Egypt needed to fear, because Joseph had more than enough food saved for everyone. By now he was governor of the land.

When the famine spread to Joseph's family in Canaan, Joseph's brothers went to Egypt to buy food. One can only imagine the mixed feelings Joseph felt when he recognized them. His brothers no longer knew who he was.

Joseph required his brothers to make many visits. At times, he turned away from them so he could privately weep from bitterness and relief. Finally he told them he was their brother. He hugged them and said he forgave them. He explained that God had sent him to Egypt to save them from starvation.

Joseph's father, brothers, and their families were later reunited with him. He gave them homes, food, clothing, and carts. God took the misfortunes in Joseph's life and turned them into a miracle of mercy.

Whatever our circumstances, God can help us shed our layers of resentment and sorrow and replace them with compassion and forgiveness.

Whatever you do, work at it with all your heart, as working for the Lord, not for men, since you know that you will receive an inheritance from the Lord as a reward. It is the Lord Christ you are serving. COLOSSIANS 3:23–24 NIV

MANY OF US have experienced working a job under less than desirable conditions. We may have felt (or feel) taken for granted, criticized, unappreciated, or abused. We may want out, but quitting may not be possible.

Monica knows what this is like. She had been working directly under her boss, Sandra, for many years. Things went well until Sandra was forced to face some family problems. Sadly, her attitude at work changed for the worse, and she began criticizing and bullying Monica. The harder Monica tried to please her, the meaner Sandra became. Even coworkers grew concerned.

Monica wanted to change jobs more than anything. Other bosses in the company requested her to work for them. But the general manager knew there would be such a battle with Sandra that it would split the company.

Monica asked God for strength, wisdom, and a way to escape. First Corinthians 10:13 assured her that He would bring her through. God helped her realize that *He* was her Boss. He wanted her to work wholeheartedly for Him. And He'd handle the problems!

Next, she purchased the book *Boundaries* by Dr. Henry Cloud and Dr. John Townsend. Its lessons and scriptures showed her how to be respectful yet firm in everything she did. She was to be a good worker, but God didn't intend for her to be a doormat. She was learning to work above the circumstances instead of under them. Monica's prayer changed from asking to leave her job to seeking His timing. He knew best.

After a while, God graciously gave Monica a new job that she didn't even search for. Now she's happier than ever and she has tremendous respect from those in her previous job—including Sandra.

"I have loved you, O my people, with an everlasting love; with loving-kindness I have drawn you to me." JEREMIAH 31:3 TLB

DO YOU EVER feel like you want to unload all of your frustrations, doubts, and fears? Bring those needs to Jesus. He has broad shoulders and understands. Do you ever want to argue with Him and tell Him you can't comprehend what He's trying to do in your life? That you desperately want your prayers answered right now—your way? He already knows how you feel. I believe being willing to open your soul to Him is extremely important. God cares about you during the ups and downs. He's listening to you and wants *you* to listen to Him.

When our burdens become so heavy that we can hardly bear them, we might toss and turn through the night, crying out to the Lord for help. Like me, you may at times feel like Jacob, who wrestled with the angel and said, "I will not let You go unless You bless me!" We may feel this most strongly when praying for loved ones.

The psalmist also went through distressing experiences. He cried out to the Lord and complained: "Hear my voice when I call, O LORD; be merciful to me and answer me.... Hear me, O God, as I voice my complaint... as I call to You for help, as I lift up my hands toward Your Most Holy Place" (Psalm 27:7; 64:1; 28:2 NIV).

What a comfort it is to know that our Lord promises us that He knows our needs even before we bring them to Him. "Before they call I will answer; while they are still speaking I will hear" (Isaiah 65:24 NIV).

He really loves us. He has broad shoulders and always helps us through.

Grant that I may never fail Thy hand to see;
Grant that I may ever cast my care on Thee.
—JAMES MONTGOMERY

[Jesus said,] "Greater love has no one than this, than to lay down one's life for his [or her] friends." JOHN 15:13 NKJV

MANY OF US love doing things for other people. When we do, the joy we give somehow brings warm feelings to our own hearts. However, sometimes we're required to graciously give of ourselves to the point of extreme sacrifice. And when we do, God gives us the ability to help others with no strings attached.

A legend has been told about two brothers whose family had very little money. As they neared adulthood, they both developed a sincere love for art, and they were both extremely talented. They longed to attend art school and pursue their lifelong dreams. Unfortunately, they couldn't afford to go.

Still, they decided that one of them would work for several years and put the other through school. After the one completed his studies and became successful, he, too, would help his brother. It's been told that they made the decision by tossing a coin. The loser went to work in the mines to pay for his brother's education.

Years passed as the faithful brother worked grueling hours. After his brother became successful and returned, it came time for the brother who had worked to achieve his dream. Sadly, it was too late.

According to the story, the continual pounding and digging in the mines had destroyed his hands. Crippling arthritis caused his once-nimble fingers to twist with constant pain. Never again would the faithful brother hold a brush or pen to the once-familiar canvas.

His reward for his labor may have been seeing his much-loved brother succeed. What greater deed could this unknown artist have done than to graciously give up part of his life for his brother/friend, with no strings attached?

[Jesus said,] "*These things I command you, that you love one another.*" JOHN 15:17 NKJV

WHEN WE GIVE sacrificially, we may wonder if it was really worth the price. We may not always see the good that comes from a kindness shown. But as God works in the heart of the giver, He develops an abundance of gracious, unselfish love, bringing about spiritual blessings that spill over to the giver and the receiver.

According to the legend of the two brothers, the successful artist noticed his brother silently praying one day with his gnarled hands clasped and decided to paint a picture of them. The painting became famous. Known as *Praying Hands*, it has been treasured by many through the years. Many of us have been blessed by having a picture or carving of this timeless masterpiece in our homes.

The brother who had sacrificed so much never could have imagined he would receive the greatest heartfelt gift of honor and gratitude possible from his brother, Albrecht Durer, one of the world's most acclaimed artists. Some say *Praying Hands* may have been a sketch of the hands of Durer's mother—or perhaps his own hands. Whatever the truth may be, the picture and the stories told about it have served as an inspiration to many.

The love associated with the praying hands symbolizes the ultimate gift. It's the kind of love that reaches beyond friendship, beyond family, beyond giving of ourselves, and touches our hearts today. It brings to mind the nail-scarred hands of our Savior and the selfless sacrifice and forgiveness that He gave because of His love for each one of us. His dying for our sins and giving us a free, abundant life in Him truly is His ultimate gift.

In His Image

For you created my inmost being; you knit me together in my mother's womb. I praise you because I am fearfully and wonderfully made; your works are wonderful, I know that full well.
PSALM 139:13–14 NIV

WHAT AN EXCITING event it is when a baby is first born. Whether we're the proud parents or a family member or friend, we take delight in peeking at fingers and toes. We enjoy comparing eyes, nose, mouth, and hair to the parents and relatives.

When my daughter-in-law Stayci carefully placed her baby Elizabeth in my arms, I was filled with awe. Liza, they would call her. She looked as though she didn't have a care in the world. At that moment, she captured my heart.

She had her mother's nose and her father's mouth. But when I looked into her blue eyes, I felt as though I were looking into a mirror. She had my eyes! I remember whispering, "Hello, little Liza. Nana loves you."

Think of how much joy our heavenly Father must have felt while He fashioned our small bodies in the warmth of our mother's womb. He created every intricate part of us. He knew what we would look like before we were even born. He knew our personalities and abilities that would develop with time. Best of all, He planted a love-seed in our hearts that would grow and intertwine with His.

The Bible says God created us in His image. I wonder if we have His eyes. I'm glad He has us near His heart.

❧

Thank You, Father, for giving us these young ones in our families and for how they seem to remind us a little bit of ourselves. Thank You for creating each of us in Your image. Thank You for giving us abilities and goals and dreams. Help us through the years to be near to Your heart—to always be a reflection of You.

He guides me in paths of righteousness for his name's sake. PSALM 23:3 NIV

GOD SOMETIMES WORKS in mysterious ways, using circumstances and people to answer prayers.

My friend Colleen Reece and I were flying to a speaking engagement. Early on, we prayed for protection and guidance. Colleen sat near the window, and I took the center seat. Soon a nervous man sat down on the other side of me. When the plane took off, his face paled as he gripped the armrests. I silently prayed for God to comfort him.

Colleen and I introduced ourselves as Christian authors. The man, whose name was Matt, was traveling to his dad's birthday celebration. He hadn't flown in years. Idle chitchat followed. Then silence.

Before long, Matt struck up a conversation. "Do you have children?" he asked.

"I have grown children and grandchildren," I replied.

Matt's eyes filled with tears. Wiping them away, he told us how he and his wife were raising two strong-willed teenagers. Although they were Christians, stress was threatening their marriage.

I listened then shared some lessons God had been teaching me. "God sees us through good and bad times. In tough times, God is often closer than ever. God loves you and your family, Matt. Trust and obey Him. He'll take care of you."

Matt's face filled with awe. "My seat was changed at the last minute. It's no accident that I'm sitting next to you, is it? I think God planned it this way."

I agreed. Our paths were meant to cross. After we landed, the three of us prayed and went on our ways.

When God changes your routine, watch for His compassionate interventions.

The Good News Is...

A new commandment I give to you, that you love one another; as I have loved you, that you also love one another. JOHN 13:34 NKJV

I DON'T HAVE all the answers to my friend's problems, Lord. But You do. Grant me the wisdom to listen and to care about how she feels. Teach me how to be gracious, understanding, and compassionate. Remind me that Your Holy Spirit has the ability to guide her and meet her needs.

I'm excited about what You did in *my* life, Lord. I went through my share of struggles in letting go of the mess that I made. The good news is that I turned the whole thing over to You. What a miracle that was! When I gave You first place in my life, it was so amazing. I still marvel at the joy and peace You gave me, how You cleansed my heart and showed me mercy and grace.

Maybe all I need to do is to tell her about how You've changed my life and still help me each day. When I read in Your Word, it tells me about the Gospels, Matthew, Mark, Luke, and John. I've learned that *gospel* means "good news." Good news I certainly have. Please make an opening, Lord, when You want me to tell about You. Then help me to be brave enough to follow Your lead.

Well, here she comes, Lord. I'm tuning in to You for direction and help.

Hmm. That wasn't so bad, Lord. In fact, it was downright exciting to see how Your Holy Spirit worked and spoke to her through my words. Thank You for showing her Your loving-kindness and mercy. And thank You for being with me.

The next time You urge me to tell Your good news, help me again. Season my words and grant me Your graciousness. And, Lord, please help another friend find a new life in You.

But as for me, I am like a green olive tree in the house of God; I trust in the lovingkindness of God forever and ever. PSALM 52:8 NASB

ABOUT TEN YEARS ago, I purchased a two-foot dwarf peach tree sapling. This little tree had barely begun growing when it was dug from its earthy nursery home and transplanted near our flower garden. We live on an old river bed, so the soil the tree was plopped into was rocky. But I was determined to help it establish strong roots and grow. It started out with no leaves and only a few branches. My son Jonathan laughed when he first saw it. He described it as a "stick in the dirt."

For years I faithfully watered and fertilized the tree. Finally, two or three peaches emerged. Now that tree regularly produces bumper crops of peaches to the point where its branches occasionally need to be propped up.

Most of us have had to move several times throughout our lives. Whether those moves are wanted or unwanted, there are adjustments to make. Yet like that peach tree, no matter where we move, we can depend on the Lord to lovingly nourish and encourage us, and help us grow spiritual fruit for Him. And wherever we go there is a common bond of Christian friendship in the family of God.

We can be assured when we read Psalm 92:12–13: "The godly shall flourish like palm trees and grow tall.... They are transplanted into the Lord's own garden and are under his personal care" (TLB).

When we move again, God will prepare the soil we'll be planted in and help us continue to bear fruit for Him.

The will of God will never take you where the grace of God cannot keep you. —AUTHOR UNKNOWN

A Firm Hold

For I am convinced that nothing can ever separate us from His love. Death can't, and life can't. The angels won't, and all the powers of hell itself cannot keep God's love away. ROMANS 8:38 TLB

WE ALL FACE challenges in our walk with God. Even when we cling to Him, things can still go wrong, but we must hold on tight to the One who sustains us.

One morning two men prepared for their window-washing job. With scaffolding and lifelines in place, they hooked the lifelines to their safety belts, loaded their supplies, and headed up the side of the skyscraper.

But when they reached the top, something gave way. Supplies and framework plummeted to the street below. Lifelines snapped taut and brought both men to an abrupt stop in midair, where they swayed precariously in the wind. Fortunately, the reliable safety clamps held them secure while rescue crews worked quickly to lower them to safety.

Can bad things happen when we're obedient to God? I believe so. There's a real spiritual battle going on. Satan is trying to break Christians any way he can. He's no gentleman. First Peter 5:8 describes him as a roaring lion, searching for someone to devour. Yet no matter how tough things get, God promises to never allow us to endure more than we can handle. When we become frazzled, brokenhearted, or worn out and feel like we're losing our grip, He's still there, firmly holding onto us.

God loves us and knows how much we love Him. He's near during the good times and bad. He's graciously holding onto us when we soar, and mercifully sustaining us so we don't crash. When our strength is gone, God's powerful grip takes hold.

As you prepare for your day, be sure to draw close to God and hook up to His lifeline. Then fear not. Keep a firm hold! For God is near.

But as for me, I trust in you. PSALM 55:23 NIV

DO YOU EVER get that "can do" feeling that makes you want to do everything? Then life's storms crash in and the Master's presence fades from view. You may become discouraged or even bitter as seemingly unfair trials are sent your way. After all, the Bible says, "I can do all things through Christ who strengthens me." Yet it is often too easy to get caught up in the moment of "I can do all things," and forget about the One who is there for us.

One night Jesus had just finished feeding crowds of people. He wanted to be alone to pray. He sent Peter and the other disciples back to the boat where they launched out to the sea. A storm sprang up without warning. Violent waves and winds tore at the boat as the frightened disciples struggled to stay afloat. The rising sun revealed an image walking on the water toward them. They were terrified and thought it was a ghost, but they soon saw that it was Jesus. He immediately called out, "Take courage! It is I. Don't be afraid."

Peter was one of those take-on-the-world kind of guys. He often acted first and thought later. He wanted to climb out of the boat and walk on the water toward Jesus, so Jesus told Peter to come. It didn't take long for Peter to feel the fierce winds and high waves around him. He was scared and started to sink. When he desperately cried for Jesus to save him, Jesus reached out His strong hand and rescued him. After they climbed into the boat and the wind quieted, Jesus reminded Peter to trust in Him.

No matter the circumstances, let's look to the Master. When we do, He will faithfully hold our hand.

He Keeps Us Safe

Do not withhold your mercy from me, O Lord; may your love and your truth always protect me.
PSALM 40:11 NIV

MOST OF US have faced danger of one kind or another. Some dangers are the result of unwise decisions. I made a poor choice several years ago while working a second job at a fast-food restaurant.

One night my shift ended at 1:00 a.m. I folded my stiff muscles into my Toyota and headed for home. Flashing lights from a police roadblock and six patrol cars kept me from getting to our house one block over. I made a U-turn, circled the block, parked in our driveway, and whispered a prayer: "Lord, I hope everyone is all right. Please help them."

Curiosity overtook common sense. The corner was only two houses away, and the obstruction, one block down near the apartments, was directly behind our backyard. I could walk down and peek around the corner. I'd lock my car when I returned.

"I can't believe I'm doing this," I mumbled. I ventured to the corner, when a *pop, pop, pop* filled my ears. It sounded like gunshots! I never knew I could run so fast. I scrambled into my unlocked car, frantically elbowed down my lock, and tried to scrunch out of sight. Why did the porch light have to be on? (Bless my husband's heart.) And why did it take thirty seconds for the dome light to turn off *after* the door was closed?

Once the shots stopped, I quietly slipped out of my car and entered our welcoming home.

I could have been seriously injured or killed that night, yet God watched over me. More than we realize, God keeps us safe from danger. Whether we are victims of circumstances or the causes of the problems, we can be grateful for His merciful intervention and protection.

The eternal God is your refuge, and underneath are [His] everlasting arms.
DEUTERONOMY 33:27 NIV

WHEN WE ARE faced with danger, God is our refuge and strength, patiently caring for and protecting us—in spite of our bungles.

That night after work, in spite of the popping noises and flashing police lights at the apartments behind us, I should have gone to bed and left everything to the Lord and the police. But curiosity spurred me on. I crept to our kitchen window, which overlooked our backyard. *Pop, pop!* I hustled to the bedroom and my sleeping husband. How far could bullets fly?

Bob raised his head. "What was that?" he asked.

"It's gunshots!" I whispered hoarsely. "Keep your head down!" I dropped my purse. With one lunge, I dove for the bed and landed with a belly flop, hoping I'd miss Bob.

"Dear God," I managed, "please keep us safe." I clung to Bob, shivering with fright. He pulled the covers over me and wrapped me in his arms.

The shots lessened and Bob fell back to sleep. I huddled under the covers, shoes and all, for an hour. My shivering finally stopped as I waited and listened. Silence. I rose and tiptoed to the window again. I could still see flashing lights. I felt God urging me to trust Him and let others do the worrying. I listened to Him as He calmed my fears. I returned to bed, thankful for God, the police, and the sweet husband I love.

The next day the neighbors buzzed. There had been a domestic dispute. The police coaxed a mother and children from an apartment where there was an armed man. They shot tear gas into the apartment and apprehended the man. Thankfully, no one was harmed.

I thanked God for His lesson that night: to trust Him and rest in His loving, caring presence.

For I cried to him and he answered me! He freed me from all my fears. PSALM 34:4 TLB

DO YOU EVER find yourself filled with fear? Perhaps it's for good reason. Fear of danger, bad influences on our children, the unknown, the future... The list goes on.

When gigantic fears loom over us with foreboding and cruel threats, we can place our trust in God and face them bravely. The longer we cringe and shy away from them, the bigger they can become. Before we know it, they are towering over us, making us feel so helpless that we can't see over, under, around, or through them! Yet no matter how big our fear-monster becomes, God is bigger.

When things are going smoothly, we might be tempted to say, "This is too good to be true. What will happen next? What if...?" When we feel like everything is over our heads, God is still near. He calms our fears and soothes our souls. As we leave our plights to His care, we can be assured that God is taking care of us and those we love.

We worship an understanding, gracious God who knows the future and is in control. We have no guarantees about what will happen next. Still, we know we can trust God to bring about good. There's no limit to His love and grace. Remember, He gave His life for us and keeps our lives for Him.

Whatever our present circumstances are, we can be sure that God is with us all the time. Instead of worrying, He asks us to leave everything with Him and others whom He assigns to help. When we completely trust Him, He helps us overcome our fears. He guides and sustains us. He whispers words of comfort to our hearts. He tenderly envelops us in His big, strong arms and keeps us safe.

Rejoice in the Lord always; again I will say, Rejoice. PHILIPPIANS 4:4 RSV

THINK OF SOME of your favorite getaway experiences. Try writing down what they were and how the Lord used them to bless you during those times of your life. Thank Him for the good memories. If you can, recall the happy memories with the ones you shared the getaways with.

One of my most treasured breakaways was with Bob on a Fourth of July weekend several years ago when our children were grown up enough to take care of themselves. We decided to climb in the car—just the two of us—and just start driving. We had no idea where we were going. We had no deadlines, no expectations. We just drove and laughed about funny things happening in our lives, enjoying the beautiful scenery along the way.

Before we knew it, we had driven from one side of Mt. Rainier to the other. It was late, and we didn't want to drive back in the dark, so we called one of our sons and told him we'd be home the next day, then found a motel in Yakima where we spent the night. Even though we had no luggage, we were content. We still talk about that spontaneous trip we took that holiday weekend. And we still remind ourselves to always keep our sense of adventure.

Sometimes *God* likes to take us on adventures, as well. Perhaps He's already done this for you. The surroundings may be familiar, or He might provide us with something brand-new. He knows what we need before we even do ourselves. He may place certain signs in our pathway, encouraging us to break away with Him. No matter what, let's not put off His beckoning call. When He does, let's be ready to go. All we need to pack is our Bible.

And He said to them, "Come away by yourselves to a secluded place and rest a while."
MARK 6:31 NASB

IN OUR BUSIEST and most stressful times, we may allow our minds to daydream about running away to relax and just have fun.

If you had the chance to escape, where would you like to go? The moon or quiet outer space? An airplane ride to watch the sun sink behind pink cotton-candy clouds? How about a cruise? Hawaii? Deep-sea diving with the dolphins? Relaxing on the beach under the warm sun while waves lap your toes? Floating down a lazy river, or riding the exciting rapids? Watching wildlife in a remote field?

I would love to do all these, but one of my favorite time-outs is catching a sunset or sunrise in my own backyard with my husband, my best friend. Years ago, our youngest son, Dave, and I used to camp in the backyard. Staying in the tent wasn't our cup of tea. We loved it under the stars. We would lie there for hours talking and straining to stay awake, knowing we could see shooting stars from midnight until early morning. Whispering with excitement, we counted them. The next day we felt refreshed and invigorated by our late-night getaways.

The greatest escapes of all are ones we spend with our dearest Friend, the Lord Jesus. He's a wonderful listener. After we talk with Him and wait a little while, He speaks to our hearts and shows us amazing things. We leave feeling refreshed.

Vacations are wonderful, but they are complete when we escape to time alone with God. No matter where we go, He is there—graciously listening and loving.

The next time you are "getting away," take your Bible so you can enjoy some quiet, pleasant time with the Lord. What a wonderful escape it will be!

My soul clings to You; Your right hand upholds me. Psalm 63:8 NASB

Bob and I have our living room recliner chairs placed next to each other. Not even a small end table is between us. During our devotions, work projects, or relaxing together, we often find ourselves holding hands—even after all these years. My hands are much smaller than Bob's. In fact, mine fit in the center of his. We often link part of our fingers so our hands will fit. I think his big, strong hands are one of many reasons why I fell in love with him.

When we're fortunate enough to sit by each other in a meeting, it doesn't take long for us to clasp hands. We frequently squeeze our hands together three times—a silent signal meaning "I love you," something we started doing when we were first engaged. When I'm ill or frightened, Bob's hand is a comfort and strength to me. I think mine is for him as well.

Holding hands makes me think of Bob's parents in their late years. Only a few months ago they went home to be with the Lord. I ponder how some good things pass down from one generation to the next. Considerate people arranged their hospital beds so they could hold hands and remain close.

Even more reassuring is knowing our loving Savior is clasping our hand all the time, twenty-four hours a day, as we love and trust Him. The longer we know Him, the more we recognize His strong, sure grip.

He holds our hand when we work, relax, or simply talk with Him. He clasps our hand when we're sick or afraid. The best part is we never have to let go. I thank my heavenly Father for clasping my hand in His. In Him I place my trust.

Take off your shoes, for you are standing on holy ground. EXODUS 3:5 TLB

PERHAPS THIS PRAYER that came to me one morning in my kitchen will bless you, dear reader, and inspire you to write one of your own to the Lord. May His gracious Holy Spirit fill and strengthen your soul.

❧

Here I stand, Lord. My kitchen sink may be my only altar, but You are so near to me that I can nearly reach out and touch You.

Through the night and early morning I have sought Your direction. At this moment, You unexpectedly shower me with Your glorious, merciful love. Your awesome presence is almost too great to bear. I feel I should remove my shoes, like Moses did, as though I am standing not on simple tile but on holy ground.

How can You be so wonderful, my Lord? All this time I have been pleading with You for my needs. Thank You for now taking them to Your Father, mercifully interceding on my behalf. Just as You prayed in the Garden of Gethsemane before dying for the sins of all humanity, You are taking my needs to the Father right now.

I praise You, Lord, that so many years ago You caused the thick curtain in the temple to rip from top to bottom, exposing the Holy of Holies to all who love and obey You. No longer are we separated from our Father's presence. I can go right in and pour out my soul to You anytime, anywhere.

Remain with me, I pray. Linger with me just a little longer, so I may bask in Your warm, refreshing presence. Teach me what I must learn, and help me obey. Fill me to overflowing with Your Holy Spirit. Thank You for Your touch, Lord, for letting me stand on Your holy ground.

I will pour out my Spirit on all people. Your sons and daughters will prophesy, your old men will dream dreams, your young men will see visions. JOEL 2:28 NIV

DO YOU FEEL God calling you to do something for Him? When we acknowledge Him, His Spirit instills a powerful vision and drive within us to do whatever He asks. Robert Pierce answered God's call, and God blessed in surprising ways.

When Robert was twelve years old, he accepted the Lord as his Savior. Little did he know what God had planned for him. When Robert, better known as Bob, became a teenager, he began preaching on downtown Los Angeles street corners. A few years later, he attended college. Though he didn't consider himself to be very talented, he became student body president. At the end of his junior year, he married a Nazarene minister's daughter. Three children blessed their marriage.

Over the years, Bob answered God's call to serve as a traveling evangelist in the West Coast Church of the Nazarene, an evangelist for World Christian Fundamentals Association, a manager of Eureka Jubilee Singers, a Christian filmmaker, and an assistant minister to his father-in-law at Los Angeles Evangelistic Center. He was ordained by the First Baptist Church in Wilmington, California. He dedicated himself to work with teenagers in Youth for Christ and became Youth for Christ's national vice president. Through his ministry, countless teenagers became Christians.

Whether God's calling for us is large or small, He gives us the vision, power, and abilities to accomplish whatever He asks. The blessings we experience for answering may exceed our wildest dreams. They might even continue from one generation to the next. Let's keep listening for His call then willingly answer. We never know what plans God has in store!

"And if anyone gives even a cup of cold water to one of these little ones because he is my disciple, I tell you the truth, he will certainly not lose his reward." MATTHEW 10:42 NIV

AS WE FOLLOW God's call, we often begin to feel the joys and heartaches of those we are helping. Though some hurts are almost unbearable to face, God gives us the mercy and strength to do so. God gave Bob Pierce a vision. No matter the sacrifice, he knew he must obey.

One day Madame Chiang Kai-shek asked Bob Pierce to bring Youth for Christ to China for a series of rallies. During those rallies, eighteen thousand people came to the Lord! The hurts of the disabled, poor, outcast, and orphaned in China broke Bob's heart. He knew he had to help these people and others like them.

Bob's ministry spread to South Korea. Through his labors, World Vision organization was born. He formed the Korean Orphan Choir, and it traveled all over the world, raising money for the orphans. Dr. Pierce's ministry of mercy expanded from Korea to Taiwan, then into other countries. His heartfelt and memorable statement still rings through history: "Let my heart be broken with the things that break the heart of God."

Sadly, the pain and poverty Dr. Pierce witnessed caused him to become so engulfed in his work to the point that he neglected his own health and died of leukemia. Others picked up Dr. Pierce's torch, and World Vision has expanded to help people all over the world. What began with his love for children and obedience to God's call far exceeded the dedicated missionary's greatest dreams of what God would accomplish. Surely his greatest reward is in heaven.

May God richly bless World Vision workers, givers, and each one of us as we continue to reach out and help others in this lost and needy world.

God's gifts put man's best dreams to shame.
—ELIZABETH BARRETT BROWNING

But I have trusted in Your mercy; my heart shall rejoice in Your salvation. I will sing to the Lord, because He has dealt bountifully with me. PSALM 13:5–6 NKJV

HOW MUCH DOES God love us? Is there a way we can possibly measure His love? When we feel we don't deserve His love, will He discontinue His care? The Bible tells us that no matter where we are placed on this earth, nothing can separate us from His love. All the troubles in the world can't. Being the poorest person on earth can't. Danger can't. He loves us with an everlasting, immeasurable love. It goes on and on forever. Though we are undeserving, God loved us so much that He sacrificed His Son and paid the price for our sin.

David's prayer describes God's love so beautifully in Psalm 36:5 (NASB): "Your lovingkindness, O LORD, extends to the heavens, Your faithfulness reaches to the skies."

All we need to do to find God's love is to open our heart's door and accept it. And when we do, His love will overflow, never to run dry.

෧

There was a time, Lord, when I felt so discouraged about the difficulties I was going through that I wondered if You had forgotten me. I questioned whether I was good enough to deserve Your love and if You were actually hiding Your face from me. No matter how hard I tried, I couldn't win the battles I tried to fight on my own. Even so, I knew You were and are the true Victor.

Then I felt Your Spirit minister to my soul. With feeble voice and heart, I pleaded for You to bring Your light back into my life. It didn't take long for me to trust in Your unfailing love. Thank You for the way You put a song in my heart and gave me new joy and victory over all circumstances!

I wait for the LORD, *my soul waits, and in his word I put my hope.* PSALM 130:5 NIV

WHEN DISASTER STRIKES, we may be tempted to lose hope and give up. However, God uses our tragedies to bring out the best in us, and He mercifully brings us through our troubles.

Dwight L. Moody told about an Englishman who lived in Chicago during the winter before the Great Fire. The man had observed rapid growth in the forty-year-old city. Impressed by its magnificent buildings, churches, and schools, he decided to report his findings to people in Manchester, England, and its surrounding areas. However, no one shared his interest about Chicago.

One day the news spread about Chicago's catastrophic fire. All seemed hopeless; half of the city had burned. Sad reports came; over 100,000 people were homeless and nearly starving.

People were shocked when they heard the news. Everyone began showing concern, with thousands responding to the need. Finally, others had become interested in the city.

It's the same with our lives. God works it all together for good. He replaces despair with hope and confidence for the future.

When my hope is nearly gone, Lord, when I feel totally cast down, I might wonder if You or others care about me in this busy world, if others even know I need help.

Yet even though everything seems hopeless, Your Word assures me that nothing is impossible when I put my trust in You. I won't allow myself to dwell on the negative. Instead, I'll leave my problems in Your hands.

Thank You for gently changing my perspective from despair to hope and confidence in You.

God is our refuge and strength, a very present help in trouble. PSALM 46:1 KJV

MANY OF US enjoy hearing about people being rescued by police, firefighters, paramedics, and sometimes everyday heroes. In the midst of danger, it's comforting to know about those who reach out and grasp the hands of others in order to help them. The rescuer may calmly say, "Relax. I've got you!" Then like a knight in shining armor, he or she skillfully takes charge and provides safety.

I recently visited one of our sons at his remote countryside home. One morning, while walking through the yard, I discovered a small green frog trapped in a five-gallon bucket of water, frantically swimming round and round. It couldn't seem to scale the smooth sides and was in danger of drowning.

The frog looked helplessly up at me. I couldn't help but smile at the creature and calmly said, "What are you doing in there? Relax. I've got you." I tipped the bucket to one side so water could slowly pour out. A gentle nudge from my fingertip and the brownish green critter was freed. It rested for a while before heading for its rightful home.

Like me, you may sometimes get ahead of God's will and find yourself stuck in the middle of a problem, running frantically in circles, unable to find a way out. Then, when all our feeble attempts fail, we cry out to God and trust Him to help. When we're finally ready to hand over our entire mess to Him and trust Him, He reaches His strong hands out to us and patiently says: "Relax. Trust Me. I've got You."

We relax and trust while He takes charge and keeps us safe.

And my God will supply every need of yours according to his riches in glory in Christ Jesus.
PHILIPPIANS 4:19 RSV

DID YOU EVER feel God nudging you to do a kindness for someone else, even if it involved giving up something you treasured?

Terry had a blue canvas duffel bag with zippered pockets in all the right places. She carried it wherever she traveled. It didn't have wheels, but slipping the handles over her roller suitcase bar made transporting it easy. But the bag was falling apart and wouldn't survive another trip. Finally, she decided to spend forty dollars for another bag—this time one with rollers.

A few days later, she felt God bringing to mind some close friends who were going through discouraging circumstances. She knew she was to give up purchasing the bag and send the money to her friends instead. She also felt she was to send exactly forty dollars. Terry's obedience left a warm feeling in her heart. Purchasing another duffel bag could wait.

Sometime later she was visiting with her friend Janice and decided to share the story with her. Janice jumped up and pulled out a beautiful blue backpack that her grown daughter Sarah had left after a visit. Sarah gave permission by phone for it to go to Terry.

Terry's mouth dropped open in surprise. It was a flexible blue canvas backpack with pockets in all the right places, complete with rollers! It appeared to hold as much as Terry's worn bag. Surprisingly, there was a smaller blue duffel bag inside. All three ladies agreed that God knew Terry didn't need the forty dollars because He already had a backpack and duffel bag waiting for her.

Isn't it amazing how God works in mysterious ways to give us His mind-boggling blessings!

Teach us to put our trust in Thee and to await Thy helping hand.
—TRADITIONAL AMISH PRAYER

May grace and peace be multiplied to you in the knowledge of God and of Jesus our Lord.
2 PETER 1:2 RSV

GIVING TO OTHERS is something most of us enjoy doing; and it brings a warm feeling to our hearts. We are practicing the Scripture that urges us to do kind deeds without expecting anything in return: "But when you do a charitable deed, do not let your left hand know what your right hand is doing, that your charitable deed may be in secret; and your Father who sees in secret will Himself reward you openly" (Matthew 6:3–4 NKJV).

There are some people who refuse to lend money. Instead, they willingly give a money gift and explain they don't want it repaid, suggesting that the receiver pass on a blessing to someone else when the time is right.

To me, giving is much easier than receiving. It takes graciousness and humility to receive a kindness. I find myself wanting to do something in return. However, a sincere thank-you is often all the other person wants.

In the story of the Good Samaritan, the man who was looked down upon by those around him didn't hesitate to help the man who had been robbed, beaten, and left for dead along the side of the road. The Samaritan not only tended the man's wounds, he took him to a nearby inn and saw to it that the man was cared for. The story never mentions that the man would have to repay the Samaritan for his generosity.

When we insist on repaying a kindness shown to us, we may be cheating the giver out of a blessing. I wonder if God wants us to be gracious receivers so the givers can enjoy the blessings of contentment that fill their own souls.

A sincere thank-you from a gracious receiver awards the giver boundless blessings of warmth and joy.

Humility and reverence for the Lord will make you both wise and honored. PROVERBS 15:33 TLB

DO YOU KNOW someone who possesses a heart of humility? Do his or her mannerisms cause you to pause and take notice?

I know a lady who has a warm and humble way that I deeply admire. Whenever I see her, I pray for my attitude to improve. She's always willing to listen and care about others. She isn't famous, nor does she hold any titles or degrees. She doesn't try to build herself up or brag about her accomplishments. Instead, she radiates the life-giving presence of the Holy Spirit. Others respect her because she loves God and is content with simply being herself. The more I get to know this lady, the more I realize she's the way she is because she reflects a peace that all is well with her soul. Her main focus is the Lord and the wisdom He gives her.

Nineteenth-century preacher Dr. T. DeWitt Talmage pointed out that many great leaders come from humble homes. They learned while still young to care for the poor and oppressed. According to his observations, great thoughts frequently come from humble people. Although many leaders begin their early years in obscure circumstances, they develop into noble leaders for humanity and axletrees that turn the course of history. Most significantly, our Savior and Lord was born of humble means in a lowly stable.

Father, I feel humbled to come before You in prayer. Help me turn my focus from myself to be wholeheartedly fixed on You. My accomplishments, my failures, I give to You. I pray that others will look past me and see You, my main source of peace and confidence. May all I do bring You honor and praise.

An attitude of peace given is gratitude of peace received.

"I have loved you, O my people, with an everlasting love; with loving-kindness I have drawn you to me." JEREMIAH 31:3 TLB

HOW MUCH DOES God love us? His love for us is so great that it can't even be measured. He who spoke creation into existence put the greatest of love and care into creating you and me.

Isn't it wonderful that we're a part of Him and made in His image, yet we're still created to be individuals? He already knew us well since He secretly fashioned our innermost parts while we were in our mother's wombs. He formed our eyes, noses, mouths, even the hairs on our heads (that He can still number).

God loves us with a wholehearted, unquenchable love. He draws us to Him and watches over us day and night. He keeps us safe in the shadow of His wings like a mother hen protects her chicks. When we fall asleep, He's with us. When we awaken, He still remains. He thinks of us all the time. If we tried to count His thoughts about us, the number would be more than all the grains of sand in the world.

Because God loves us, He wants us to wholeheartedly love Him in return. Deuteronomy 6 tells us that God wants us to acknowledge His presence in our everyday lives, to talk about Him with our children while sitting at home, going for walks, tucking them into bed, and waking them in the morning.

God wants us to write about His love on our walls, our door frames, and our gates, and to store His love in our hearts. When we do, He provides us with peace and understanding that go beyond all else.

All the money we could ever give, all the sacrifices we could ever make can never compare to our returning to Him the wholehearted love He gives to us.

For God did not send His Son into the world to condemn the world, but that the world through Him might be saved. JOHN 3:17 NKJV

THE TROUBLES AND anxieties of this world press in around us daily and batter the doors of our lives. Because of the crises in our world, we may hesitate to even turn on the news. When disaster strikes and we mourn, we often rush to our churches in search of comfort and strength.

Whose side is God on during these troublesome times? Where can we find peace? Is God watching over us? How strong is our military power if we aren't depending on God? I believe God isn't on our side or the sides of those we unite with. Neither is He taking the sides of our enemies. God is graciously on the side of right.

When God gave His Son Jesus to die on the cross, He didn't make the sacrifice for one certain group of people. We're all unworthy of His love and mercy. No, He gave His Son for every one of us. Let's take our focus off the troubles of this world and center it on Jesus. Let's pray fervently for world peace and for people to know Him as their Savior—whether they're friend or foe.

God really does answer our prayers. Isn't it astounding that we can pray for people clear across the world? Our prayers are free and unrestrained! The Bible says a righteous prayer is filled with His power. God is here and on the other side of the world at the same time. All we need to do is open our battered doors and communicate with Him.

The next time we turn on the news or experience disaster, let's stop and pray about the problems. As we do so, we become the peacemakers. While we continue focusing on the things of God, He will mercifully keep us in His perfect peace.

Snatched Away

May peace and blessing be yours from God the Father and from the Lord Jesus Christ.
GALATIANS 1:3 TLB

"I WISH I could have some peace." How often have we mumbled these words? We long for peace but may miss the opportunities God sends us.

God gave me such an opportunity in the form of my husband's persistent voice one spring day. When I arrived home from my teaching job on the last day of school, Bob met me at the door with a big smile, puppy dog eyes, and a tall glass of ice water. "Let's run away," he urged. "Grab your tablet and pen. We'll find a quiet place for you to write."

Even though I was tired, I wanted to dive into writing and catch up on house and yard work. I didn't have time to take a break. But Bob wouldn't take no for an answer. Minutes later, we were heading down the road.

"Mountains or water?" Bob asked.

"Um, water," I mumbled.

We drove for hours. Soon my body relaxed and I began enjoying the scenery. It was late when we arrived in a town called Belfair, so we spent the night. The next morning, we drove to Twanoh State Park where we enjoyed a gorgeous view of Hood Canal. Bob offered to read at a picnic table near the car and give me a couple of hours to write. I found a table by the water and was amazed at how a good night's sleep and the serene setting made the words fly onto the page.

Two hours later I heard Bob approaching the table. We held hands and thanked God for the opportunity He gave us, with still enough time to enjoy the rest of the day together. How blessed I felt that God compassionately snatched me away and provided peace.

Peace comes from God's gracious direction. Watch for its beckoning call.

"Are not two sparrows sold for a cent? And yet not one of them will fall to the ground apart from your Father.... So do not fear; you are more valuable than many sparrows." MATTHEW 10:29, 31 NASB

NO MATTER HOW hopeless childhood may have seemed, how difficult life has been, or what we've made of our lives, Jesus is near. Through it all, He watches over us as much or more than He does a tiny sparrow. And He calls us to be His own. That's exactly what happened to the lady in this story.

She was born with the help of a Polish midwife; her African American mother had been raped. For a long time, her mother didn't love her, so she was shuffled from place to place as a child. Her grandmother and Aunt Ide watched over her the most.

Dr. and Mrs. Bell were neighbors of Aunt Ide who always made her welcome in their home. Dr. Bell was the pastor of a small church in downtown Philadelphia. When she visited them, she enjoyed learning gospel songs. Yet in spite of Dr. and Mrs. Bell's attempts to be a good influence, the allure of Philadelphia's mean streets was too powerful. To survive, she had to be tough. She beat up anyone who crossed her and soon gained a bad reputation. By age twelve, she had become a ringleader for a street gang.

Still, her love for music kept her in church. The influence and prayers from those who cared about her slowly paid off. One Sunday morning in a little Chester, Pennsylvania, church, the struggling adolescent girl gave her heart to the Lord. Her life changed immediately. Between her Christian friends and the beloved Dr. and Mrs. Bell, she finally realized what it meant to be loved.

Jesus constantly watches over us and loves us just as we are. He's asking us to release everything to Him and to invite Him into our hearts. When we do, He begins a brand-new life in us.

Because it is written, "Be holy, for I am holy." 1 PETER 1:16 NKJV

BEING A CHRISTIAN isn't always easy. Along with facing temptations, we may also struggle with hurt feelings from others.

Shortly after the girl from the previous devotion accepted Jesus, she was ridiculed by another girl who was jealous of her singing. The two almost got into a fight. Instead, our heroine walked out the church door. Angry and deeply hurt, she stopped going to church. During the following years, she became a successful singer in prestigious nightclubs and, eventually, on television. Still, she longed for a closer walk with God.

Many years later, while in New York, she began attending a Billy Graham Crusade in Madison Square Garden. She'd previously performed there in front of thousands of people. This time she clung to Billy Graham's messages. She felt like a hungry baby bird receiving one morsel of spiritual food at a time.

One night the crusade's choir sang a song she'd sung with the little church in Chester. She recognized that God wanted her to sing for Him but money was scarce. How could singing for God become a reality?

Suddenly a voice rang over the speakers, inviting her to sing "His Eye Is on the Sparrow" for the crusade. Although she'd performed the song many times before, this was different. Despite being scared, her professional experience took over. She stepped to the microphone... and then something happened. She realized she was living two lives. In God's eyes, she couldn't be on both sides of the fence.

Ethel Waters finished singing, sat down, and rededicated her heart to Jesus. The Lord had a new plan for her life.

Lord, take my lips and speak through them; take my mind and think through it; take my heart and set it on fire. —WILLIAM H. AITKEN

Looking at them, Jesus said, "With people it is impossible, but not with God; for all things are possible with God." MARK 10:27 NASB

LIKE ETHEL DID that night at the Billy Graham Crusade, we, too, need to dedicate and rededicate our lives to the Lord—giving Him our worries and wants, our goals and dreams. God never asks the impossible from us. He knows the whole picture. When He calls, He makes a way. As we take each step of faith, the Lord graciously opens doors and makes the impossible possible.

After Ethel rededicated her life to the Lord, she felt a marvelous, forgiving presence fill her. She discovered a peace she'd never known. The hurt and bitterness she'd stored up throughout her life melted away.

Ethel continued singing at the crusade meetings instead of returning to work. Even though she didn't know how she could make a living by singing for the Lord, she fought her doubts and kept committing everything to God. She knew one thing: He *would* provide. When she returned home, she cancelled her club engagements.

Many people heard Ethel Waters sing on national television with the Billy Graham Crusade. She sang for Youth for Christ Crusades and the Tennessee Ernie Ford and Roy Rogers and Dale Evans Show TV variety series. Each time Ethel sang "His Eye Is on the Sparrow," she told how she loved God and what He'd done for her.

She sang "Deep River," "Just a Closer Walk with Thee," and many spiritual favorites.

Because of God's love and mercy for Ethel Waters, she was able to use her inspiration and influence to pass on His love—a message that spanned several generations and reached millions of lives, young and old.

Perhaps God is tenderly calling you. Know for sure that when He does, He always makes a way.

Love your neighbor as yourself. ROMANS 13:9 NIV

LOVING ONESELF IS often a difficult thing to do. We may be disappointed with our weight, our talents or intelligence, or how we compare to others. But when we're unable to love and care about ourselves, what do we have to offer to the Lord or others? When we ask Jesus to be our Savior, He claims us to become His very own sons and daughters. He doesn't love us because of our merit. He loves us because of His all-encompassing mercy and grace.

A woman I'll call Patty was miserable and angry with the world. She didn't trust other people and wouldn't allow herself to get close to anyone. Because of her attitude, few people wanted to be around her. Nevertheless, God graciously surrounded her with Christian people who prayed for her. They were able to befriend her, and she began to feel comfortable telling them how she felt about herself. One day a friend showed Patty a Scripture that changed her life. It's found in Matthew 22:37 and 39: "Love the Lord your God with all your heart and with all your soul and with all your mind.... Love your neighbor as *yourself*" (NIV; emphasis added).

Patty accepted Jesus as her Savior, and she learned to love herself as God already loved her. Now she isn't afraid to love others as well.

Lord, help me to love myself as You love me. Show me how to forgive myself for my wrongs, because You have forgiven me. I'm no longer afraid to love others because You taught me how to love.

God can do wonders with a broken heart if you give Him all the pieces.
—VICTOR ALFSEN

Ever-Living Laughter

A cheerful heart is good medicine, but a crushed spirit dries up the bones. PROVERBS 17:22 NIV

DEEP-DOWN JOY THAT can only come from the Lord plays an extremely important role in our lives. It gives us hope for each day and contributes towards our feeling better emotionally and physically.

There's much we can do to improve our health: proper food and rest, exercise, regular physical check-ups, etc. One that's essential to me is a deep-down dose of ever-living laughter from the belly.

The Bible tells us: "A cheerful heart is good medicine" (Proverbs 17:22 NIV); and "The joy of the Lord is your strength" (Nehemiah 8:10 NIV).

The gift of laughter helps improve our well-being. Medical studies prove that good old-fashioned belly laughs make us breathe deeply and send more oxygen to cells of our body. They reduce adrenaline and other stress-related substances, easing tension and calming emotions. They make us more alert. A hearty laugh sends natural painkillers through our stressed-out be-ings, helping to relieve some of those "knot-in-the-neck" headaches. Did you know a few minutes a day of deep belly laughing also burns calories and helps relationships?

On the day Bob and I were married, my future father-in-law drove me to the church to check on the catering equipment. He gave me some advice that has stayed with me for almost fifty years. "Always keep your sense of humor, Neat," he quipped. "It will carry you and your love for Bob a long way. When I get in trouble with Ma, I stick my head in the door and ask if I can throw my hat in first. Ma and I always burst out in laughter."

We live in a complex world. Life may not always be happy, but it can still be filled with God's wonderful joy. So let yourself relax, and enjoy a good laugh.

A true friend is always loyal.... PROVERBS 17:17 TLB

FRIENDSHIP IS ONE of our greatest blessings. We may enjoy many friends, but we often have only a few who are close.

Loyal friends remain near and help us weather the good and bad in life. When one of my friends struggled for several years with her rebellious teenage daughter, some people deserted her. But others remained close, praying, sharing Scripture, having her over to tea, and simply giving her hugs.

Good friends overlook our faults. They are also willing to speak honestly when asked. A couple of my close friends manage to do both for me. They tell me truthfully what they think, yet they are compassionate enough to understand my needs and feelings. They look for the best in me and expect me to do my best.

We all long for true, dependable friends who stick closer than a brother or sister. These kinds of friends believe in us and hold us up in prayer. They remain loyal and are willing to stick up for us when things go wrong. But we unfortunately also have "friends" who only pretend to be our friends. When things go wrong, they may not show that they care.

A treasured friendship is like a two-way street. Both care about the other and are willing to talk and listen. The enjoyment gained from the friendships spring from earnest counsel and understanding. This kind of sweet company is like perfume and incense that bring joy to our souls.

Luke 6:31 tells us, "Do to others as you would have them do to you" (NIV). May we offer to our treasured friends the same faithful, gracious love that Jesus, our Friend, gives to us.

A true friend is somebody who can make us do what we can.
—RALPH WALDO EMERSON

Lord, what do You want me to do? ACTS 9:6 NKJV

HEAVENLY FATHER, I love coming to You in prayer. Here at this simple worship center in my home, I bring You my thanksgiving and praise. Thank You for surrounding me with Your loving presence. The more we commune with each other, the more I love and appreciate You.

My heart's longing is to be more like You. I long for You to lay out one at a time the wonderful lessons You want to teach me. I take delight in You as You answer the desires of my heart to know You better every day. To You I commit my ways and trust in You completely. I will not worry about how You meet my needs when I bring them to You. You know what's best. In Your good time, You answer in the right way.

What comfort and exceeding joy You give me, my Father. May my meditations be as a sweet-smelling fragrance to You. You are my God, yet still my dearest friend. In You I place my hope and dreams for the future. May all of them bring glory to You.

As I go about my duties today, may praises, requests, and thanksgiving to You continually spring forth from my heart. Thank You for what You have taught me. Help me to remain within Your will in all I do and say.

Thank You for fulfilling my heart's longing to become more like You. I love You above all else, Father. In the name of Jesus, amen.

In the secret of His presence how my soul delights to hide!
Oh, how precious are the lessons which I learn at Jesus' side!
—ELLEN LAKSHMI GOREH

I will say of the LORD, "He is my refuge and my fortress; my God, in Him I will trust."
PSALM 91:2 NKJV

HOW OFTEN HAVE our plans been altered, delayed, or even cancelled due to circumstances beyond our control! Perhaps it happens because we're distracted by other things or because of obstacles we encounter. We may not always recognize God's hand in it to protect us from disaster.

Linda was delighted to be able to take her daughter and friend, who were visiting from out of town, to see the local sights in the mountains. While driving toward a special spot she wanted to show them, they somehow missed their turnoff. Eventually they realized their mistake and turned around. When they finally found the correct turnoff, they realized it was getting late and decided to head back home.

Imagine their surprise and gratitude when they returned home and learned that their delays and detours had saved them from being caught not only in a rock slide but also in a huge landslide that blocked the road and filled the nearby river. God had a surprising part in watching over them and keeping them safe.

We can be thankful for the ways He sometimes sends angels or redirects our paths away from danger or harm.

God moves in a mysterious way
His wonders to perform;
He plants His footsteps in the sea,
And rides upon the storm.

Ye fearful saints, fresh courage take;
The clouds ye so much dread
Are big with mercy, and shall break
In blessings on your head.
—WILLIAM COWPER

He Draws Us Back

I have strayed like a lost sheep. Seek your servant, for I have not forgotten your commands.
PSALM 119:176 NIV

A FEW MONTHS ago a young man named Jeff was substituting as a recess teacher when he noticed a large group of children running aimlessly around the playground like a bunch of lost sheep. Their leader captivated them with loud shouts and flamboyant actions. It was clear to Jeff that their reckless behavior spelled impending trouble.

A quick tweet of his whistle and beckon of his index finger caused the group to stop in their tracks. A firm warning to make better choices helped most of the kids to change their behavior. Still, Jeff carefully watched the child who wanted to rebel. Eventually he had the child stay with him for the rest of the recess.

We adults can become like lost sheep and get sidetracked without being aware of how the whims of some influential people affect us. We may even get to the point where we lose our sense of right or wrong. When we allow the opinions and lifestyles of other people to overshadow the wonderful purpose-filled life God has to offer, it doesn't take long for chaos and heartbreak to take over our lives. We soon become lost. We're confused as to how we can get back on the right path, and we wonder if there is any way out of our predicament.

It's never too late to ask the Savior to draw us back into His loving care. Think of how a shepherd gently yet firmly calls out to his lost sheep and uses the crook of his staff to draw it close. In the same way, Jesus the Shepherd calls us back to Him and keep us close. There with us by His side He leads us back to a new life with Him—a life filled with joy and peace and purpose.

The testing of your faith develops perseverance. Perseverance must finish its work so that you may be mature and complete, not lacking anything. JAMES 1:3–5 NIV

HAVE YOU EVER told yourself during trying times to cheer up, that things could be worse—and then discovered that sure enough, they did get worse?

Sometimes we bolster our courage and trust God only to find things growing more discouraging than ever. We then fall on our knees amongst the mucky confusion and uncertainties and plead again for God's help.

When I go through discouragement, I take a deep breath, stubbornly grit my teeth, and once again yield to His plan for me. Then, in His perfect way, God graciously continues to lead. Each time I trust Him with the good and bad in my life, I experience fantastic victories and thank Him for bringing me through.

Had the man in John 9, blind since birth, been hoping and praying that the Savior would stop and heal him? Jesus could take away his infirmity.

How did the man feel when Jesus came up to him? Frightened? Confused? Excited? What if he hadn't allowed the Savior to put *saliva-filled* mud on his eyes?

The man was undoubtedly eager to wash off the muck in the Pool of Siloam. He must have been overwhelmed to see for the first time and yet ecstatic that he had obeyed Jesus. Was he now afraid to tell others of this great thing Jesus had done for him? Perhaps his faith was being put to the test.

Often God asks us to tell other people what He's done for us, even though some who don't know Him may think we're strange. Still, our obedience is an essential link to the mercy He provides. We'll find that God takes the muck and turns it into something good, filled with His blessings.

Blessed is the man [or woman] who perseveres under trial, because when he has stood the test, he will receive the crown of life that God has promised to those who love him. JAMES 1:12 NIV

IT'S SCARY WHEN we go through challenges and uncertainties. We may even wonder why they happen. Yet God uses a mixture of the bad and the good, the muck and the water, to accomplish His perfect will.

In spite of controversy over Jesus healing people, the formerly blind man couldn't wait to tell everyone what had happened—"The man they call Jesus put mud on my eyes; I washed, and now I can see!" (Paraphrased from John 9.)

When the Pharisees hurled insults at the man, he refused to back down. He wouldn't deny the miracle. What a letdown, to be mistreated by presumably holy men of God after being healed. Why would God heal him and then allow him to go through all this? He received an answer when Jesus came to him again: "[Jesus] said, 'Do you believe in the Son of Man?' 'Who is he, sir?' the man asked. 'Tell me so that I may believe in him.' Jesus said, 'You have now seen him; in fact, he is the one speaking with you.' Then the man said, 'Lord, I believe,' and he worshiped him" (John 9:35–38 NIV).

Perhaps he even became one of Jesus' followers.

The next time you face difficulties and criticism, keep in mind that Jesus loves you. Hand the uncomfortable muck over to Him. Allow Him to touch and lead you. Trust in Him to answer your prayers in *His* way. We must totally yield to Him, no matter what.

It may get worse for a while. But God takes the mucky bad times, works them together in His hands, and achieves greater things than we can ever imagine. Later, you can tell everyone who will listen about the gracious things God does for you—but remember to thank Him for the help *and* the muck!

Blessed are those who have learned to acclaim you, who walk in the light of your presence, O LORD. PSALM 89:15 NIV

I'M SO GLAD I could have this chance to come to You in prayer, Lord. In the quiet of this morning hour I get a chance to bask in the light of Your love. The only noises I hear are the birds and the cars passing on the street. I'm pleased I was able to rise early so You and I could talk—and listen. I sip on a cup of tea, even as the thirst of my soul is being satisfied by the pure, sweet waters of Your Holy Spirit. How I rejoice in Your gracious presence.

How dear You are to me, Lord, as You minister to my soul. I praise Your name for filling me to overflowing with Your faithful love and care. I open my Bible and read of Your lessons that are tried and true. As I ask for Your guidance, Your Holy Spirit leads me to Scriptures and gives me the wisdom I need. Thank You for Your promise of hope and direction. No matter how important or insignificant my concerns might be, You have a remarkable way of solving each one.

Lead me this day, I pray. Help me to be mindful of Your constant presence. Keep me calm. Help me to be gracious and courteous on the freeway, at traffic lights, in my workplace, and especially with my loved ones at home. From the beginning to the end of my day, Lord, may I be an encouragement to others and bring honor to You. In each circumstance, I give You gratitude and exalt Your holy name.

Thank You for the time I get to have with You and for allowing me to bask in the light of Your love. In You I delight. In You I place my trust. In Your presence I rejoice.

Cravings

Oh...give thanks to the LORD *for His goodness, and for His wonderful works to the children of men! For He satisfies the longing soul, and fills the hungry soul with goodness.* PSALM 107:8−9 NKJV

IT HAS BEEN said we women have a vital need for a specific food element in our bodies: chocolate! I like to think this is true. When the pace picks up, stress attacks, fatigue sets in...and chocolate calls, it just *has* to be a dietary need.

When deadlines flood the workplace, employees strip the break room snack stand of its chocolate. Before significant holidays when our everyday pace kicks into high gear, chocolate shows up everywhere. I like a nice cup of hot chocolate, especially at the end of a long day. Its warm, smooth liquid soothes and relaxes me.

Whether these things are good or bad remains to be determined. However, when our bodies like something, our minds attempt to fit it into our diets.

God gave us the greatest ingredient of all to meet our needs no matter what life brings our way: the warm presence of His Holy Spirit. As Christians, our souls periodically become drained. We grow weak and irritable. Before long, we crave precious time with the Lord so we can be strengthened by His calming presence.

God refreshes and rejuvenates us. His gracious presence is more satisfying than hot chocolate or a good night's sleep. Our minds quicken and our emotions lift and remain intact as we drink in His presence. It isn't like an instant fix. Experiencing God's presence requires avoiding the distractions and tuning in to Him, where we allow nothing to come before Him.

When we take time with God, He exceeds all else! Unlike material solutions that soon fade away, we have a holy God who loves us and showers His mercy on us when we pray. Whether we're relaxed or stressed, His presence meets and surpasses *all* our needs.

There is a friend who sticks closer than a brother [or sister]. PROVERBS 18:24 NKJV

MANY OF US enjoy good friendships, yet we might have just a few close friends that are like soul mates and true blessings from the Lord. They are the kind of friends we love talking with by the hour, the kind we can let down our guards with and simply be ourselves. When we're fortunate enough to have friends like this, we are truly blessed.

One day I stopped by to see one of my friends, planning to stay only a few minutes. Neither of us felt well that day, but when she grinned at me and suggested we run away to a natural zoo called Northwest Trek, I just had to say yes. We wandered all over the countryside, enjoying the animals and nature. Our spirits lifted as we laughed and visited about whatever came to mind.

Another friend of mine lives a couple hours from our home. She always keeps a bed waiting for me for whenever I want to run away and write. There in her wooded backyard, she and I enjoy brainstorming what we can write next for the Lord. Hours fly like minutes while we enjoy our time, friend-to-friend.

I have another friend who's dear to me and has been my friend since we were young girls. Whenever I knock at her door, she welcomes me in and shares a cup of tea. There at her kitchen table, we share our concerns and secrets. The past and present blend while we lift each other's needs up in prayer.

Each time I get to be with my friends, I'm reminded of how precious our time is. Life goes too fast. The next time you're weighing the options of work or play, consider running away with a friend.

For you were bought at a price; therefore glorify God in your body and in your spirit, which are God's.
1 CORINTHIANS 6:20 NKJV

HOW DEAR YOU are to me, heavenly Father. I come to You in prayer and bask in Your warm, loving presence. How comforting is the way Your Holy Spirit fills my heart's cup to overflowing. Your love for me is more rewarding and satisfying than anything or anyone else. Thank You for treasuring me, for calling me Your child. I really am a child of You, my King!

As You know, Father, there was a time when I didn't realize how much You loved me. I allowed myself to think I was worthless to others, myself, and sadly even to You. Because of the way I had been treated, I couldn't imagine any kind of a future for me other than one filled with heartache, despair, and fear.

That was before You got my attention and kept whispering to my heart that You were there for me every single moment, every single day. No matter how frightening things were, You assured me that You would make ways of escape and help me through. Then You showed me through Christian friends and Your Word that I didn't need to remain in such hopeless circumstances. You had something better planned for me.

You made the conditions for my getting help very clear. You showed me that I must love You with all my heart, soul, and mind, and put You above anyone or anything else. Thank You for graciously helping me to escape the sinking sand of my abusive past and setting my feet on Your solid rock. Through You, I've learned to build a firm foundation for my life. How grateful I am that You saw worth in me, forgiving me and treasuring me as Your own.

But now the Lord who created you, O Israel, says, "Don't be afraid, for I have ransomed you; I have called you by name; you are mine." ISAIAH 43:1 TLB

NONE OF US manage to make it through life without facing heartache. One of those heartaches is the painful experience of divorce. Perhaps you or someone you care about has or is facing a divorce. Someone who went through a divorce once told me that it's more painful than losing someone by death; she said she felt like surgery had been done on her with a dull teaspoon.

Those who are going through a divorce often wonder how in the world they will ever make it through. For better or worse, their spouses have been a large part of their lives, and they feel the tremendous loss. Piece by piece was ruthlessly cut away until there seemed to be nothing left of themselves. Some felt they were living a barren existence. They didn't think they were loved or beautiful anymore.

The best way to survive the hurt of divorce is to depend on the understanding, compassionate love of our heavenly Father. As we turn to Him and ask Him to take our despondency and carry our grief, our Father replaces our shattered feelings of nothingness with His blessed, holy Presence. Through it all, He becomes our Guide. When we're unable to solve the problems, He gives us strength and goes where we can't.

He comforts and loves us. He will never, ever leave us. He shares our grief and carries our sorrow. He tells us He loves us and that we are worthy of His love. He reminds us that we can love ourselves the way He loves us. He teaches us to forgive and go on. Through the stripes He received on the cross, He restores us and begins the healing process.

As we walk day-by-day in His pathway, we gain a new life through Him that's filled with joy and peace.

O Lord, when You favored me, You made my mountain stand firm. Psalm 30:7 NIV

My friend Charlene, a dedicated Christian and a leader in her church, felt her life was shattered by a tragic, unwanted divorce. After meeting with her divorce lawyer to make final arrangements, she reeled with emotional pain. She had to take her daughter Jessie to an eye doctor's appointment, so after signing Jessie in at the desk she waited for her in the car. She leaned back and closed her eyes. Gloomy thoughts filled her mind. It must all be her fault. How could she be worthy of love?

A holy Presence jerked Charlene out of her stupor. She realized those degrading thoughts weren't of God. He loved her. She sat up straight and haltingly cried out, "Lord Jesus, take control of my mind and emotions. Help me to forgive my husband, and speak to his heart."

Soon God's presence surrounded her like a soft, warm breeze. She noticed a huge cedar tree towering proudly over the doctor's office, its strong branches spreading over its surroundings. "Jesus, that tree has weathered lots of storms," she prayed. "It's firmly rooted, when trees around it have been cut down. It's a survivor. I want to be like that, Lord. I'm sinking my roots deeply in You. Through You I can stand tall despite what my children and I are going through. Right now I feel rejected, Lord. Still, I know You're helping me. Grant me wisdom and graciousness to be a blessing to those I love."

Amazing peace enveloped Charlene. She knew His understanding mercy and grace made her worthy of His love, and that He would always remain with her.

As He was with Charlene, our gracious Lord is also here for us, helping and leading us.

And I will ask the Father, and he will give you another Counselor to be with you forever—the Spirit of truth. JOHN 14:16–17 NIV

FATHER, HERE I am in gridlock freeway traffic, hemmed in on all sides. I've been going full-speed ahead lately and have barely taken time to spend with You. My only excuse? There's been so much to do.

Now I'm at a standstill. I don't know what the problem is ahead, but these cars aren't moving. I switch off my engine. In the sanctuary of my car, all grows silent. The world around me stops. It reminds me of those scenes in movies when everything is frozen in motion.

Anxiety and stress leave me as I think of You. I pull out my Bible from the glove box and read Your Word. I open my mind to Your presence. Your Scriptures saturate my thirsty soul. Forgive me, Lord, for putting off this precious time with You. Take hold of my deeply rooted faults. Prune them. Grant me freedom from wrong motives and actions.

Let me hear the winds of Your Holy Spirit speak to me. Teach me Your lessons. Reveal Your secrets to me so I may triumph over life's daily challenges. Allow me to dream Your dreams and see Your visions.

Thank You for causing Your winds to whisper to the center of my soul and fill my being. You, Lord, are great and mighty. I can barely contain Your love as You fill my heart to overflowing. Thank You for the way Your righteousness and power surround me.

The world suddenly returns from freeze mode to the present. Traffic edges forward. Thank You for stopping me in my tracks so I can take in the lessons of Your Word. I praise You for helping me draw close and listen to Your leading. Thank You for enabling me to hear the winds of Your Holy Spirit stirring within my soul.

The LORD will guide you continually, and satisfy your soul in drought, and strengthen your bones; you shall be like a watered garden, and like a spring of water, whose waters do not fail.
ISAIAH 58:11 NKJV

DO YOU EVER feel like you're stretched so thin that you don't know which way to turn? Do you long to get your spiritual batteries recharged by God's ever-present Holy Spirit?

Some time ago a hectic schedule had left me worn out physically and mentally. I needed an escape, even if only a short one. I slipped on my sweats and tennis shoes, grabbed my Bible, and trudged to the riverbank.

I sank to my knees at the gnarled base of a huge maple tree. I considered how its roots must have gone beneath the soil as deep as the tree was tall, drawing in water for strength and growth. "I'm used up, Lord," I prayed. "Please refill me and bring back the joy and vitality I so desperately need from You."

Time was no longer an object. There I knew He understood my every concern and addressed my needs. As I read from His Word, He filled me with His cleansing Spirit and restored my vitality and strength. Like the tree I knelt under, I sank my roots down deep into the soil of His compassionate love and grace.

His calming presence helped me to get just a glimpse of how long and wide and deep and high His wonderful love really is. No matter how hard I tried to measure that love, I realized I could never fully comprehend it, never see its beginning or end.

As I drank from His cleansing water, He filled and restored my parched and wearied soul. I rose from my knees, replenished with God's power and love.

"Thank You, Lord," I prayed. "I look forward to talking with You more at the end of this day."

Take time with the Lord. His grace and mighty power will meet your every need.

For I know whom I have believed, and am persuaded that he is able to keep that which I have committed unto him against that day. 2 TIMOTHY 1:12 KJV

LET ME TELL you about a Christian young lady I will call Kim. While she was in college, she dated several Christian guys. Although her boyfriends were different, each one loved the Lord, and Kim wondered whom she would marry one day. Yet the more she dated and wondered who would be her lifelong mate, the more confused she became. After a while, she seriously took her quandary to the Lord in prayer. Shortly before she graduated, she met Lawrence, a dedicated Christian man from her church. Before long, she and Lawrence knew God had brought them together. Now they are happily married and serving the Lord.

In a similar way, as newly born Christians we are excited about living for the Lord. If we don't already worship in a church congregation, we're anxious to find one we can attend. We may begin visiting one church after another, trying to find the one we feel most comfortable in. However, the more we "shop around," the more confused we may become. Some people "church hop" their entire Christian lives, rather than committing to stay faithful to one.

Ephesians 4:14–15 wisely tells us: "That we should no longer be children, tossed to and fro and carried about with every wind of doctrine...but, speaking the truth in love...grow up in all things into Him who is the Head [of His body, the Church]" (NKJV).

As we ask God to lead us, He faithfully helps us find a church that teaches the gospel of Christ where we can grow in Him. Just as in a marriage, we learn to grow spiritually, work together, and love our new brothers and sisters in the Lord. Soon we develop a steadfast faith in God's Word and become consistent and strong in Him.

Then Jesus told him, "You believe because you have seen me. But blessed are those who haven't seen me and believe anyway." JOHN 20:29 TLB

FINDING FAITH TO believe in God can be difficult. Some doubts arise from hurts and disappointments, others are a result of today's variety of beliefs and worship. Most people want proof before believing. Charles experienced several reasons to doubt.

As a child, he enjoyed listening to adults telling Bible stories. But as he grew, he noticed people drawing away from God and the Bible. Their spiritual fervor cooled and they disregarded God. Charles became deeply discouraged. Perhaps others' lack of Christian commitment caused him to doubt all he'd learned.

Years later, Charles began reconsidering his disbelief. Was there a God after all? Was Jesus Christ more than a man? Was He really the Son of God? He decided to see for himself. He traveled to the Holy Land and studied its history during Bible times. When he returned home he began reading everything he could about God. Could the Bible really be true?

After many hours of prayer and study, Charles opened his mind and heart and invited Jesus to enter his soul and remove his disbelief. God lovingly answered Charles' prayers. He sought the advice of Christian leaders and started writing a story about the most powerful thirty-three-year life in history: that of Jesus Christ.

Charles Fulton Oursler touched countless hearts and helped remove doubts about God when he gave the world his inspiring classics, *The Greatest Story Ever Told* and *The Greatest Book Ever Written.*

In spite of the doubts and confusion that cloud our minds, God still showers us with His mercy today and ignites our hearts with the flame of love and trust. He overcomes adversity and affirms that He dwells within us.

Overflowing Joy

Oh, the joy of drinking deeply from the Fountain of Salvation! ISAIAH 12:3 TLB

TORNADOES OF TROUBLE often surround our lives. We wonder if our joy is being consumed by storms and droughts like barren, wasted gardens. Our positive attitudes plummet to despair. Perhaps we mumble, "All is lost, and the whole world's one big, bad place." Yet God has a way of positioning a positive Christian in our path just when we need one most. Where do these Christians find their source of strength and joy? The answer reminds me of when Bob and I and our young sons lived on a small farm in eastern Washington.

Our only source of water was a small well. We had to be careful not to pump the well dry. If we did, we had to crawl into the well's upper opening with a metal pitcher of water, lean against one wall, drizzle in some water, and prime the pump.

Cooking, laundry, and watering our little garden often caused me to use the water to the limit. Imagine our surprise when the well eventually tapped into a strong underground rivulet. The more I used it at a conservative pace, the more it increased.

It's the same with us. Everywhere people are thirsting for Christ. We want to water and nourish them, but if we're not careful, we feel drained and our spirits become parched. So we pause, read God's Word, and pray. We prime the pump to His living water, our source of joy and strength. Soon His Spirit blesses and fills us again to overflowing. When we draw from His bottomless well, we feel refreshed and energized in the Lord. Afterward we can encourage others.

From drought and discouragement, after priming, pumping, and seeking God, our wells spring up and overflow with joy.

The next time you feel drained, remember to prime your pump with prayer.

Always be full of joy in the Lord; I say it again, rejoice! Let everyone see that you are unselfish and considerate in all you do. PHILIPPIANS 4:4–5 TLB

FATHER, THIS IS one of those days when I'm forced to contend with a grumpy person for who knows how long. Their bad attitude is getting me down. Please help! And in the process, please help me bring some joy to this person's life.

When sour-grapes attitudes are passed my way, they make me shudder and grit my teeth, like the taste of vinegar. Help me not to get caught up in this downbeat mind-set. Remind me instead to fix my thoughts on You and to reflect Your love and graciousness.

When someone passes me sour grapes, show me how, I pray, to stir those offensive little morsels into the pure, winning sweetness of Your love—and to make grape jelly! Not the sickening, phony sweetness of this world, but the unselfish, thoughtful kindness and compassion that comes from You.

No matter what happens during my day, remind me to live life in the fullness of Your grace, as You intend. Teach me to pass on kindness and gentleness to others. Grant me the strength to do so through the power of Your love.

When troubles surround me, help me not to be anxious but submit everything to You in prayer. I know I am Your child. I will trust in You and give You thanks as You help me with each day. All I need to do is tell You my problems and ask for Your help and Your peace to stay with me.

I am determined in Your strength that whatever I think on will be true, noble, just, pure, lovely, positive, and praiseworthy. Thank You, Father, for showing me how to experience abundant life and for teaching me how to make sour grapes into Your pure, sweet Holy Spirit–filled jelly.

August 15 | Love Is Patient

Be humble and gentle. Be patient with each other, making allowance for each other's faults because of your love. Try always to be led along together by the Holy Spirit and so be at peace with one another. EPHESIANS 4:2–3 TLB

RAISING A FAMILY can be rewarding and challenging at the same time. It's good to know when our patience is tested that God is helping us just when we need Him the most. We learn to pray for guidance and strength.

It seems like yesterday that our kids were growing up. Being a large family, we never had a dull moment. Sometimes my patience was stretched to the limit—and that of our kids as well. More than anything, I wanted them to know I loved them then and forever.

As the years flew by, our patience matured. Our love for the Lord and each other brought us through each test and cemented bonds between us. Still, this patience doesn't compare to what Jesus showed toward His disciples, especially Simon Peter.

After Jesus rose from the grave, He and his disciples were sitting around a warm fire where He had prepared fish and bread for them to eat. By this time, His disciples knew He was God's Son and that He loved them.

After they ate, Jesus looked directly at Peter. "Simon, son of John, do you love Me more than these?"

Peter replied, "Yes, Lord; You know that I love You."

He said to him, "Feed My lambs."

Jesus asked Peter two more times if he loved Him and instructed Peter to "tend My sheep" and "feed My sheep." He had forgiven Peter for denying Him three times only a short while back. Now He patiently waited for Peter's three replies that he loved his Master most of all.

Peter must have felt humbled when Jesus affirmed His disciple's love by saying, "Follow Me." In the same way, Jesus asks us to patiently love those around us and says, "Feed My Sheep" and "Follow Me."

[Love] bears all things, believes all things, hopes all things, endures all things.
1 CORINTHIANS 13:7 NKJV

IN TODAY'S SOCIETY, so much of what we have is disposable, but the quality of steadfast love endures. The marriage vows "to love and cherish, in sickness and in health, for better or for worse, as long as we both shall live" imprint themselves on the minds of husbands and wives. The words replay through the best and worst of times, keeping a marriage strong and true.

Joseph's love for Mary must have been severely put to the test when she told him she was expecting a baby that was conceived of God. Such a thing was too difficult to comprehend. But Mary explained how the angel Gabriel told her the power of the Holy Spirit would overshadow her and that she would conceive a baby boy. Even though she was a virgin, she knew this was so. She took God at His word.

Joseph must have been beside himself. What was he to do? He loved Mary, and though he would have to tragically end their engagement, he would do so secretly so Mary wouldn't be ridiculed or put to shame. While he earnestly thought about all that Mary had told him, an angel of the Lord appeared to him in a dream. The angel told Joseph to take Mary to be his wife, assuring him that her baby truly was conceived of the Holy Spirit.

Joseph must have felt relief and joy. He immediately took Mary to be his wife. He loved her with a steadfast love. No challenges in the future would take that love away.

Through the tests of time may our marriages also be strong and true.

I love things that bear the touch of time, chips and all—they are more beautiful than perfection. —Victoria Magazine

Therefore, if anyone is in Christ, he [or she] is a new creation; the old has gone, the new has come!
2 CORINTHIANS 5:17 NIV

ONE YEAR IN early spring I asked a teenaged boy named Stephen to weed our flower gardens. After he finished, I did a quick walk-through with him to see how everything looked. The gardens appeared clear of weeds, and new colorful flowers I had purchased were neatly arranged where I instructed Stephen to plant them.

After Stephen left, I allowed gardening responsibilities to drift to the back of my mind. One day when I pulled into our driveway, I was shocked to see six-inch quack grass growing everywhere in the front flower spot. When I tried to remove the grass, I discovered I would have to dig up most of the flowers so I could free their roots from the weeds. This appeared to be the end of the colorful garden Stephen had made, but it had to be done.

It took me a couple of hours with pitchfork and shovel to clean out the area. Some flowers were half-dead from being strangled by weeds, and I had to replace them with new ones. Yet after I finished the job, it was more beautiful than ever.

Sometimes we allow the good things God has placed in our lives to be strangled and crowded out by negligence and crippling sin. When this happens, we may be shocked and dismayed when we discover how we've allowed our relationship with God to deteriorate. When we call on the Lord, He faithfully works hand-in-hand with us to dig out and bring an end to our old undesirable traits. It is then He generously offers us a clean, fresh beginning, one where He causes us to become new like beautiful spring flowers, free from weed-like wrongs, replaced with His glorious, creative love.

Teach me your way, O LORD; lead me in a straight path. PSALM 27:11 NIV

SOME PEOPLE WELCOME change in their lives as an adventure, seeing it as a new chapter full of opportunity where God is leading the way. Unanticipated changes, however, cause some to feel insecure and threatened.

One day several years ago when I was facing unexpected changes that concerned me, Bob and I went to visit some close friends at their home on the beach. I had an opportunity during the afternoon to take a walk and be alone with God while He ministered to my heart and calmed my spirit.

Small shells crunched in the pebbled sand beneath my feet as I walked. After trudging a few miles I sat down on a log and gazed across the calm water. The tide was out. An elegant blue heron stood in shallow water a safe distance from shore. Winds rippled the water, causing sea life to adjust to nature's rhythm. I breathed deeply, filling my lungs with the clean, salty air.

A purple mountain range surrounded the area as far as I could see. To my left, the Dungeness Spit stretched its huge finger out into the water for miles. Near the end of the spit was a red-and-white lighthouse. It shone brightly, in contrast to the blue of the sky and water.

A feeling of peace came over me as God assured me that He was graciously directing my path. In the same way He had control over the balance of nature, He also had special plans for what would happen to me around the next bend.

Lord, the task is impossible for me but not for Thee. Lead the way and I will follow. Why should I fear? I am on a royal mission. I am in the service of the King of kings. —MARY SLESSOR

I waited patiently for the Lord; he turned to me and heard my cry. PSALM 40:1 NIV

WHEN WE BRING our needs to God during uncertain times in our lives, He speaks to our hearts and assures us that all is well. He's in control. That day by the water, He listened attentively to my concerns and assured me that He cared about me. All I had to do was trust Him.

I stirred the toe of my tennis shoe in the sand and watched the beachfront change before me. I'd been told that when storms hit, strong waves can move ten-foot logs up and down the beach. I thought of some of the changes I'd faced, how God stilled my storms. Like the sea life, I had to develop a rhythm through the wavering ups and downs and adjustments. I had to allow His leading to ripple though my everyday life—cleansing, shifting, and refreshing me.

I pulled out my journal, pen, and small Bible and began to read Ecclesiastes 3:1: "To everything there is a season, a time for every purpose under heaven" (NKJV).

As I leafed through my journal, I could see God's hand at work. I read about prayers that were answered, problems that were solved, spiritual splinters that felt as big as the seashore logs that were removed. Sometimes I had felt battered by troubles and wondered if I would survive, but now I could see how God's finger had created a long protecting bulwark for me, buffering me from harsh storms. Whenever I asked for His guidance, God's unmistakable voice directed the way, slicing through my uncertainties like a foghorn cutting through the mist.

I turned to a clean page and wrote: "I don't know what the future holds, Lord, but I know You are here every step of the way. Guarding. Guiding. Keeping."

I run in the path of your commands, for you have set my heart free. PSALM 119:32 NIV

TALIA'S PARENTS AND older siblings loved their curly-headed little girl. Everything she did was cute. Everyone knew she loved her binkie and blankie. She carried them everywhere. She was often asked to remove her binkie from her mouth when she talked so people could understand her.

The time came for Talia to stop depending on her two favorite things. Every time her parents tried reasoning with her, her lower lip stubbornly jutted out. But with much persuasion, she let go of her habits and was free to move on to more grown-up interests.

We all have habits; some are good, some bad. Reading the Saturday paper. Sitting in the same place in church. Driving the same streets to the store. We may sing in the shower, plant kisses on our loved ones every morning, and pray together before we go about our days. But other behaviors can ruin our lives. Those who love us may even suffer because of them. Our children often copy our example, whether we want them to or not. What goes into or comes out of our mouths is habit-forming. Routine attitudes and body language form our character. What we read, listen to, or watch on TV often shows up in our behavior.

As we saw with Talia, these habits are sometimes too difficult to break on our own. We can get help from instruction books, doctors, counselors, and friends, yet our supreme Helper is our gracious heavenly Father. As we give our habits to Him, He showers us with His mercy and provides us with direction and strength. Then we can be set free to enjoy victorious lives in Him.

Let him have all your worries and cares, for he is always thinking about you and watching everything that concerns you. 1 PETER 5:7 TLB

NO MATTER WHAT challenging, stressful, or discouraging things press in on us from every side, we can be assured that God possesses complete knowledge and wisdom concerning them.

We often recoil when we see the sin that overtakes so many lives. Sometimes we can help and influence people, but we're only human and don't have the answers to all of life's problems. As we see the unpleasant and sometimes frightening actions of others, we must view these people as possible miracles in progress and faithfully pray for their salvation.

There's something far more powerful than our limited efforts to win souls for the Lord. That's when we faithfully hold up in prayer each person we brush shoulders with and ask God to save them through His grace.

Today I was told about an amazing way God worked from all directions to help a family I've been fervently holding up in prayer for months. The father just got out of prison and accepted the Lord. The mother, who has been hooked on drugs, is seeing hope. Their child, who has been suffering because of his broken family, is gaining new joy. God has truly been moving mountains in order to bring this whole family to Him.

God never gives up on His people, so must we not give up either. He has a miraculous way of using the most unlikely people to bring about answers to prayers. He works back and forth, up and down, inside and out to accomplish His will. As we continue praying, God hopes all things, sees potential good in all things, and accomplishes the impossible in all things.

So don't give up. Keep praying, keep hoping, and keep trusting. God is still in control!

Behold, like the clay in the potter's hand, so are you in My hand. JEREMIAH 18:6 NASB

LORD, I BRING my aspirations and dreams to You. I've had these dreams for a long time, and I'm working hard to fulfill them. So why is everything at a standstill? Am I doing what's right? Or am I trying to do everything my way, rather than submitting to Your plans for me? Help me to become like clay in Your hands.

"My child, you turn your life upside down and harden your heart toward Me as though you presume you are the potter and I am the clay. Can't you comprehend who made you in the first place? Don't examine what I am making of you. Instead, trust Me" (paraphrase of Isaiah 29:15–24).

Lord, this is going to be difficult. Sometimes I'm stubborn and want to have control. Take this hardened block of clay of my life. Work it in Your hands until I become soft and pliable, yielding to You. Place my life on Your potter's wheel. Pour the waters of Your Holy Spirit upon me. May Your hands work within and without, over and around me. Press me into Your vessel, Lord. The more I yield, the more You can accomplish in me.

Isaiah 64:8 becomes my prayer: "Yet, O LORD, You are [my] Father. [I am] the clay, You are the potter; [I am] all the work of Your hand" (NIV). I want to be a beautiful vessel, Lord, and do mighty things for You.

"[My child,] does not the potter have the right to make out of the same lump of clay some pottery for noble purposes and some for common use?" (Romans 9:21).

I surrender all, Lord. Mold me, trim my rough edges. Painful though it be, refine me with Your fire. You are the Master Potter. Let me be used by You.

Have Thine own way, Lord! Have Thine own way!
Thou art the potter, I am the clay.
—ADELAIDE A. POLLARD

Facing the Unknown

Trust in the LORD with all your heart, and do not rely on your own insight. In all your ways acknowledge him, and he will make straight your paths. PROVERBS 3:5–6 RSV

ONE OF OUR greatest fears may be of the unknown, yet we need not allow fear to dominate our lives. We can take the uncertainties that have been dealt us and snip away the negative "un." No matter how frightening things may appear, God is our protector. He capably handles our concerns as we trust and obey Him.

A woman in the Bible named Hadassah faced uncertainty far more serious than any of us ever will. An orphan living with her cousin Mordecai (who was like a father to her), she was forced to leave him when King Ahasuerus of Persia summoned her to be in his harem. Though she didn't know what lay ahead, she knew she must obey and follow the path God had laid before her.

Hadassah must have trembled as she entered the king's palace. She remembered Mordecai teaching her to be faithful to the one true God. In order to be safe, he told her to carefully hide her identity as a Jew. Soon after she entered the royal harem, her name was changed to Esther. It meant the star of Venus, because she was so beautiful. Esther's loveliness and grace won King Ahasuerus's heart, and she knew he loved her above all others. God honored Esther's faithfulness to Him and she was crowned queen of Persia.

What would happen to her next? No matter what her future held, she would trust completely in the Lord.

In the face of our uncertainties, we need not fear. We can be confident as God maps out the course He has prepared. He watches over us each step of the way.

Willing to Give All

To You, O my Strength, I will sing praises; for God is my defense, my God of mercy.
PSALM 59:17 NKJV

ABOUT THE TIME we think our situation is getting better, we might discover there's no easy way out of our troubles. The Lord may need to push us out of our comfort zone. We may have to be willing to give up the most treasured things in our lives for His cause. Even if we should be forced to face poverty, ridicule, or danger, the Lord goes before us and helps us to make it through.

Perhaps Queen Esther felt all was well because of the honor bestowed on her. She must have been shocked to discover that a courtier named Haman hated her cousin because Mordecai had refused to bow down to him. The enraged man decided to get even by dishonestly convincing the king to give him his signet ring, then issuing a decree that all Jews were to be killed.

Mordecai immediately sent the news to Esther. No matter what happened, she had to be true to her people and her God. She returned a message through Mordecai, asking all their people to fast and pray—to take no food or drink for three days. In spite of her fear, Esther must reveal her Jewish identity to her husband and tell him about Haman's wicked plan. If he refused to receive her, she could be put to death.

After three days of fasting and praying, Esther approached the king. Once again, God showed favor to her. The king held out his golden scepter and touched the top of it. Then she invited her husband and Haman to a banquet without telling them why, followed by a second banquet. The king and Haman accepted her invitation.

Esther trusted God to defend and protect her during this crucial time. Surely He had a plan.

A Time to Fast and Pray

Commit your way to the LORD; trust in him and he will do this: He will make your righteousness shine like the dawn, the justice of your cause like the noonday sun. PSALM 37:5–6 NIV

MANY OF US start our day by thanking God for His blessings. We tell Him we love Him, and pray about our needs. He gives us direction and peace.

However, when trouble hits, our prayer life might take a different course. Instead of praying from our chairs, our burdens may drive us to our knees before the Lord. We may pray and wait, still finding no answer in sight. It is then that we may decide to fast as well as pray.

Esther and her people continued to fast and pray. In the meantime, the king read how Mordecai had once saved his life, and ordered Haman to honor Mordecai. Haman reluctantly complied.

During the second banquet, when King Ahasuerus asked Esther why she invited him and Haman, Esther told her husband about Haman's evil command. She begged for protection for herself and her people. The king ordered Haman to be hanged on the gallows intended for Mordecai then gave Mordecai his signet ring. Esther put her cousin in charge of the house of Haman.

Esther pleaded once more with her husband, asking that Haman's order to destroy the Jews in all the king's provinces be reversed. Haman's order couldn't be overturned by law, but the king gave permission to Esther and Mordecai to do what they could.

Esther probably continued praying, while Mordecai decreed that the Jews be allowed to fight for their lives. With God's help, the Jews won an overwhelming victory.

The Lord rewarded Esther's prayers, obedience, and willingness to give her all by blessing her with a king's love, a reunion with Mordecai, and the salvation of her people. The Lord listens to an earnest heart.

Hang in There

Now choose life, so that you and your children may live and that you may love the Lord your God, listen to His voice, and hold fast to Him. For the Lord is your life. Deuteronomy 30:19–20 NIV

IN OUR WALK with the Lord, we experience many of His blessings, but we also get our fair share of bumps and bruises. At times the blows are so severe that we feel like our spiritual roots are being knocked away from the comforting holy presence of the Lord.

It may be that we're being wrongfully accused or misunderstood at work or painfully struggling with a faltering marriage or trying to hold on for dear life to a rebellious child. Whatever the trial, when these things happen, God assures as that as we trust in Him and turn to Him in prayer, His presence never leaves us—even when we are unable to feel Him near.

We have a two-foot-wide dishpan garden on our backyard patio filled with chicken-and-hen cacti that my dad gave me after my mother passed away. You would think these hens and chicks would survive only if they were in the desert, but after years of living on the deck of my parents' western Washington home, they have become accustomed to the climate. In spite of the blustering winds, pouring rain, and freezing snowfalls, the cacti keep thriving.

Occasionally, when I walk past it, I notice a little chick cactus has been either blown or knocked off the dishpan, separating it from the rest of the plant. Each time I discover it, I gently pick it up and place it back near a hen cactus. Amazingly, its roots hang on tightly and it keeps growing.

When we are bumped and bruised, the Lord faithfully gathers us up and securely nestles us in His arms. There He tells us to hang in there and keep trusting everything to His care.

Learning to Understand

Now it happened, as He was dining in Levi's house, that many tax collectors and sinners also sat together with Jesus and His disciples; for there were many, and they followed Him. MARK 2:15 NKJV

WHEN GOD CALLED Bob and me to the mission church we are now pastoring, He abruptly pushed us out of our comfort zone. I was used to worshipping with people who lived average lives, Christian workers grounded in God's Word. We thrived on Christian leadership and strong church families.

This time it was different. When we first came, we asked God to help us to reach out to our neighborhood. Little did we know our neighborhood would be full of people from broken homes, recovering alcohol and drug addicts, and abused women and children. It was obvious the challenge was far greater than our human abilities could handle. We could only be effective through the power of God's grace and love.

Jan has been a treasured friend and board member for years. I'll always remember the lessons she taught me early on of unconditional love and compassion. After services, Jan sat in a quiet area with ladies who were broken and ruined, some covered with tattoos and scars. Jan took time to listen, care, and try to understand. It didn't take long for me to learn to do the same.

Leadership is developing in our church now. We are blessed to have a congregation full of people who are putting their lives back together. As they experience victory, I see them doing the same thing Jan did—listening, loving, and trying to understand our new "neighbors" who walk through the church doors.

My life is so different from the lives of some of these people (even children). I pray that the Lord would give me His discernment and love while I genuinely care for them. May He show me how to inspire them to grow stronger in Him and give them double portions of His help and grace.

As far as the east is from the west, so far has he removed our transgressions from us. As a father has compassion on his children, so the LORD has compassion on those who fear Him.
PSALM 103:12–13 NIV

AS WE WALK with the Lord, we experience an amazing power from Him that we never knew before He was our Savior. Now His love for us and our love for Him come first in our lives. We enjoy going to the Lord in prayer. When we ask for His guidance, He's always there to help. He gives us the ability to love, forgive, and make sound decisions that are within His will.

Sadly, we may have lacked the ability to love others unselfishly before we invited Jesus into our hearts. Unselfish, merciful love comes from God. Now and then our past bad behavior comes back to haunt us. We are so sorry for our failures and wish there was some way we could turn back the clock and make things right.

We learn to forgive others for wrongdoings but often have difficulty forgiving ourselves. This feeling is not planted by God. It's another one of Satan's tactics to get us to think we aren't worthy to be forgiven.

Whenever we are confronted with these thoughts, we can claim this Scripture in the Lord's prayer: "Forgive us our debts, as we also have forgiven our debtors" (Matthew 6:12 NIV). I believe that when we sin, we not only sin against God and others, but we also sin against ourselves. Jesus wants us to forgive ourselves, release those guilt feelings, and turn everything over to Him.

We may have to repeatedly take it all to the Lord. Each time we do, we can claim the victory of forgiveness in the name of Jesus. He has power to forgive us. He provides the power for us to forgive ourselves. When we do, all guilt and regret are replaced by His Spirit of unlimited joy and grace.

In thee, O LORD, do I put my trust: let me never be put to confusion. Deliver me in thy righteousness, and cause me to escape: incline thine ear unto me, and save me. PSALM 71:1–2 KJV

HOW CAN WE experience perfect fulfillment in God? Is it possible for us to get to that point by trying harder to be a better person? We can take our confusion and concerns to God in prayer and ask for His direction. He is always willing to listen and help us in areas where we need to improve. Yet in our daily struggles to measure up to His perfect will, we find we still fall short.

How about our good deeds? Because of our love for the Lord and for each other, we are frequently driven to help and encourage those around us, giving us a warm, contented feeling inside. Whenever I'm feeling down, helping someone else lifts my spirits and brightens my day, even if it's a little thing. But the Bible tells us that no matter how much we try to be right in God's eyes or how many good deeds we do, they're like filthy rags and we fade like a leaf. (See Isaiah 64:6.)

Perfect fulfillment in the Lord comes as we learn to totally lean on Him and depend on His merciful, saving grace. Above all else, He asks us for our wholehearted love and devotion. When trouble comes, He lifts us up. He is our Rock, our Guide, our Shield. His strength shows up best in our weaknesses. Through Him we receive His absolute, irrefutable grace and enjoy perfect fulfillment, feeling complete in Him, peace of heart and mind, and the knowledge that He's our best Friend, our Savior, and our Lord. His love is measureless. His grace is sufficient. His mercy endures forever. Remember, *He* is our perfect fulfillment.

The LORD is good, a refuge in times of trouble. He cares for those who trust in him. NAHUM 1:7 NIV

WE ARE ALL regularly faced with challenges, large and small. Yet when new hardships come our way, our stress levels climb. And often just when we manage to solve one problem, another one crops up, leaving us grateful when things calm down for a while.

I wonder how Noah felt when God instructed him to build the ark. He must have been thankful that he had family around him. Even so, being instructed to build a huge boat in the middle of the desert must have brought plenty of stress. Can you imagine being Noah's wife, trying to believe in and stick up for her husband?

In spite of everything, the ark was built, the animals were loaded, and the door was slammed shut. Then the waters began to rise. Now they were with a bunch of noisy, hungry animals, floating around in the middle of nowhere for who knew how long.

The day finally came when Noah and his family looked out and saw a beautiful rainbow in the sky. After awhile, they spotted a landscape of glorious mountains, lush valleys, trees, and flowers. They watched the sun rise and set on the new land that spread before them. Finally they could rest.

When we face challenges, the Bible reminds us in 2 Corinthians 4:8–9 of God's encouraging promise: "We are hard-pressed on every side, yet not crushed; we are perplexed, but not in despair; persecuted, but not forsaken; struck down, but not destroyed" (NKJV).

God cares for us and faithfully brings us through each large and small trial. Afterward, we can look to the sky and praise Him. Through raindrops, we see His rainbows of promise, His sunrises and sunsets reminding us that He is with us anywhere, all the time.

Be of good cheer. God is always near.

He Sheds His Grace

Blessed is the nation whose God is the LORD. PSALM 33:12 KJV

MORE THAN ANY other mode of travel, my favorite is taking a road trip. Somehow I've always managed to pack twice as much in our economy car as Bob or my dad. With each trip, I feel the adrenaline rush through my body as we pray for safety and pull out of the driveway. The farther we drive, the more we appreciate the way God lays before us His constantly changing beauty. It's almost like a priceless painting, spanning thousands of square miles.

English teacher Katherine Lee Bates also felt blessed by the loveliness in this vast country. During the summer of 1893, she took the opportunity to journey across the United States. At one stop, she made her way to the top of Pike's Peak in Colorado.

As she stood on the breezy mountain summit, the beauty she had seen along her trip vividly returned to her mind. She recalled the purple haze hanging over the Rocky Mountains, the fruitful Colorado plains, the golden grain fields in Kansas, and much more. Everywhere she had gone, she had witnessed fertile country that spread from one shining sea to the other. She returned to her hotel room and composed the words to "America the Beautiful."

Along with our country's natural wonders, Katherine wrote about the pilgrims from long ago who landed on Plymouth Rock and about those who gave of themselves to help make our country safe and great. It was then Katherine wrote her plea that in spite of our flaws, God would teach us brotherhood, nobleness, and self-control, and that He would shed His grace upon this land undimmed by human tears.

May the Lord's grace continue to shine on us!

At this I awoke and looked around. My sleep had been pleasant to me. JEREMIAH 31:26 NIV

NIGHT SHADOWS HAVE fallen, Lord. It has been a long, stressful day. Troubles and unanswered questions whir through my brain like an endless recording. My head throbs as I try to solve each one. What should I do? What should I say? How can I handle this problem? Where can I find the energy? The list goes on.

Take my thoughts, my concerns, my questions, dear Lord, and carry them for me while I sleep. Change my focus from the events of this frenzied day to Your blessed, calm assurance and peace of heart and mind. My thoughts turn to Your tender care. I sense Your holy presence around me like the soft, warm blanket upon my shoulders. You are even in the air I breathe. The noise of passing cars and neighborhood music fades, and my thoughts drift toward Your holy presence and songs of praise and assurance.

All through the night, my holy Savior, I dream of how wonderful You are. An orchestra fills my thoughts. It's almost audible to me. I think of lines from hymns: "Perfect submission, all is at rest...." "He leadeth me, O blessed thought...." "Now I belong to Jesus...." How good You are, Lord. Your mighty love and power reach deep into my soul.

I sense morning approaching. You bless me with another song. "When morning gilds the skies, my heart awakening cries: May Jesus Christ be praised...." I awaken rejuvenated, ready to face a new day. I feel relieved to discover that so many of my concerns and questions seem to have fallen into place during the night. Thank You, Lord, for Your concert in my dreams.

Direct me in the path of your commands, for there I find delight. PSALM 119:35 NIV

LIFE GOES FAST, especially when raising a family. My best description for the child-rearing days is "organized confusion." Best-laid plans require masterminding, coordination, and a whole lot of flexibility.

Shortly after we moved to Auburn, Washington, we enrolled our kids in four different schools. Since we often raced the clock to get them to school on time, I ended up driving the troop. Talk about chaos.

Our house constantly jumped with activity. And at the end of the day, we enjoyed crowding around one of the kids' bunk beds to read a Bible story and just talk. Peace settled in. Soon silence filled the home.

Although I loved our kids—and still do—I treasured my quiet moments with God. I often smiled when I recalled how Marjorie Holmes described those busy years: the only things she could call her own were the ironing board and her toothbrush. And she sometimes wondered about the toothbrush!

How thankful I was to sense the Savior's voice giving me direction and helping me to calm down.

ಇ

Lord, this was a crazy day. Thank You for noticing my hurry and fuss and for calming my heart and mind. Thank You for reminding me during the frustrating moments to react politely, especially to my family. Please keep me from running ahead and help me to follow You.

God is above, presiding; beneath, sustaining; within, filling.
—HILDEBERT OF LAVARDIN

Nothing will ever be able to separate us from the love of God.... ROMANS 8:39 TLB

WHEN WE BECOME trapped in difficult circumstances, we want to escape immediately. We might feel like prisoners. But when all seems hopeless, God is still helping while we trust and follow Him.

Imagine being a woman born on a Maryland plantation to a family of slaves. She was mistreated and beaten, but even when things were most discouraging, she trusted that God would help her escape to freedom.

One day, a white Quaker lady waited in a buggy at the edge of the woods. The lady supplied an escape route for the young woman through the Underground Railroad to freedom.

With very little food, the woman walked from station to station, through swamps and woods, following the North Star. Quaker families provided much-needed rest, food, warm clothing, and prayers. After walking 140 miles, the slave made it to freedom.

She later returned and helped free other slaves. Many called her "Moses." Like the biblical hero, she led her people out of captivity.

A reward of forty thousand dollars was offered for her capture. She made nineteen trips to free slaves, including her own family—a total of over three hundred slaves.

Eventually Harriet Tubman and her family settled in Auburn, New York. She crusaded for women's rights and started a home for needy people. She never stopped thanking God for helping her fulfill her vision of being free.

It takes a lot of courage to free ourselves from people and situations God doesn't want for us. But as we take each step and follow God's sure, merciful guidance, we really can find a better life. Perhaps when we do, we can help and encourage others.

Because of his kindness, you have been saved through trusting Christ. And even trusting is not of yourselves; it too is a gift from God. EPHESIANS 2:8 TLB

HOW DO YOU feel when you bungle things? Annoyed with yourself? Frustrated with whatever you are working on? Ready to tear everything apart and start over? Or do you want to give up entirely?

When I make mistakes, I'm often hard on myself. Whenever possible, I try going back and correcting what I'm doing until it comes out right. And if I can't make it right, I usually do the entire thing over. However, as I've been experiencing God's loving-kindness in my life, I've been learning to be patient and gracious with myself. No matter how hard I try, I can't always get things perfect. Whether I'm working on a project or relating to another person, I'm bound to fall short and sometimes even hurt someone else's feelings. And when I do, I've learned to own up to my shortcomings, ask for forgiveness, and then learn from it.

One day a first grader in my class was attempting to draw a picture. He tried and tried but couldn't get it perfect. Finally, out of frustration, he broke his pencil and began to cry.

I sat down beside him, handed him a new pencil, and placed my hand next to his. "Would you like for me to help you?" I asked. He nodded. I moved my finger back and forth across his paper, gently directing him. When he finished drawing and coloring, he had turned his scrawl into a beautiful flower—one that was filled with crazy colors. It was beautiful to him and to me.

Whenever we bungle things, we can have faith in God to make them better. He graciously takes the good intentions that are hidden in our bungles and turns them into something beautiful blessed by Him.

Grace freely given often extends to grace freely received.

Be kind and compassionate to one another, forgiving each other, just as in Christ God forgave you.
EPHESIANS 4:32 NIV

WHEN WE THINK of compassionate love, we may think of a love that goes beyond concern, beyond sympathy, beyond kindness. Perhaps it's a deep, empathetic love and sorrow felt and received.

I wonder what Jesus was thinking as He and His disciples traveled to Bethany where Lazarus, Mary, and Martha lived. He'd heard that Lazarus was seriously ill but delayed going for two days. Bethany was in Judea, near Jerusalem, where people wanted to stone Jesus; nevertheless, He would go. Before he arrived in Bethany, Jesus knew Lazarus had already died, yet the Son of God would be glorified by having waited two days.

Lazarus had been in the tomb four days by the time Jesus arrived. Martha went out immediately to meet Him and lamented that if Jesus had been there, Lazarus would have lived. Even so, she believed her Lord knew best.

Jesus assured her: "Your brother will rise again."

Soon Mary came to Jesus and fell at His feet. She reflected Martha's intense grief. She, Martha, and their friends began weeping. This moved Jesus with deep sorrow and love. He asked, "Where have you laid him?"

There amongst mourners, doubters, and spectators, Jesus ordered the tomb stone to be removed. He looked toward heaven and prayed, "Father, I thank You that You have heard Me.... Because of the people who are standing by I said this, that they may believe that You sent Me" (John 11:41–42 NKJV). Then Jesus called Lazarus from the grave. He instructed that the grave clothes be removed and Lazarus be set free.

What could compare to the compassion Jesus felt that day for those who mourned? How comforting it is to know He shows us that same compassion today.

'Twas grace that taught my heart to fear, and grace my fears relieved.
—JOHN NEWTON

Blessed are those who mourn, for they will be comforted. MATTHEW 5:4 NIV

HOW CAN WE comprehend the loss of a loved one we hold dear? We want to pick up the phone, but no one's there. An unborn baby is taken before we can hold him or her. A broken marriage brings a sense of failure and sorrow. A rebellious child causes anguish and despair. Loss of a job leaves us fearful and helpless. We feel alone.

We long for comfort, but it's slow to come. There's no measurement of time for healing. We're appreciative of family and friends who offer sympathy, but our greatest comfort comes from the refuge we find by nestling in the arms of our Father. God knows the whole picture. He cares and understands.

God holds the key of all unknown, and I am glad;
If other hands should hold the key, or if He trusted it to me,
I might be sad, I might be sad.

What if tomorrow's cares were here without its rest!
I'd rather He unlocked the day; and, as the hours swing open, say,
"My will is best, My will is best."

I cannot read His future plans; but this I know;
I have the smiling of His face, and all the refuge of His grace,
While here below, while here below.

Enough! This covers all my wants, and so I rest!
For what I cannot, He can see, and in His care I saved shall be,
Forever blest, forever blest.
    —JOSEPH PARKER

I waited patiently for the LORD; He turned to me and heard my cry. PSALM 40:1 NIV

GRIEF IS A God-given tool to help us survive our losses. The steps are like peeling an onion, one layer at a time. There are no shortcuts, no rules, no timetables. Here are some steps I've learned.

☙ Denial and isolation. We don't want to believe what's happening. Denial acts like a buffer, allowing loss to sink in slowly. Gradually, we turn to the Lord, then our family and friends for comfort. (Read Deuteronomy 33:27.)

☙ Anger. "Why me? I feel cheated." It's best to tell the Lord exactly how we feel. We may even become angry with God, but He has broad shoulders. He never tires of listening. When we allow anger to burn out, things slowly fall into place. (Read John 16:33.)

☙ Bargaining. Considering options and searching for easier ways are no strangers to us. We beg and argue with those around us, ourselves, and God. Finally, we ask Him for direction and strength. (Read John 14:1.)

☙ Depression. We feel abandoned and alone. No one seems to care or understand. Why should we care, either? We may not always feel God's presence, but Jesus knows our hurts and brings them to His Father in heaven. (Read Matthew 11:28–30; Romans 8:26.)

☙ Acceptance. God shows us how to accept the loss. We may wonder what the next step will be. It is then that God lovingly takes our hands, ready to lead us on.

☙ Hope. Jesus is our resurrection and life. He brings us through our grief. He offers hope for tomorrow. There's no hopelessness in Christ. He helps us visualize our future: an abundant life in Him. (Read John 10:10.)

The future belongs to those who belong to God. This is hope.
—W. T. PURKISER

Just as Christ was raised from the dead through the glory of the Father, we too may live a new life.
ROMANS 6:4 NIV

FROM THE MOMENT we draw our first breath as babies, we have a God-given determination to make these mortal bodies of ours live, grow, and thrive. Life is precious. We want to hang onto it for all we're worth. We seldom desire to give up this world we know. When we're about to die, however, I believe God will be with us every step of the way through the valley of death.

It is interesting to note that some refer to the Kidron Valley, located on Jerusalem's northeastern slope, as the valley of death. In winter the Kidron Valley floods with deadly torrents. In summer it is dry and unbearably hot. Its steep, naked banks hug dreary burial grounds no one has ever wanted to walk through.

When Jesus left Jerusalem on the night of His betrayal, He might have crossed the northern end of the Kidron Valley to reach the Garden of Gethsemane. Those brave enough to walk the twenty miles south to the other end of the valley find the Spring of Gihon filled with pure, sweet water.

When we are about to leave this world and approach the valley of death, we need not fear. Jesus has gone before us. He will be there, ready to take our hands and safely lead us to His living water and life eternal.

These frail bodies we have hung onto so tightly will no longer matter. In light of His glory, we'll shed our mortal shells and realize we aren't dead at all. We shall have new lives that will never end.

We won't feel sickness or pain. Sadness and tears will be no more. We will begin a brand-new life of joy and peace. We will become complete with indescribable blessings from our Lord.

But they that wait upon the LORD shall renew their strength; they shall mount up with wings as eagles; they shall run, and not be weary; and they shall walk, and not faint. ISAIAH 40:31 KJV

DO YOU EVER wonder where strength comes from after it disappears? It may return during an exhausting work day, what some people refer to as a second wind. It may come back after we've been sick. When we don't know where we'll find the energy to do what needs to be done, we pray for help and marvel that we made it through the day then whisper a prayer of thanksgiving.

We can also become drained emotionally and spiritually until our stamina is gone. We call on God for help. Some answers come immediately; other times we have to wait. Still, every so often God gives us a sign that He's taking care of everything.

My elderly father and I were visiting my uncle in Montana when concerns about Dad's well-being caused me to feel emotionally and physically exhausted. Early in the morning, before leaving my uncle's home, I knelt by the bed and asked God to assure me that He was providing the strength and wisdom I needed.

A short way out of St. Regis, Montana, I spotted an eagle's nest on top of a tall telephone pole alongside the highway. I was baffled and slowed down the car to take a second look. How could it possibly remain there, exposed to everything?

I felt God reminding me that He made the eagle strong and clever enough to build a nest that would last. He also gave me assurance that He made me strong enough to endure. Should my wisdom and strength fade, all I needed to do was wait on Him just as I did that morning. As He has many times before and since, He lifted my spirits and restored my strength.

Don't despair, dear reader. No matter our challenges, God is near, supplying the strength we need for each day.

Finally, be strong in the Lord and in the strength of His might. Put on the full armor of God.
EPHESIANS 6:10–11 NASB

FRIGHTENING TIMES REQUIRE strong prayers, great faith, and mighty miracles. If you or others close to you are facing the dangers of war, this prayer is for you.

❧

Lord, I thank You for being with those who are fighting to protect our freedom. Thank You for Your protective grace and mercy, for comforting and caring for us and our loved ones far from home.

Speak to our hearts through Your Word. Surround us with Your love and protection. "The angel of the LORD encamps all around those who fear Him, and delivers them" (Psalm 34:7 NKJV).

Keep us safe from dangers and uncertainties. You, O Lord, are greater than all else. You are fighting these battles for us. Right now we put on Your full armor. Through Your strength, we will stand for truth and right. "Stand therefore, [gird] your waist with truth" (Ephesians 6:14 NKJV).

Grant us Your holy righteousness. "Put on the breastplate of righteousness" (Ephesians 6:14 NASB). Help us to carry Your peace to those who desperately need it. "[Shoe] your feet with the preparation of the gospel of peace" (Ephesians 6:15 NASB). Protect us, Lord! "[Take] the shield of faith with which you will be able to extinguish all the flaming arrows of the evil one" (Ephesians 6:16 NASB).

Keep close to our hearts Your promises that You provide us Your saving grace and eternal life through Jesus. "Take the helmet of salvation, and the sword of the Spirit, which is the word of God" (Ephesians 6:17 NASB). Help us to stand firm, fully believing in You! "Having done everything...stand firm" (Ephesians 6:13 NASB).

Thank You, Lord. We completely put our trust in You. In Jesus' name, amen!

If my people, who are called by my name, will humble themselves and pray and seek my face and turn from their wicked ways, then will I hear from heaven and will forgive their sin and will heal their land. Now my eyes will be open and my ears attentive to the prayers offered in this place.
2 CHRONICLES 7:14–15 NIV

THE MORNING BEGAN like any other. As I drove to work, the traffic bogged down. I glanced at people in their cars, riding the busses, and walking. Some shook their heads. Others cried. It was September 11, 2001, the day our country was attacked by terrorists.

You may remember where you were when you received the devastating news. As a nation, a part of our heart was broken by shock and fear. The scars may never totally heal. People began to pray. Some went to church. Almost every eye was glued to the news. Others flocked to stores to purchase flags of all sizes they could hang in their yards. Surprisingly, flags are still flying at homes all over the country.

This tragedy makes me think of the trauma our country faced 187 years earlier during the bombardment of Fort McHenry in 1814. Just as Francis Scott Key dramatically described his glimpse of the Stars and Stripes through the haze of battle in "The Star-Spangled Banner," *we* were thankful to know "our flag was still there."

When I see the flag hanging by our front door, I'm keenly aware that freedom isn't free. I used to take freedom for granted, but now I pray for the Lord to protect it. Although I don't always agree with our leaders, I sense God's urge to pray for them and our people in the military.

❧

Thank You for our country, Lord, and for the freedoms You provide. Watch over us and keep us safe. May we, through Your protection and care, be able to always say, "Our flag is still here!"

Therefore...clothe yourselves with compassion, kindness, humility, gentleness and patience.
COLOSSIANS 3:12 NIV

LIKE YOU, MY days are filled with endless responsibilities. After praying for help and guidance each morning, I jump into my routine full-speed ahead. In the process, I'm amazed by the special blessings God imparts to help make my workload a little lighter. It may be a kind action, a genuine smile, or a hug from someone that warms my heart and brings a smile to my face.

Early one morning I was substituting on a vision health-screening team at a local middle school. Sleepy teenagers patiently stood in line while our team tested each student's eyesight. I had started my day with prayer, asking God to help me to be a blessing. Little did I know He would do that and bless me in return. During the testing, I glanced up in time to see a tall, lanky boy named Paul. I recognized him immediately. He had been in my Sunday school class when he was in fourth grade. He came from a troubled home, and even though he didn't come to church anymore, I kept praying for him.

Paul looked at me with surprise then pointed at me with his arm outstretched, never saying a word. A slight smile and a twinkle in his eyes told me he was saying, "I remember you, and I'm okay." I pointed back at him with my arm outstretched and gave him a big smile in return.

I didn't get to test Paul's eyes that day. Obviously I couldn't give him a hug like I did when he was in my Sunday school class, yet that thoughtful gesture from him was worth a thousand hugs to me.

Enjoy giving and receiving an act of kindness today. It may become a special blessing that makes a world of difference to you or someone around you.

For He Himself has said, "I will never leave you nor forsake you." HEBREWS 13:5 NKJV

TRULY YOU ARE my Shepherd, Lord Jesus. Thank You for how You care for me and generously supply my needs. You speak and I hear Your voice. I listen as You teach me how to be a Christian shepherd to others.

You make me stop amidst my busyness to lie down in green pastures. I drink of Your pure, sweet, living water from quiet streams and feel Your peace. I pour out my concerns and give You my hurts. I feel Your healing presence as You tenderly restore my soul.

I praise You for leading me to make wise and righteous decisions. Thank You for reminding me to put Your will before mine. Your way is always sure and true. I long to do Your will, Lord. When the tasks I face are far beyond my wisdom and abilities, I draw on Your guidance and strength.

When I face loss, grief, and even death, I am comforted. You have already walked that valley before me and paid the price to bring me through. No matter how frightening the situation, I need not fear. You are with me.

Thank You for Your comfort and mercy, Lord, for guiding me through the challenges and changes in my life. As I learn to obey, You give me blessings beyond measure, even in the presence of those who are thoughtless and cruel. I praise You as You anoint and fill me with Your powerful Holy Spirit until my cup overflows.

I know Your goodness and mercy are with me my whole life. Because of Your love, I will always be a part of the family of God. I will serve You all of my days and look forward with great joy to the day You graciously take me home to be with You.

I urge you to live a life worthy of the calling you have received. Be completely humble and gentle; be patient, bearing with one another in love. EPHESIANS 4:1–2 NIV

DO YOU FEEL God calling you to accomplish something that seems impossible? When He calls, He also provides the means we need to follow Him.

Years ago God gave Gladys, a tiny English woman in her twenties, a challenging call. Responding obediently, she went to a missionary society and told them that God had called her to become a missionary in China. They bluntly told her that she didn't meet the educational requirements and wouldn't be able to learn the Chinese language, but she didn't let that dissuade her. She worked hard to earn money for her transportation, and a few years later she boarded a train. She had nothing but a suitcase filled with cooking supplies, a little food, and a rug to keep her warm.

After a perilous journey by train, boat, and mule, she reached Yangcheng, nestled in the northern China mountains. There she joined an elderly missionary woman. Gladys had no money and received no support, but the older woman purchased an old house and converted it to an inn. God somehow provided their food. When mule trains stopped at the inn to rest and eat, the women told the men Bible stories. One at a time, roughhewn men were won to Jesus.

Sadly, the older missionary became seriously ill and died, but Gladys had learned how to take over the work. She was beginning to understand that the reason God called her to China was to continue what the older missionary had started. Although the tasks were difficult, God's mercy provided for her daily needs.

Like this young missionary, God sees potential in us to do great things for Him. Whatever His call, may we say, "Here am I. Send me."

May you be able to feel and understand...how long, how wide, how deep, and how high his love really is; and to experience this love for yourselves.... And so at last you will be filled up with God himself.
EPHESIANS 3:18—19 TLB

AS WE SERVE God, we may find our abilities stretched to the limit. We might face challenges from people with hardened hearts or see terrible suffering. Doors may close. Dreams may be shattered. But God always understands the whole picture. In it all, He promises His help and grace.

The missionary to China in our last devotion kept her focus on God's call to tell everyone who would listen about Jesus. The work became increasingly difficult, and little money was coming in. Again, she prayed for help. The help came when a Chinese official and soldiers came to her for advice. The government had ordered women to stop binding their feet as they had in the past. The missionary was the only woman with large feet, so the official requested her to become a foot inspector. They would pay her in money and food.

Not forgetting her calling, she told them she would inspect feet if she could tell people about Jesus. The official agreed. By day she inspected feet; by night she told about God's love. God blessed her with enough to keep the inn running.

This lady, Gladys Aylward, not only learned the Chinese language but fluently spoke several different Chinese dialects. God used her to calm a prison riot and improve prison conditions. She started an orphanage, cared for the wounded during World War II, helped bury the dead, and guided numerous orphaned children to safety.

From the time Gladys entered China until she went home to be with the Lord, she gave of herself and reflected God's grace and love.

But God hath promised strength for the day,
Rest for the labor, light for the way,
Grace for the trials, help from above,
Unfailing sympathy, undying love.
—ANNIE JOHNSON FLINT

"It shall be done to you according to your faith." MATTHEW 9:29 NASB

AT TIMES WE wonder if life is really worth living, perhaps because too many hard things have happened. A long-term illness, losing a loved one or a job, facing a surprise pregnancy, making an unwanted move—any of these can make us feel like giving up on life. We want to stay in bed and pull the covers over our heads, attempting to shut the world out.

Yet through it all, it's wonderful how God can take our struggles and give us a renewed life when we allow Him to do so. Years ago I suffered intense pain in my lower back that wouldn't go away for even a few minutes. After trying various unsuccessful treatments, the doctors recommended that I go to a pain clinic.

I'll never forget one lesson the instructor taught me: in order to get rid of the pain, I had to first stop fighting it. Then I had to let the pain go. In the same way, we can learn to stop fighting our hurts and disappointments, no matter how small or severe. Then we must be willing to take them to our Savior, place them in His healing hands, and leave them there. Each time we do this, He patiently speaks the same life-giving words to our hearts that He said to His disciples so long ago: "I have come that [you] may have life, and that [you] may have it more abundantly" (John 10:10 NKJV).

Then we can fling open our curtains, open wide our doors and windows, smell the fresh air, listen to the rain, and simply let life shine in. Even better is when we open the windows of our hearts and allow the Lord to give us a life, renewed in Him.

As the rain soothes and heals the parched earth, so the grace of God brings renewed life and healing.
—JANICE LEWIS CLARK

Let us not become weary in doing good, for at the proper time we will reap a harvest if we do not give up. GALATIANS 6:9 NIV

AN ACT OF kindness may inspire hope and lead to a better life for another, but because of the ups and downs of life's circumstances, sometimes we may wonder if what we do is making much of a difference. Galatians 6:9 talks about doing good even when we're weary, but the rest of the scripture says: "For at the proper time we will reap a harvest if we do not give up." Wow! This promise just gave me a shot of spiritual adrenaline.

While traveling by bus to Omak, Washington, I had a forty-five-minute layover in Wenatchee. I ordered a cup of tea in the coffee shop and sat down at a quiet table. I had my laptop and tablet handy so I could do some writing. However, God had a different plan.

A lady I recognized from the bus came over to my table. After introducing herself, she told me her story. Kari had spent some time in prison for drug possession and dealing. In prison, a lady chaplain kept after her to accept the Lord. This irritated her; she just wanted to be left alone. But finally she became a Christian and dedicated her life to serving Him. Shortly before her release, she told the chaplain she felt called to get an education so she could help people in a recovery program.

The chaplain spent her own money to travel to Othello where she helped set Kari up in a Christian program in order for her to gain her education and find a job. At present, Kari's about to graduate and find work. She's asking God to lead her to the organization where He wants her to be. All because of the perseverance and kindheartedness of one prison chaplain.

If I should err, I would rather it be on the side of compassion.
—ROBERT DONIHUE SR.

The LORD watches over all who love him. PSALM 145:20 NIV

WHEN THINGS GO wrong and we feel down and out, we may wonder where the Lord is. Is He really watching over us each day?

Elementary teacher Sylvia had been going through some hardships. Though she trusted the Lord to help her, she was haunted by discouraging doubts. She was doing the best she could and knew deep inside that God was near. Still, she needed His assurance that He was with her and would see her through.

Sylvia had a boy named Elliott in her class that no one else wanted. Every time Elliott turned around, he was getting into trouble. He attracted trouble like a magnet. Still, Sylvia loved him and was determined to change his defeated attitude to one of self-confidence.

One day Sylvia and another teacher watched Elliott complete a language arts project and look at it with pride. The other teacher asked Sylvia if she thought Elliott might get lost in the "educational cracks." "Not on my watch he won't," she responded with conviction. "I'll stick with him for as long as he's in this school."

Her own words hit her like lightning. She knew God cared about her and was graciously helping her each day. She could almost feel Him smiling and whispering to her heart: "Not on my watch, Sylvia. I'm sticking with you for as long as you live."

Later, during her lunch break at her desk, Sylvia quietly thanked God for reminding her of His faithful love.

He who climbs above the cares of this world and turns his face to his God, has found the sunny side of life.
—CHARLES HADDON SPURGEON

You have also given me the shield of Your salvation; Your right hand has held me up.
PSALM 18:35 NKJV

HAVE ANY MIRACLES taken place in your life? Did they come about through a gradual process, or were they more dramatic? Miracles happen everywhere, and they all have one thing in common: when God decrees a miracle to take place, nothing is impossible.

I know a woman who was born to a couple running from the law. Danger, uncertainty, and fear threatened her throughout her childhood and teenage years. She was bounced from family member to family member, foster home to foster home. Still, dedicated Christians were simultaneously placed in her life all through those years. One person planted the seed to trust God; another person watered that little seed of faith. Some protected her and intervened; others nourished, loved, and gave timely advice. Remarkably, she was given enough encouragement and godly love by different people that she recognized the loving, saving hand of God and became a Christian.

God has taken the good and bad this woman experienced and transformed them into powerful blessings that she is now passing on to children all around her. Through her work, He's using her to help transform hopeless situations in children's lives into incredibly real possibilities for them to become future leaders for Him. Very likely many will in turn spend their lives carrying on miracles of encouragement and love to the next generation, and the next...and the next.

God makes a miracle when He takes hopeless impossibilities in our lives and turns them around into powerful possibilities through Him.

I can do everything through him who gives me strength. PHILIPPIANS 4:13 NIV

THE THOUGHT OF taking on a huge project that's been put off for a long time can seem overwhelming. The more we look at what needs to be done, the more defeated we become. We may be tempted to just put off the project a little longer.

A friend of mine that I'll call Marilyn felt this way about a spare bedroom in her home. Every time she had things she didn't know what to do with, she tossed them into that room. She kept telling herself that some day she would get in there and organize everything, but "some day" never seemed to come.

One evening when Marilyn glanced in the room, she was shocked to see stuff piled knee-deep. She had to do something. She sat down on a chair near the door and nearly cried. From that level, the piles of stuff looked mountainous.

She stood up in dismay and prayed for help, asking God to give her the determination and means she needed to make the room clean. The next morning while at work, she decided to bring home five boxes that would help with her project: a box for carrying stuff into the hallway for sorting, one for keeping, one for thinking about what to keep, one for trash, and one for giving reusable things away. She even began emptying dresser drawers one at a time so she could reorganize what she kept.

Marilyn worked at her project for a couple hours each day. The more progress she made, the more she began thinking about how she could redecorate the room when done. After she finished, she thanked God for giving her a new perspective and helping her to rise above the mountainous mess by using five cardboard boxes.

But they that wait upon the Lord shall renew their strength; they shall mount up with wings as eagles; they shall run, and not be weary; and they shall walk, and not faint. ISAIAH 40:31 KJV

SOME TIME AGO Bob preached on the groundhog and the eagle, explaining that as we deal with life's problems, our attitude and perspective can cause us to make mountains out of molehills like the groundhog, or soar above our problems like the eagle. We may be facing challenges that God wants us to let go of and give to Him. We might be struggling with weaknesses that hinder our walk with Him. God wants us to view our problems from a higher perspective, not to be buried under them. He wants us to accept His help so we can overcome them one by one.

Through His guidance and strength, we can learn to soar above the rubble like the eagle and experience His victories.

WOULD YOU RATHER GRUB WITH THE GROUNDHOG?
Man was made to soar like an eagle, to take risks,
Dream big dreams and seek the sky,
If you're lying in the rubble concentrating on your trouble,
Chances are that you're not learning how to fly.

You may think you're protected in your tunnel,
Safe and sound underground in the dark,
But your shadow sets you quaking; it's a ghost of your own making.
Better raise your eyes up to a higher mark.

In the good book God made me a promise,
And I know I can take Him at His word:
Though the storms of life wash over me, He'll lead me on to victory
If I just keep my eyes fixed on the Lord.

Would you rather grub with the groundhogs?
Hit the dirt or try your wings, it's up to you.
Whether crawlin' or a-flyin', it's the Lord we must rely on.
If you trust in Him, you know He'll see you through.

—JANICE LEWIS CLARK

"Be still, and know that I am God." PSALM 46:10 NIV

FATHER, LIFE IS getting way too hectic. Strife and tension are all around me. People are impatient and rude. There are too many demands upon me. What more do they want from me? I'm doing my best, but it never seems to be enough. Besides that, I feel totally unappreciated. I, too, must be showing frustration.

Every area of my life is rush, rush, rush. I find myself gritting my teeth while waiting impatiently in long lines. When I'm driving, I catch myself gripping the steering wheel until my knuckles turn white. Little things are becoming major to me. My head is pounding. The knots in my shoulders and neck feel like giant ropes that are getting tighter and tighter. It seems like I don't have control of life anymore. It has control of me.

Here I am, Father. I'm desperately seeking Your merciful presence. I can't remember when I last broke away from all my responsibilities and distractions and took time with You. Please help me. I don't know how to get out of this whirlwind of my life, but I know You understand my needs.

My body relaxes as I sense Your gracious love ministering to my heart. Thank You for encouraging me to let go of things I can't handle on my own. I trust You to guide me through each one of these problems as they arise.

Whenever I'm tempted to take on more than I should, I pray that You will give me a new perspective about what is most important. When the pressures come, let me roll over my worries and place them in Your compassionate, faithful hands.

Thank You for Your merciful kindness. I love and appreciate You.

O Lord, how manifold are Your works! In wisdom You have made them all. PSALM 104:24 NKJV

SOMETIMES WE GET so busy that we allow God's simple blessings to pass us by. If we aren't careful, we miss out on things He has planned for us.

Not long ago, I visited my son and grandkids at their remote countryside home. During that time, we traveled forty miles round trip to spend two days at Ferry County Fair. The kids entered exhibits, and I sold my books and shared God's love with some delightful people. The next day, we went to town for church. I spoke a few words in the service, and we enjoyed worshipping with friends. By the end of three days, we were happy but exhausted.

Yet early Monday morning as the sun barely peeked over the trees, I was wide awake. I was ready to witness God's simple blessing that I'd looked forward to for months. I grabbed my Bible and tablet and slipped outside to my favorite spot: the picnic table near the side of the house.

Mist hung over the pastureland of a neighbor's farm. The rising sun kissed the surrounding foothills. It was absolutely quiet. "Oh, Lord," I whispered, "You are so good. In wisdom You have made all of this. Thank You for Your simple blessings of calmness and beauty."

Then to the left I saw what I'd been waiting for. A doe, two small fawns, and a buck walked slowly out of the woods a few feet away and began grazing in the front yard. I was so excited I could barely move. At that moment, I forgot about being weary. I felt truly refreshed in God's presence. The simple blessing that morning continues to replay in my mind.

Look for the simple blessings God has in store for you. You never know what He has planned.

How does a man [gain knowledge and] become wise? The first step is to trust and reverence the Lord! PROVERBS 1:7 TLB

THERE'S A WONDERFUL thing about thirsting for knowledge. It opens doors and answers questions about everything in our world. One of my greatest pleasures is watching the students I teach in school and church soak up knowledge like sponges. Their minds are fresh, eager to find pieces to fit into the puzzle of life.

In addition to what we learn in school, we gradually gain experience through trial and error and the school of "hard knocks." Some people say their most valuable lessons were learned the hard way.

There's another priceless education we can obtain. It comes from seeking wisdom from God. Proverbs 9:10–12 explains that when we learn from God and His Word, we receive lifelong instruction, knowledge, and wisdom that help us make wise choices. When we're willing to listen to what God and wise Christians teach us, more years will be added to our lives. We'll also be able to avoid a great deal of heartache.

A student named Kim in the college I attended wanted to know how education could answer her questions regarding her daily life. One day a kind lady in her church had her over for tea and biscuits, and Kim told the woman her dilemma. Her hostess opened her oven door to check the biscuits and closed it again. "Honey," she said, "you're like these biscuits. You're just not done in the middle yet. It takes time, prayer, and searching for wisdom to help you find your answers."

True wisdom comes from God. It's a gift we can ask for and receive that will help the whole thing to make sense.

I will study and get ready, and perhaps my chance will come.
—ABRAHAM LINCOLN

"For I know the plans I have for you," says the Lord. "They are plans for good and not for evil, to give you a future and a hope. In those days when you pray, I will listen. You will find me when you seek me, if you look for me in earnest." JEREMIAH 29:11−13, TLB

DO YOU LOVE the Lord? Do you wonder if there's something you can do for Him? More than ability, what matters most is that you have a willing heart to love and serve Him.

During a Sunday morning worship service, Bekah stepped up to the pulpit and stood by Pastor Bob. Everyone was silent while she told how she went with our youth group to a "Dare to Share" conference in Seattle. They went door to door asking for canned goods for the Salvation Army, telling people about God's love, and even leading some folks to accept the Lord as their Savior.

When I met Bekah a year before, she was a quiet Christian girl who came to the youth nights. She soon began attending church and helping me in my Sunday school class, but her shyness held her back from speaking in front of people.

One Sunday I asked my students to close their eyes. I invited them to ask Jesus into their hearts if they hadn't already done so. I also encouraged them to pray to be filled with His cleansing Holy Spirit. They could pray either silently or aloud. Later Bekah told me that she asked the Lord to fill her with His Holy Spirit and use her in any way He wanted. And He did.

Now in her quiet way, Bekah shares her love for the Lord with everyone who will listen. No matter their age, she's able to relate and care. God has given her a passion to tell how He changed her life and given her a call to serve Him.

What does her future hold? The adventure has only begun.

Consider giving Him *your* willing heart, and see what wonderful things He has planned for you.

Teach me Your way, O LORD; I will walk in Your truth. Unite my heart to fear Your name.
PSALM 86:11 NKJV

WHEN WE SEEK God first and His righteousness, we will discover the most wonderful relationship with Him that we could ever imagine. He begins teaching us how to live a holy life, grants us wisdom, and provides for our needs. (See Chronicles 1:11–12.)

When Josiah sought God's will first, God gave him the wisdom to make powerful and authoritative decisions. By the time he was twenty, he had purged Judah and Jerusalem of its idols. When he was twenty-six, he cleansed the temple of anything that was offensive to God; then he cleaned and repaired the precious house of God. All of his life, Josiah loved and served the Lord. He accomplished great things simply by asking God for righteousness, wisdom, and grace.

I believe righteousness and wisdom are found by anyone who seeks God's right and wise way with an open heart and cautious mind. When making important decisions, we can ask advice from discerning, respectful, God-fearing people. Most of all, we must continually hunger and thirst for God's righteousness and not compromise our standards. Stepping outside of God's will in the slightest can spell serious heartache and disaster. When we do obey God, He will fill our spiritual cups to overflowing.

As we ask, God generously gives answers. As we seek His will, He helps us find the right way. When we knock, in search of His guidance, He will open doors to right choices and sound wisdom. Then He will infinitely bless us with His grace, peace, and everlasting joy.

More important than where we stand on the issues of life is what we are doing with the time on earth we've been given.

I will take up the cup of salvation, and call upon the name of the Lord. PSALM 116:13 NKJV

LORD, I'M FACING another dilemma; I don't know which way to turn. All the experience and knowledge I possess don't seem to matter right now. My heart's racing and my emotions are in turmoil. I want to do what's right, but I'm not sure what right is! I've asked advice from those I respect and have received a variety of opinions. I'm at a loss as to what to do. Please help me, Lord. Calm my spirit and show me the way.

I come before You with an open heart, seeking Your will. How I yearn for You to teach me Your righteous way and grant me Your wisdom. Although I long for a quick and easy solution, I know You understand the whole picture. As I read Your Word, I feel my mind clear. Ever so slowly, things fall into place. How I delight in Your love and guidance. I want to meditate on Your teachings day and night.

Though all seems uncertain and difficult, I will sink my roots deeply into Your streams of living water. When discord parches my soul, I will not wither, for You are with me. I trust that whatever wisdom and surety I need, You will give it to me. My heart interlocks with Your will. I praise You for filling my spiritual cup until it spills over to those around me. Thank You for helping me to focus on You and synchronize my thoughts with the directions I read in Your Word.

I sense myself being filled with Your merciful gift of peace. No longer is my heart troubled, neither am I afraid. I trust You and thank You for remaining with me, guarding, guiding each step along the way.

Do not be overcome by evil, but overcome evil with good. ROMANS 12:21 NASB

SOMETIMES WE ARE blindsided by people who cut us down for being Christians, but we can still be winners even when we appear to lose.

Hot tears welled in Patty's eyes as she left her workplace. Beth, a coworker, had constantly criticized her for living a Christian life, and her lies had caused Patty to be fired. Patty never wanted to see Beth again. *Doesn't everything work out for good when we love the Lord?* she wondered. She took her bitterness and her need for work to God.

She immediately found another job that was better than the first one. Through God's help, she managed to release her hurts and forgive Beth. Her new job required more responsibility, so she took classes to improve her skills and threw herself into her new position. Before long, she was promoted to assistant manager.

One day at work, Patty glanced up in time to see Beth walk through the door. Both were surprised to see each other. Old anger boiled in Patty until she felt God speak to her heart. She offered Beth a seat. Beth was applying for a job. She'd been caught lying at her old job and was fired. She hung her head in shame and asked for Patty's forgiveness. God nudged Patty to forgive and give Beth another chance. It proved fruitful. Beth became one of Patty's most faithful employees.

Best of all, Beth finally prayed with Patty and accepted Jesus as her Savior. Patty's experience proved that things really do work together for good when we love the Lord.

Let's remember when we're mistreated, love really does conquer all. When we do our best to follow God's lead, He gives the right mixture of wisdom and grace to us just at the time we need it.

The fear of the LORD teaches a man wisdom, and humility comes before honor. PROVERBS 15:33 NIV

IS THERE SOMEONE you love and respect because of their humility? Are you drawn to humble people? I know I am. They don't seem anxious to impress others. When they speak, their words are weighed and worth listening to. Wherever they are, they are willing to love and care about those around them, rather than try to draw attention to themselves.

John the Baptist was this kind of person. His focus was on glorifying God, his heavenly Father. His lifestyle was simple. He never seemed to want to impress others, nor was he self-seeking. Instead, he spent his energy preparing the way for his cousin, Jesus Christ, the Savior.

People from miles around came to John asking him to baptize them. Still, he sought no recognition. Some asked him if he was the Savior promised to them. He emphatically replied, "I indeed baptize you with water unto repentance, but He who is coming after me is mightier than I, whose sandals I am not worthy to carry. He will baptize you with the Holy Spirit and fire."

When Jesus asked John to baptize Him, John said, "I need to be baptized by You, and are You coming to me?" John did as Jesus instructed and baptized his Savior. How marvelous it must have been for him to witness the Holy Spirit descending upon Jesus like a dove and God saying, "This is My beloved Son, in whom I am well pleased." (See John 1:19–34.)

I imagine God was also pleased with John's humility.

We, too, can be a blessing for the Lord when we humble ourselves before Him. When we do, He is truly pleased. May the Lord take our lives and make them His. Let His glory shine through us.

We know that we all possess knowledge. Knowledge [without God] puffs up, but love builds up.
1 CORINTHIANS 8:1 NIV

MANY OF US can recall a happy experience when we were recognized for an accomplishment well done, only to have someone's jealous attitude or cutting remark steal that happiness away.

The opposite happened a year ago when I took my books to sell at a county fair near the home where some of my grandchildren live. All four of the kids made special things to enter in the fair. That year, Ian entered a beautiful bowl made of one piece of wood. He had spent hours working with the lathe, smoothing every little grain. Along with a few other items, Ian's younger sister, Talia, decided the night before the fair to enter one more project. She spent half an hour crocheting an attractive pink hat. She planned to later donate the hat to an organization that helps children with cancer.

At the end of the weekend, the judges announced their decisions. All four of the kids won ribbons. Ian earned second prize for his bowl, and Talia became a grand-prize winner for the crocheted hat. Ian was very disappointed. He went off to one side where Talia couldn't see him and took time to think. After a few moments, he walked up to his sister and congratulated her for her accomplishment. It was an act of unselfish love.

In today's society, we are programmed to think of incentives and awards for our achievements. These things are good, yet the Lord encourages us to also recognize the worth we see in those around us.

I wonder how much of a difference we would make in the lives of others if we were to look for three people each day and offer them encouragement and praise. I wonder if such positive actions might multiply like ripples in a pond. I wonder...

For the eyes of the Lord are on the righteous and his ears are attentive to their prayer.
1 PETER 3:12 NIV

ONE SUNDAY AS I stood in our Sunday school classroom overflowing with rambunctious students, I had trouble getting their attention. They couldn't stop talking long enough to hear what I was trying to tell them. I had an especially important and fun lesson planned for them that Sunday, and I knew I couldn't talk above their voices because I'm a soft-spoken person. I could feel my frustration building, yet God gently reminded me to not show my impatience but to think about their feelings.

With a big smile, I stood before them with arms outstretched, palms down. I slowly moved my arms from side-to-side while quietly saying "*sh-sh-sh.*" The Holy Spirit was at work. The kids immediately stopped talking and were ready to find out what we would be doing. We ended up having a great time together learning about Him.

There may be occasions when we wonder if God is really paying attention to what we're doing or if He's too busy with other things. Does He listen each time we come to Him in prayer? The Bible says: "For the eyes of the LORD run to and fro throughout the whole earth, to show Himself strong on behalf of those whose heart is loyal to Him" (2 Chronicles 16:9 NKJV).

Like a good parent watching over his children, God is with us all the time, helping with our concerns and needs. The moment we speak His name in prayer, He is right there with us, ready to listen to our every word. What's even more wonderful is the way He responds by speaking to our hearts.

What blessings we can enjoy when we are attentive to His presence and commune with Him as Friend with friend.

Show me Your ways, O LORD; teach me Your paths. Lead me in Your truth and teach me, for You are the God of my salvation; on You I wait all the day. PSALM 25:4–5 NKJV

THE MOST IMPORTANT times in our lives as Christians are when we go to God in prayer. Not hurried moments but blocks of time when we can share our joys and sorrows, victories and concerns with our dearest Friend, our Lord. The more we talk with Him, the more we know how He feels about all that's going on in our lives.

Can you imagine rushing through conversations with your husband, your children, or your best friends day after day? There would be no bond, only distance and discouragement. Neither are we able to have a closeness with God unless we really take time to talk.

It's tempting in this fast-paced world to rush through our prayer time the way we gobble breakfast or take morning vitamins. We need to find time to savor the moments with God. Talk and talk some more. Laugh with Him about the funny events; cry on His shoulder about the things that break our hearts. Tell Him how much you love Him. He wants us to accept His grace and mercy in return. What relief we feel when we ask God to search our hearts for attitudes that shouldn't be there. What peace we experience when we turn those things over to Him and leave them at the foot of His cross.

After this, it's important to not just go on our way. There's more. The most precious time of all with God is yet to come. It's when we pause and listen. And listen. Then listen some more. Effective and fruitful prayer with God must be a two-way conversation.

When we're willing to do this, we're getting to know the heart of God and learn what *He's* concerned about. What a full, triumphant life we experience when we do so!

You will fill me with joy in your presence, with eternal pleasures at your right hand.
PSALM 16:11 NIV

HOW GOOD IT is when we can take time with God and snatch a few quiet moments away with Him. We may find a favorite spot or a comfortable chair where we can meet, where we get to talk with our best Friend. As we focus on Him, the noise around us fades to where we think only about our wonderful, caring Lord.

When we come to God in prayer, we may begin to realize how much our parched souls have been desperately thirsting for His compassionate, gracious presence. Soon we're able to open our hearts and minds to Him. As we do, He makes Himself known to us. He fills and satisfies us with the pure, sweet waters of His Holy Spirit. How good it is to be in His presence. Here in our simple place of worship, He ministers to us. He understands how we feel and showers us with His indescribable love.

We have the chance to open our Bibles and read about His countless wonderful ways. In wisdom and love He lays them out before us. He shows us His promises of hope, courage, and guidance. There is nothing too great or small for Him to handle. We offer Him our tiny morsels of faith and place each of our concerns in His capable hands.

With all our hearts, may we thank the Lord for His gracious, abiding care. From the beginning to the end of each of our days that lies ahead, let us lift our hearts to Him in quiet songs of praise. May our words and actions exalt Him and reflect His goodness and grace. In Him we take delight. In Him we eagerly place our trust. In Him we find assurance that His presence is always near.

O LORD our Lord, how excellent is thy name in all the earth! PSALM 8:9 KJV

IT'S NEAR THE end of the day, Father. I kick off my shoes and climb out of my car. A feeling of tranquility sweeps over me as I dig my toes into the warm sand. Here with You, I sit down and relax. I gaze out toward the water. The low tide causes the wet beach to stretch out for what seems like miles, reflecting the sun's golden rays. I breathe in the fresh, cool wind and sense Your Spirit restoring my soul. A shift in the breeze causes a soft salty spray to caress my face.

Father, when I think of Your creation, I feel like I'm only a tiny dot on this planet, Your footstool. The hours seem like minutes while I sit here with You. Before I know it, You display Your glorious sunset. I marvel at the shades of blue, red, orange, and yellow. How exquisite is Your creation! How can I take it all in?

Here I give You my thanksgiving and love. Here I pour out my joys and share my concerns. I commit my needs only to You. Your words of compassion and love strengthen my heart.

Praise You, Father, for Your heaven and earth. Praise You for Your angels. Praise You for Your sun, moon, and stars. Praise You for Your seas, rivers, and lakes. Praise You for Your refreshing rain, for thunder, lightning, and hail. For seasons filled with clouds, snow, and blustery winds. Praise You for Your mountains, hills, and trees. For all the creatures You have made. Praise You most of all for taking the time to make me, and for tenderly keeping me near to Your heart.

Thank You, Father. It's nearing dark. I'm ready to return to my room and enjoy a restful night with You.

Not that I speak in regard to need, for I have learned in whatever state I am, to be content.
PHILIPPIANS 4:11 NKJV

THERE'S SOMETHING PRECIOUS and sacred about the contentment the Lord gives us while we nestle in the care of His loving arms. Though illness, oppression, and hopelessness may press in, we have the joy of experiencing God's goodness. Though sin and others' ill regard try to drain the strength from our souls, God helps us to stand firm on His sure foundation. No amount of adversity or discouragement can remove this satisfaction we experience when we live for God with a grateful heart.

If anyone had reason to be discouraged, it was a girl named Fanny who was made blind when she was a baby by a doctor's incorrect treatment. When she grew up, she attended and later taught for eleven years at the New York Institute of the Blind. While there, she met and married Alexander van Alstyne, a blind musician.

Even as an adult, tragedy was no stranger to Fanny. Her only child died as an infant, and after many years of marriage, she lost her husband to death and had to live alone for the rest of her life. In spite of everything, Fanny resolved to enjoy life and be thankful for God's blessings. Her positive attitude shined brightly through everything she did.

One day Fanny visited a friend named Phoebe Knapp. Phoebe played a melody for Fanny that she had recently composed and asked Fanny what the words should be. Fanny dropped to her knees in prayer. What she visualized in her mind was clear. There in Phoebe's home Fanny wrote the lyrics to the melody, and the hymn "Blessed Assurance" was born.

The Lord inspired Fanny Crosby to write numerous hymns throughout her life. They all reflect the contentment she enjoyed in Him.

Surely he has done great things. JOEL 2:20 NIV

IF YOU COULD sit and talk for hours about what God has done for you, what would your favorite stories be? Would they be of happy childhood memories? Would some be about the transformation that took place when you accepted Christ as your Savior? Perhaps you have stories of how God moved mountains and amazingly brought certain people into your life when you desperately needed help.

I love hearing my friends and loved ones tell how God is doing everyday, remarkable things in their lives. Their stories bless me. I also enjoy telling everyone who will listen about the marvelous things He's doing for me. It's like a daily adventure in Him. There's a term for this; it's called "good news." Another word for "good news" is *gospel*. What a blessing it is to read about the gospel in Matthew, Mark, Luke, and John.

Have some fun spreading your good news to people around you, and watch the blessings flow.

Blessed assurance, Jesus is mine!
Oh, what a foretaste of glory divine!
Heir of salvation, purchase of God,
Born of his Spirit, washed in his blood.

Perfect submission, perfect delight,
Visions of rapture now burst on my sight:
Angels descending bring from above,
Echoes of mercy, whispers of love.

Perfect submission, all is at rest,
I in my Savior am happy and blest:
Watching and waiting, looking above,
Filled with his goodness, lost in his love.
—FANNY J. CROSBY

A gossip betrays a confidence; so avoid a man who talks too much.... A gossip betrays a confidence, but a trustworthy man keeps a secret. PROVERBS 20:19; 11:13 NIV

HAVE YOU EVER been the victim of gossip? Sometimes a morsel of information can be expanded out of proportion until it's barely recognizable.

When this happens, we are often tempted to become bitter. After all, our treasured reputations are at stake. We wonder if the best way to handle the problem is to spread news *about* the gossiper or attempt to correct the misinformation. However, these can only add fuel to the fire. Rather than making the situation worse, we can gain wisdom from the Bible and stay away from those who spread words of slander. Instead, we can pray for God's help and grace.

Although we may be the victims, God is the Defender. When we take these problems to Him in prayer and set a Christian example, He goes before us and defends us. He is our Guide and makes our paths sure and true.

Through it all, the truth often comes out and we become victors through our Lord, Jesus Christ!

❧

I come before You, Father, searching my heart as to whether I deserve to sit in Your presence. I slipped up once again when I carelessly gossiped about someone I know. Why couldn't I have mentioned something kind when the rumors began to fly? I should have refused to listen, said how much I detest slander, and walked away.

Forgive me, Father, for my wrongdoing. Please guard my lips and help me to refrain from such talk. Grant me Your grace while I pray. Please give me insight and discernment to understand this one being talked about. Guide me, Father, as to what I should or should not do.

Love Is Kind

"God sees not as man sees, for man looks at the outward appearance, but the LORD *looks at the heart."* I SAMUEL 16:7 NASB

IS IT TRUE that you can't judge a book by its cover? Some tend to categorize people according to their appearance, but actions and words reveal what they are really like.

While traveling by train one day, Bob and I sat a short distance from a man with long, unkempt hair and arms covered with tattoos. Some may have been turned off by his appearance—until an elderly gentleman across the aisle from him began choking. While everyone else just watched, the young man immediately came to the gentleman's aid. When he had recovered, the older man thanked his rescuer and stated that he could have died.

"Not on my watch," the young man returned with a smile.

Jesus told about a man traveling from Jerusalem to Jericho who was robbed by bandits, stripped of his clothes, and left to die. A priest happened by. When he saw the man, he crossed the road and went on. A Levite callously did the same. Sadly, priests and Levites were the religious men of the day.

Then a Samaritan man came along. Samaritans were rejected by the Jews and looked upon as untouchables. Noticing the injured man and feeling sorry for him, he cleaned the man's wounds with oil and wine then wrapped them in bandages. He lifted the man onto his animal and brought him to an inn. He cared for the man through the night then left enough money with the host for the man's lodging until his return. Should the cost be more, the kind Samaritan would make up the difference. Who do you suppose showed the most love?

This story reminds us to look for the best in others and to show kindness wherever we can.

The things which you learned and received and heard and saw in me, these do, and the God of peace will be with you. PHILIPPIANS 4:9 NKJV

AS PARENTS OR children's leaders, we enjoy blessings, but we also go through our share of struggles and discouragement. Remember, God has amazing plans for our youth.

Dwight was the son of a Massachusetts farmer and stonemason. The seventh in his family, he held little promise of greatness. When he was only four, his father died, but his courageous mother provided for her children and kept them together. She gave Dwight a foundation of perseverance and self-reliance. He didn't do well in school, but he loved to learn about life around him.

At age seventeen, he moved to Boston with little money. There he sold shoes and attended Sunday school. His love for God was nurtured by a dedicated Sunday school teacher who saw something special that would one day blossom into a God-given ability to win souls.

When he was grown, *he* became a Sunday school teacher and missionary to sailors in Chicago. He found another job selling shoes and rented a room in a run-down part of town. He visited hospitals and prisons and ministered to homeless adults and children. Soon the Sunday school attendance grew to over six hundred. He quit his job and became a full-time evangelist. During the Civil War, he helped countless men in Camp Douglas near Chicago. He was also a missionary in the Young Men's Christian Association, now known as the YMCA.

Because of a mother's and Sunday school teacher's commitment and God's compassion, Dwight L. Moody followed God's call. May God send you children to influence and inspire. When discouragements occur, don't give up. God is helping. You never know when you plant seeds how bountiful will be the harvest.

October 10 | Rising from the Ashes

His mercy extends to those who fear [and reverence] him, from generation to generation.
LUKE 1:50 NIV

WHEN WE HEAR God's call, we may be excited and eager to get started. Yet as we experience setbacks and struggles, we may be tempted to give up. God might change our calling to something different, but as long as He leads us to keep going, we must trust Him, press forward, and claim the victories as we go.

Dwight Moody married a woman who shared his love for missions, and two children blessed their union. With the help of their Sunday school congregation, he built a large church for the still-growing numbers attending. But a few years later, the building tragically burned to the ground in the Great Chicago Fire.

Rather than give in to disappointment and defeat, he saw the fire's tragedy as the next step of a huge opportunity God was providing. He held revivals in Brooklyn, Philadelphia, and many other cities. God blessed him with enough money through offerings to build a mammoth new tabernacle in place of the church destroyed by fire. Not counting adults, the Sunday school now exceeded one thousand!

His evangelistic work miraculously expanded to other cities, states, and even countries. Christian song writer Ira Sankey joined him with his motivating songs as they won thousands of souls to the Lord. The two men held some of the greatest revivals of the nineteenth century. Evangelist Dwight L. Moody and long-revered Ira D. Sankey are still remembered as amazing soul winners who saw great opportunities to serve God.

When you're discouraged, God never gives up. Keep trusting in His mercy and faithfulness. Remain true. He'll show the way.

We have different gifts, according to the grace given us.... If it is encouraging, let him [or her] encourage. ROMANS 12:6, 8 NIV

THINK OF A time when you've felt exhausted and prayed for encouragement, and how God answered your prayer. Let me share a time when God did that for me.

It was less than two weeks until the end of the school year. As usual, there was still a lot of work to do. Although I loved teaching my students, exhaustion had set in. I longed to have more time to write. As I had many times before, I prayed for strength and encouragement. It arrived in the form of a letter from a reader in New Zealand. I was thrilled to read that she had just become a Christian. Her letter reminded me of what God was accomplishing with others throughout the world.

Then I received a note from my father-in-law. I had recently told him and Mom how my books were doing and asked them to pray while I wrote. This is the letter they sent back:

Dear Neat,

Your letter of information about the books arrived a few days ago. We want to say how proud we are of you. As you look back over the years of hard work, long hours, sweat, and, no doubt, tears, you must feel blessed in the journey God has set you on. A job well done.

Through the times while some doubted and ignored your calling, you continued to hang in there. With the great help from the Lord Himself, your efforts were blessed and are being used by Him.

We are proud of you, Neat. Now get to work and get the next one out.

As always, we love you,
Dad and Mother Donihue

Write upon your heart to seize the opportunities God gives you every day. Be a blessing for Him with rightly seasoned words, filled with wisdom.

A soft answer turns away wrath, but a harsh word stirs up anger. PROVERBS 15:1 NKJV

LATELY I'VE BEEN noticing more people making an effort to be polite to each other. I don't know if it's my imagination or that I'm just looking for the best in others. At our local gas station the other day, a man stopped to hold the door open for me. I didn't hesitate to say thank you. The best part was his smile, realizing his good deed was appreciated.

But what of those who aren't polite? Our natural tendency when hearing a rude remark is to retaliate with a negative response. I'm tempted to give "the teacher" look when someone behaves that way. But is my attitude right?

Several years ago I was sitting near the hospital bedside of my friend and couldn't help hearing a conversation taking place in a room across the hall. Two doctors were talking with a man who had a terrible attitude. They were trying to get information from him so they could help him. Every time they asked a question, he shot back a flippant, negative remark. Every time he did, the doctors treated him with courtesy and respect. Suddenly there was silence. Then with tears in his voice he asked why the doctors were being so kind. Their response was that they cared about helping him. The man's attitude changed. What made the difference? Two men who showed unconditional love.

I'm often tempted to react rather than listen to God's direction to be polite. I find this most difficult when I'm with those closest to me. Yet who deserves my best manners more than they do? May the Lord help me to respond with gracious words and actions.

To be of a peaceable spirit brings peace along with it.
—THOMAS WATSON

Therefore be imitators of God as dear children. And walk in love, as Christ also has loved us and given Himself for us, an offering and a sacrifice to God for a sweet-smelling aroma.
EPHESIANS 5:1–2 NKJV

LORD, I DID it again. I spoke in anger before asking for Your help. Some people call this "just spouting off," but spouting off can hurt and burn deeply into the soul. Without forgiveness, those hurts can last for years.

I'm so sorry, Lord. Please forgive my foolish words. Teach me patience and self-control. Proverbs 15:18 says: "A hot-tempered man stirs up dissension, but a patient man calms a quarrel" (NIV). When tension builds, remind me to stop, think, and pray. Help me to find time alone. Calm my emotions so I can think clearly and understand another person's point of view. Teach me to be quick to listen, cautious to speak, and slow to become angry, so my attitude pleases You.

Sometimes, Lord, I bottle up my anger and refuse to say anything. If I go off and brood, resentment builds. You were angry when You were in the temple, but You used Your anger in a good way. Show me how to use my anger in a good way in order to talk out the problem.

At times I want to change the past but am unable to do so. In my grief, I ask why former days couldn't have been better. But do I have to convince others that I'm "right" when I know I really am right? Show me how to resolve things or simply forgive and let go.

Are You ever hurt or angry when I do wrong? If so, You are compassionate and merciful. Thank You for Your love, for being quick to forgive my repentant heart, and for throwing away my wrongs as far as the east is from the west. Your anger lasts for a moment, but Your favor lasts for a lifetime. (See Psalm 30:5.)

Prepare the way and guide me, Lord, as I go to this person to make peace.

Finally, all of you be of one mind, having compassion for one another; love as brothers [and sisters], be tenderhearted, be courteous. 1 PETER 3:8 NKJV

WE'VE ALL HAD someone tell us we've erred. Perhaps it was a simple mistake. Or perhaps it was because of a careless word or action on our part. Our human nature might be to recoil and try to defend ourselves. As we well know, a cutting reply usually makes matters worse.

A lady named Marcie hurriedly cleaned up her Sunday school classroom as people bustled in and out. Her class had a great time that morning, yet she was frustrated by the chaos near the end. She quickly gave her students last-minute instructions in hopes that they would all arrive at the worship service on time. She knew she was a little abrupt with one girl but mentally wrote it off as justifiable.

After church, Marcie's friend Sandra came up to her and asked if they could pray together. Sandra had overheard Marcie's careless remark and said she felt the girl's feelings were hurt. Marcie's heart sank at the very thought that she had done something wrong. She was tempted to disregard Sandra's comments until the Holy Spirit spoke to her heart to be open-minded and gracious. She accepted her friend's offer to pray, and after praying for forgiveness and wisdom on how to correct the problem, Marcie thanked Sandra for gently pointing out her shortcoming.

It isn't easy to be gracious, especially when we want desperately to do everything right. Yet we can be thankful for those who love us enough to pray with us when we've done something wrong. God blessed Marcie that day. He taught her what His graciousness is all about and He taught her to appreciate an honest Christian friend.

The LORD is my light and my salvation; whom [or what] shall I fear? The LORD is the strength of my life; of whom shall I be afraid? PSALM 27:1 NKJV

WHEN WE'RE GOING through dark times, we may wonder if there really is a light at the end of the tunnel. We try to find our way through overwhelming problems but sometimes wonder if we'll ever make it. Yet no matter how great our struggles are, we must remember that Jesus is our light and our salvation. Even when we trip and fall, He's there graciously reaching out His hand and helping us to our feet. He's the One who pierces our darkness and despair. He's the One who faithfully lights our way.

Throughout time, God has provided light to our world. He created light even before He made the earth. The sun, moon, and starts burst forth and pierced the endless darkness, reflecting His magnificent glory. It was the beginning of countless powerful things to come.

When the Israelites left Egypt in search of the Promised Land, God led them with a pillar of cloud by day and a pillar of fire by night. When God's tabernacle was made, lamps filled with oil were placed inside to change darkness to light.

Job recalled the light God had shed upon him before he was forced to suffer, and he never lost hope that it would once again shine on him. Through all his heartache, he remained faithful. God in turn blessed him abundantly.

David prayed for the light of God's face to shine upon him and his people. He recognized God was truly the light of his salvation and his source of joy.

Today we can still depend on God's gracious lovingkindness to light our way in all circumstances. Keep trusting Him to lead. He is the light at the end of our tunnel. He is the light that pierces our darkness, our hope, our strength, our all.

"Watch out that the light in you is not darkness. If therefore your whole body is full of light, with no dark part in it, it will be wholly illumined, as when the lamp illumines you with its rays."
LUKE 11:35–36 NASB

IF YOU ARE going through dark times, don't lose heart. Jesus is here to light your way every single day. When hopelessness, sadness, or depression threaten to overcome you with heavy darkness and despair, all you need to do is turn to Jesus, grasp His hand, and hold on tight.

Jesus teaches that He was and is the Light of the world. He wants us to not only follow His light but reflect that wonderful light and hope to those around us. As long as we pursue His righteous and holy ways and put Him first in our lives, we won't walk in darkness. When we trust in Him, our entire being will be full of His light with the Holy Spirit illuminating our way. If we begin to stray, His light helps pull us back to the right path. He paves the way to help keep us from stumbling. Yet if we should fall, He is always there to help us up so we can start over again.

Jesus has a remarkable way of leading us through discouragement, fear, and uncertainty. On those days when everything seems to go wrong, we can fall asleep with a prayer on our lips and awaken to the promises of a new day. We can know full well that God is always in control. He is the Way, the Truth, the Life, and the Light.

He is the One who helps us overcome regrets, hurts, and loss. He is the master healer. All we need to do is keep putting one foot in front of the other and following the light He provides us. We will one day look back and marvel at how He has victoriously brought us out of the darkness into His light.

"If anyone would come after me, he must deny himself and take up his cross and follow me."
MATTHEW 16:24 NIV

LORD, I OFTEN long to take life's easy road. I want everything to be predictable and in order. That's why I'm having trouble with what You're asking of me. It's definitely outside my comfort zone. I don't mean to complain, but I'm not good at this sort of thing. Why me? Couldn't You give this job to that nice person who would do it so well? The very thought of my taking on this project makes me cringe.

I know this isn't the way You want me to feel. Please forgive me for my reaction to Your request. I recognize that I must be willing to do anything You ask of me. How can I complain about being inconvenienced after all You've done for me? I'm so sorry, Lord.

I read in Your Word how important it is to always be open to Your leading, whether it's "in season or out of season," convenient or not—even when I feel unsure of myself. Help me to open my heart and mind to You. Fill me with love, tenderness, and compassion.

As You help me to acknowledge the urgency of obeying You, I realize there may not be a second chance for me to accomplish what You want me to do. Your ways must become mine. Let me become willing to endure hardship, Lord, and keep my attention on what You have for me to do. When I'm weak, please make me strong. When I'm worried, ease my insecurities. When I'm tempted to become impatient, grant me patience. When I run out of love, fill me with Your love.

Thank You for changing my attitude of excuse making to an attitude of willingness to do anything You ask of me. Most of all, Lord, thank You for Your patience and love.

"I tell you the truth, whatever you did for one of the least of these brothers [or sisters] of mine, you did for me." MATTHEW 25:40 NIV

SOMETIMES GOD WORKS in mysterious ways and performs unusual miracles to help our faith in Him grow. Kristina experienced a surprising miracle while praying for her sister Star to understand God's love.

One evening as Kristina, her baby, and Star were at Kristina's home watching television, they noticed frequent commercials for chicken wings. The wings were definitely calling to the ladies, so they headed to a fast food restaurant for chicken wings to go. At the restaurant, they overheard a teenage boy asking people for a ride. Kristina felt sorry for him but wanted to keep her family safe. Meanwhile, they discovered the wings wouldn't be ready for twenty minutes. While deciding what to do, they noticed the boy still asking for a ride. Everyone avoided him. Kristina felt God coaxing her to help. More wings would be ready when they returned. Surprisingly, the boy's destination was a supermarket twenty miles away. Still, Kristina agreed to take him. Star watched, not expressing an opinion.

As they drove, the boy thanked Kristina for the ride. He said he knew God had sent her to help him. All through the trip, Kristina and the boy talked about the Lord. Star listened quietly. After they dropped off the boy and were driving home, Star burst into tears. God had given her a glimpse of His love and mercy—a mercy she was beginning to understand. Kristina explained to her sister that God sometimes arranges a "divine appointment" to answer a prayer.

Soon the ladies arrived at home with their juicy morsels. Kristina thanked God for using chicken wings to help a boy—and touch Star's searching heart.

God's surprising calls often lead to miracles.

You can lie down without fear and enjoy pleasant dreams.... "Come with me by yourselves to a quiet place and get some rest." PROVERBS 3:24 NLT; MARK 6:31 NIV

IT USED TO be that when I tried to fall asleep, my mind would fill with worries for those around me. I allowed the "what-ifs" to crowd in and overshadow the peace of heart the Lord had for me. Then I decided to wholeheartedly commit my concerns to Him. Maybe you have also experienced this.

My son Dan reminds me to never speak or even think the negative possibilities into existence, but to focus on the assurance that our all-knowing God is in charge. Even before we ask, the Lord is aware of our requests and is taking care of them.

As we pray, we can leave our concerns with Him and shift our thoughts to thanksgiving—fully trusting that the Lord is taking care of each one. When we do, He will grant us peace and guard our minds while we sleep.

We can find comfort in Proverbs 3, that as we trust the Lord, we can rest and not be afraid. He promises to make our sleep sweet. We need not fear sudden disaster or ruin, because He is our hope and confidence.

❧

Father, I rest my head on my pillow and tell You about the good and bad things going on in my life. I'm thankful for the people I pray for who love You and have Your joy and sureness in their lives, but I grieve over those I try to reach for You who refuse to listen. Change their hearts, Lord, so they also can experience Your peace and hope.

My eyes grow heavy as I pray. Guard my mind, Lord. Help me to reflect on Your loving care. I give You my concerns and thank You for taking care of them.

Good night, Lord. I really love You.

Our Father...forgive us our debts, as we forgive our debtors. MATTHEW 6:12 KJV

THROUGH THE YEARS, I've talked with a lot of people who suffer from past hurts in their lives. Unfortunately, most of us have experienced our ample share of heartache. Some distress may be from a poor childhood, a bad marriage, or an unpleasant work situation. In all, grief and heartache are often severe.

Many people try to forgive and let go of the mistreatment that once overtook them. Sadly, some nurse their hurts, perhaps feeling that silent resentment helps to soothe their wounds. Yet in the process, they let the pain grow deeper, rather than allowing God to heal.

We may desperately want to go back and make things right. Often, however, no amount of effort can reverse the wrongs. Nothing can change that except a repentant heart. I believe we don't have to forgive the action committed against us, nor should we allow it to happen again. Sin is sin. But we must forgive the offender even if he or she isn't repentant, then pray faithfully for that person.

I used to think forgiveness was a one-time thing. If past hurts came to my memory, I wondered if I hadn't forgiven in the first place. Trying to block them out didn't help. Instead, I learned that I could bring it all to Jesus again and ask for His comfort and healing. He's there as often as we need Him.

When I am hurt and angry over things of the past and can't forgive on my own, I ask the Lord to change my heart and heal my wounds. I pray that He will help me to let the hurts go and put the past in His hands, and that He will encourage those involved to turn their hearts to Him. I thank Him for His healing and grace.

Hatred stirs old quarrels, but love overlooks insults. PROVERBS 10:12 TLB

HAVE YOU EVER tried to befriend someone who was difficult, but you couldn't get anywhere? Could you do no more than pray?

That happened to Pat. She had a neighbor who had gotten herself into all sorts of messes. Pat tried bringing the neighbor delicious treats, buying birthday gifts for her daughter, and visiting with her, but the woman always gave a brief reply and went her way.

One day the woman's mother insulted one of Pat's family members. Nothing prompted the mean remark; it just popped out. Pat's relative wisely said nothing, but it hurt Pat more than if she'd been insulted herself. For weeks she didn't want to even look at her neighbor. She felt she didn't need such mistreatment in her life.

Then God dealt with Pat's unforgiveness. She realized that she might not be able to befriend the woman, but she could wave and smile. She chose to love her neighbor with a low-key, genuine *attitude* of love, and she started praying for her every time she saw or thought about her.

Now when she notices her neighbor's frustration and anger aimed toward others, Pat prays. When arguments build, she prays some more. No matter what's happening, good or bad, she continues to pray.

Pat's early attempts at being friendly were more surface actions, not reflecting the "real" love God taught her to feel for her troubled neighbor. Although Pat's prayers still aren't totally answered, warm smiles and brief comments are being exchanged between the two of them. Best of all, God knows, and He's already working.

LOVE CONQUERS ALL
A genuine prayer filled with love conquers all.
It opens closed doors.
It melts hardened hearts.
It bridges gaps from hurts.
It untangles the tangled.
It corrects mistakes.
And it heals the wounded soul.

Blessed is every one who fears the LORD, who walks in His ways. When you eat the labor of your hands, you shall be happy, and it shall be well with you. Your wife shall be like a fruitful vine in the very heart of your house, your children like olive plants all around your table. PSALM 128:1–3 NKJV

FATHER, I HAVE been rushing all week. It seems like everything I'm doing is for a worthy cause, but I'm hitting overload and don't have enough time with the ones I love the most. Now I've cancelled a meeting I was to attend tonight so my husband, children, and I can have an evening together. Perhaps we'll even go out for a bite to eat, head to a park, and get away from the constantly demanding phone.

I want to serve You by helping others, but I know my family comes first in my life. The meeting can manage without me. Thank You for my family. How dear they are to me. I look at my loving husband and my "olive shoots," big and small, and praise You for these priceless blessings. Even when there are footprints on the rug, sticky stuff on the door knobs, and handprints on the windows, help me to reflect Your graciousness and love. They are my greatest treasures. During chaotic and fun-filled times, they fill my heart to overflowing. Help me never to take them for granted. Time passes too quickly.

Remind me of my priorities, Father. Help me remember my foremost mission is at home. Teach me to first keep the home fires burning. Guide and help each day to be a beacon of light to the ones I love the most.

If I get too carried away with added responsibilities (no matter how good they may appear), draw me back so I put the ones I love first.

Place a spiritual hedge of protection around them, Lord. Protect them from evil and harm. Please shine Your mercy and love upon us, and always keep us close to You.

The days of the blameless are known to the LORD, and their inheritance will endure forever. In times of disaster they will not wither. PSALM 37:18–19 NIV

SOME OF OUR tests in life are physically or spiritually dangerous. No doubt we've all been blessed by God's rescuing hand more than once. Although we may earn a few of His blessings, all of them are given by His gracious love.

How thankful we can be for those who risk their lives for others, especially for strangers. We can be grateful for the faithful, everyday prayer warriors who quietly care and love and give of themselves.

The graciousness and love God bestows on us are far greater than the good things we do. In spite of our good-hearted efforts, the only way we can gain His favor or our way to heaven is by accepting Him and actively acknowledging Him as our personal Savior and Lord.

He is the Creator of all. He is the One who placed within us the love and compassion we share with each other. When bad things happen and we as rescuers experience more trauma than we can take in, God is near. His merciful love envelops and comforts us in our times of need. He really is our refuge and strength, our very present help in times of trouble. (See Psalm 46:1.)

We don't understand or have control of our futures, but one thing we can know for sure is that God rescues and cares for us. No matter what turn our lives take, we can seek Him. As we open our hearts, we soon discover that He is our ultimate rescuer and is ready to help us in every area of our lives. The more we submit to His will, the more He's able to work through us so we can also help others. Amazingly, He brings about good in what we don't understand—especially when we give everything to Him.

Keep me safe, O God, for in you I take refuge. PSALM 16:1 NIV

WHEN OUR LIVES get crazy and we fear the challenges we're confronted with, we can depend on the Lord to help and protect us. We belong to Him; He is our refuge and strength.

A roughneck rooster named Sasquatch reigned over my dad's compliant hens. The obnoxious, beautiful bird often strutted about, brightly colored feathers on his neck bristling, his tail royally swaying behind him. The comb on his arrogant head and the tip of his curved tail feathers often touched. He had been transported to Washington from Iowa, and farmers labeled him an exotic bird. Neurotic was more like it! Back and forth he marched, like a decorated army sergeant.

Almost everyone was afraid of the intimidating beast. Yet every time Dad approached Sasquatch, the rooster fluttered to his shoulder and nestled up to him like a dove. Because of his fondness for the watchdog rooster, Dad tolerated Sasquatch's misbehavior.

At the time, our son and daughter-in-law lived next door to Dad. Our two-year-old grandson Harrison didn't handle Sasquatch very well. He watched him with saucer-shaped eyes every time the rooster came in sight. Sasquatch soon picked up on Harrison's fear and chased him every chance he got. The rooster's intimidating feathers rustled and he squawked and crowed. Each time, Harrison frantically ran for his front porch, with Sasquatch gleefully padding behind him. When Harrison reached the refuge of his porch, he knew he wouldn't be bothered there.

Like Harrison, when we face frightening challenges, we can run straight into our Savior's comforting arms.

If God be for us, who can be against us? ROMANS 8:31 KJV

THERE COMES A time when we get tired of running and hiding. Like David faced Goliath, we might feel the Lord leading us to stand firm and fight the giants that threaten us. However, when we do, we must remember to do so as God directs—and only in the power of His strength.

In the last devotion, I mentioned how frightened my two-year-old grandson was of an intimidating rooster. One day while he was playing in the front yard, out came Sasquatch, neck feathers bristling. Harrison determinedly stood his ground. Sasquatch menacingly raked his spiky feet in the dirt. Though trembling in his sneakers, Harrison stood tall. The little guy never said a word; he just stared that rooster right in the eye. The bird slowly turned and sauntered away. Harrison looked surprised. Sasquatch glanced back one more time. The saucy bird seemed to be looking past Harrison.

When Harrison turned around, there was big, tall "Chicken Grandpa" (that's what the grandkids called him) standing behind his little great-grandson. With his hands on his hips, Dad made it clear to the rooster that he was to let his great-grandson be! Soon after, Sasquatch was traded to another farmer to rule over his chicken flock (and probably the farmer).

We as Christians face roughneck roosters in our lives. Sometimes they're scary and intimidating or cause us grief. But we can remember that we are not alone. Our heavenly Father is with us, fighting our battles. All we need to do is stick close to God, remain true, and allow Him to help us. When we're mistreated for living Christian lives, we must remember that the Lord is our defense. He faithfully remains near and shows us a way of escape.

The earnest prayer of a righteous man has great power and wonderful results. JAMES 5:16 TLB

LORD, I'M ASKING for Your help regarding some neighbors who moved in down the street from our home. Ever since they came, we've been assailed by loud, booming music. They yell at each other in their yard so that the whole neighborhood is forced to hear their words. (Keep their children safe, Lord.) Cars are constantly going to and from their home that stay only a few minutes, then leave. Neighbors nearby are afraid of the men because of their offensive behavior and mean dogs. To make matters worse, they have been seen dealing drugs. How many lives are they destroying, Lord?

The man in the family squeals his tires while speeding forward and backward on our street. There are children playing around here, Lord, and I'm getting worried. Through all of this, I sense You speaking to my heart to fervently pray for this family's salvation— especially the man. So I bring each one to You in prayer. Make an opening for a Christian neighbor to tell the family about Your love, even if that person has to be me. If one of them is arrested, I pray for Christians who work in the jails and prisons to lead them to You.

The Bible tells of Matthew, or Levi, the tax collector who was considered dishonest and undesirable. Yet You called him to repentance and helped him to completely change his life. So right now I commit this family to You, Lord, and pray for You to talk to each heart. I'm thankful that You are greater than any forces of evil holding onto this man and his family. I trust You in faith, believing You will work in their lives as You see fit. To You I give honor and praise. In Jesus' name, amen.

I waited patiently for the LORD; *He inclined to me and heard my cry.... He put a new song in my mouth, a song of praise to our God.* PSALM 40:1, 3 RSV

DO YOU EVER ask God to help you with a need and your prayers never seem to be answered? No matter how you plead with Him for help, His answers don't appear to come? You may be praying for loved ones to become Christians, or your prayers may be for material needs, a job, or making the grade in work you're already involved in. Some of you may be facing layoffs at work. Whether our prayers are for the needs of others or ourselves, God is still faithful and is working things out in the ways He knows are best.

When a loved one hasn't yet accepted the Lord, we can be assured that God is already answering our prayers by constantly, patiently pleading with that person's heart. Still, He doesn't force people to accept Him. The person we're praying for has the freedom to make his or her own decisions. The good thing to remember is that God honors our prayers, even if whispered only once, throughout that person's entire life. He acknowledges our prayers not only throughout our lives, but even after we've left this earthly home and gone to be with Him.

Uncertainty and loss are terrible things to experience when we're concerned about material needs. We may not understand why we lose a home or a job. Stress from an impending layoff can stretch us to our limit. But as we do our best and trust Him, He will bring about good and provide for our needs. He loves us with a gracious, merciful love. Someday, praise God, we'll be able to look back and be absolutely surprised *and* grateful how He has brought things together for good.

Don't be afraid to completely, without reservation, leave your burdens and cares at His feet.

The Lord delights in those who fear him, who put their hope in his unfailing love.
Psalm 147:11 NIV

MOST OF US have had experiences where multiple things have gone wrong at once, only to discover later that while we were praying, the Lord was already providing for our needs.

Dana experienced God's help during a difficult time. One morning she hustled out the door for the school where she taught an elementary class. She unhooked the battery charger under her car hood, put the charger away, pushed the hood shut, and was on her way. In spite of the battery problems, she loved her little car and was thankful for it. She and her husband, Wes, were planning to buy an alternator out of their next paychecks.

Dana wheeled into a parking spot. Even though she appreciated her car, she felt embarrassed to park it near the shiny new beauties in the staff lot. She locked the doors and went into the school. When she returned to her parking spot after school, she stared in disbelief. Her little car had been stolen!

She phoned Wes. He immediately came to help her. Police and insurance reports were made. The couple carried only the necessary liability insurance on the little clunker. What would they do?

When payday came, they had still received no news about her missing car. They sat at the kitchen table and prayed together about their need. They were determined to still give their tithe to God and trust Him to help them find another car. After cutting corners and figuring to the penny, they managed to scrape up a thousand dollars. They didn't want to go into debt and hoped it would be enough to buy something reliable.

They didn't know how, but they knew God had already set His compassionate plan in motion.

Reward for Faithfulness

May Your unfailing love rest upon us, O Lord, even as we put our hope in You. Psalm 33:22 NIV

Isn't it amazing how God already knows what we need even better than we do?

Wes and Dana diligently searched for a car within their price range to replace her stolen car but without success. When would God answer their prayers? One evening Dana told her friend Sherry about the stolen car. Sherry explained that her grandmother wasn't able to drive anymore and would have to sell her car for twenty-five hundred dollars. Dana had once met Sherry's grandmother and felt she deserved full price for her car. Buying it would be out of the question.

To Dana's surprise, Sherry's grandmother agreed to one thousand dollars! She wanted her car to go to someone special who would take good care of it. Dana was thrilled when Wes and Sherry's husband pulled into the driveway with a mint condition, fully automatic silver Toyota. It had power everything. Dana thanked Sherry, her grandmother, and God for the wonderful gift. The Lord had supplied Dana's needs and more than met her wants.

The police located her stolen car right after Wes and Dana bought the new one. It had been wrecked and was worthless. Wes and Dana are glad they were faithful in tithing to God and remained out of debt. Most of all, they are thankful for God's supplying their need.

❦

Here I am again, Lord, presenting my needs to You. I think back on times You remembered me with Your mercy and favor. Now I hope in You as I wait on Your answer. Thank You for Your gracious blessings to come, beyond measure, pressed down, shaken together, and overflowing.

In the fear of the LORD there is strong confidence, and His children will have a place of refuge. The fear of the LORD is a fountain of life. PROVERBS 14:26–27 NKJV

THE RESPONSIBILITIES WE carry can be difficult and overwhelming. But no matter the circumstances, we can completely depend on God's help.

Years ago, my husband was a truck driver. One night he was dispatched to haul a trailer filled with nine thousand pounds of gasoline up a steep mountain highway in midwinter. Before he left, our family prayed together for safety. Being dispatched that evening, he'd head to the end of his run, stay overnight, and return the next day.

The roads appeared clear with a little snow falling as he started into the mountains. There were no notices saying to put on chains, so Bob kept driving. Soon snow accumulated to four or five inches. By now, there was nowhere to turn around. A steep cliff on his right dropped about two hundred feet with no guardrail. "Almost to the top," he sighed.

Without warning, his truck wheels started to spin and lose traction. The truck and trailer came to a stop, began sliding backward, jackknifed, and slid directly toward the highway's edge. Saving the truck seemed hopeless. Bob had the driver's door open, ready to bail as he made a last-ditch effort to bring the truck back under control. If it continued to slide, the gas-filled giant would crash to the river below and probably explode.

"Lord, help me," he gasped.

Within seconds and for no logical reason, the truck regained traction and straightened out. When he reached the summit, Bob thanked God for watching over him. He completed his journey on faith and a prayer.

During his trucking years, Bob had many other close calls. We look back now and thank God for answering our prayers and bringing Bob safely home.

May grace and peace be multiplied to you in the knowledge of God and of Jesus our Lord.
2 PETER 1:2 RSV

ARE YOU FACING a problem that's too difficult for you to handle? Take it to God in prayer. More than telling Him about Your problem, ask for His strength, wisdom, and guidance. Study His Word. You can find some great advice while reading the Bible. If others give you advice, make sure it measures up to what's in God's Word. Take time to listen to God speaking to Your heart, and be willing to make wise choices that are within His will.

There's a framework God gives us in our walk with Him. It's different for each one of us. No matter how He lays it out in guiding us, it's important to work within His boundaries. We may plan and labor and plan some more. We do all we can to meet our own needs, but when we have exhausted our resources, we must remember the guidelines He has set for us. No matter what, we need to remember not to step outside His will. Somehow God gives us the shred of faith we desperately need at the time so we can trust in the grace and love He wants to bestow upon us.

There's something greater than our needs: the necessity of God's presence in our lives. When we do all we can to solve our problems and present our insufficiencies to Him, we must seek His presence and ask Him to take over from there. The Lord knows what we need before we even ask. He has a better understanding of everything than our finite minds can fathom.

The next time you're faced with a seemingly impossible situation, don't hesitate to let Him take over. His way is always best. As we trust and obey Him, we can relax and watch His miracles happen.

November 1 ‖ We Know His Voice

When he has brought out all his own, he goes on ahead of them, and his sheep follow him because they know his voice. JOHN 10:4 NIV

IF YOU ARE a parent, teacher, or someone who loves and watches over children, your primary concern is to guide those kids in the right way and to protect them from harm. Isn't it a wonder how in the midst of chaos, we can distinguish the voice of a certain child? Equally amazing is the way our voice—loud or soft—cuts through everything around us and reaches the ears of the child.

Jesus does the same for us. He explains how we can recognize His voice by describing Himself as a faithful Shepherd and us as His sheep. When we become distracted by the needs and concerns around us, we can listen for Him helping us put things in perspective.

The more we know Him, the more we learn to hear His voice above the clamor and stress that crowd in on us every day. Unlike an audible voice, His reaches into the depths of our minds and souls, encouraging, warning, guiding, and comforting. When He calls, we learn to answer. When He cautions us, we learn to stop and focus on what He's trying to tell us.

We may become bogged down or, as the Bible says, "cast down" from overwork and cares. It can even get to the point where we aren't able to get up and keep going. But when we call out to Him for help, the Lord hears our feeble cries. In less than a split second He is by our side, ready to lead us back to safe ground.

Thank the Lord for how you're learning to know Him well and for hearing you when you call His name. The more you know Him, the more you hear Him speaking to your heart and guiding you.

Now faith is the substance of things hoped for, the evidence of things not seen. HEBREWS II:I NKJV

DOES IT SEEM sometimes like nothing is going right? Do you struggle to see the far-off light at the end of the tunnel but can't find a glimmer? You may ask the Lord to assure you that He's with you no matter how difficult things appear. Like me, you pray for one more blessing as a reminder of His loving care. What surprise we feel when His answers come.

Several years ago our prayer group discovered another way God helps us build our faith. Our friend Laurie noticed the way certain Scriptures seemed to jumped off the page regarding concerns and needs in her life. When she found one that applied, she underlined it in her Bible and wrote a two- or three-word prayer and current date in the margin. Later she noted the answered prayer in the same spot with a new date.

Susan did something similar. In her journal she wrote God's promises from Scripture next to her prayer requests and dated the request. Later she returned to the same page and recorded and dated her answered prayers.

I started doing this. I'm amazed how when I flip back through my notes, the Holy Spirit often uses the same prayer requests and promises when I need them the most. Each time this happens, I thank Him for using them to build my faith.

Almost everywhere I look, I find negative things happening. I refuse to dwell on discouraging thoughts. I thank the Lord for graciously being my faith builder and for encouraging me through the Scriptures He provides.

When one door closes another opens. Expect that new door to reveal even greater wonders and glories and surprises. Feel yourself grow with every experience. And look for the reason for it. —EILEEN CADDY

Pressed-Down Blessings

"Give, and it will be given to you; good measure, pressed down, shaken together, running over, will be put into your lap. For the measure you give will be the measure you get back." LUKE 6:38 RSV

MANY OF US have experienced the scene I'm about to describe: The end-of-the month bills arrive. We are about to figure our budget. Times are tough and we wonder how we're going to make ends meet. Before we tackle the project, we pray for help. Then we take a deep breath and write out the first check as an offering to the Lord. Somehow during the process He makes the money stretch. We don't know how, but He provides more than we anticipated.

When Bob and I were raising our family in Spokane, an older couple in our church told us about a farmer's way of tithing. Each year during green bean harvest, the couple and our family drove to Post Falls, Idaho, where we could gather beans behind the picking machines. We were grateful that there was no charge. Since we had a large family, we gathered about one hundred pounds of beans. Later we all pitched in and prepared them for freezing, but in the process, we learned to give 10 percent of our pickings to someone else in need.

I was surprised when some other farmers who raised carrots gave us all the oversized ones we wanted or when another family in the church shared an abundance of tomatoes with us. Before we knew it, God had given us vegetables that were pressed down and running over.

It's a test of our faith to put the Lord first, but when we do, we discover we can never outgive what He supplies. These are difficult times we are living in. When we don't know where the money will come from, God has the answer. We give Him a portion of our income and trust Him to take care of us, and we can thank Him for giving us His blessings—pressed down, shaken together and running over.

And my God will supply every need of yours according to his riches in glory in Christ Jesus.
PHILIPPIANS 4:19 RSV

WHAT PRAYERS WILL we bring Him today? Are the numbers too great to count? Do some of our burdens go beyond description? God knows. We may come to the Lord asking Him to provide a job, heat for our homes, or food for our tables. We may plead for Him to heal a child or mend a broken heart. Whatever our prayer may be, the Bible assures us there is no problem we bring to Him that's too great or small. He cares enough to notice a fallen bird, help a frightened soldier, or save a struggling soul. His mercy and kindness are immeasurable.

God not only loves us with an everlasting love, He makes available to us the same power that once raised Jesus from the dead. His love and presence abide with us every day. His empathy for our hurts and needs surpasses all else.

Whatever the situations we face, we can come to Him with open, trusting hearts and let them go. When we do, He has a way of picking our problems up, turning them around and inside out, washing them clean, and transforming them into unquenchable victory and joy.

GOD HAS A WAY
What countless ways the Lord provides.
*   Yes, God has a way.*
He stops our storms and turns our tides;
*   for He has a way.*
He may not work the way we want;
*   but God has a way.*
It may not be in our own time;
*   still He has a way.*

When you are burdened down with care,
*   our God has a way.*
He takes our loads and answers prayer;
*   for He has a way.*
Just stretch your faith and trust in Him.
*   Yes, He has a way.*
And soon the victory you will win;
*   for God has a way.*

All your sons will be taught by the LORD, and great will be your children's peace. ISAIAH 54:13 NIV

ONE OF OUR greatest challenges as families is to stay closely connected. In our fast-paced society, we're sometimes spread throughout the nation and world, yet determination, along with the blessing of modern communication and transportation, can help us remain close.

We need to hold onto the desire to stick together no matter where we live, and to show that we really care. Some family members are faithful, while others are closer to friends than family, who need their love the most. Anger or resentment may cause problems, but empathy, understanding, and forgiveness can heal wounds.

Life's short. It's important to nurture this priceless gift God has given us. In the blink of an eye, we can lose any one of our loved ones, and then it's too late.

There's a classic Aesop fable about an ailing elderly father and his four sons. One day the father called his sons together. He showed them some sticks he had tied together and invited each son to break the bundle. After many tries, they found no one could do it. Finally he instructed them to loosen the cord and told each son to break only one stick, which they did easily. He then explained that keeping close together like the bundle of sticks would help to make the family strong.

More important than our staying closely connected, the Bible tells us to pray together, love each other, and set good examples for our children. When we do, we discover God is the Author of harmony and love. It may not happen immediately, but don't give up. Keep trying. It begins with you and me.

Love sought is good, but given unsought is better.
—WILLIAM SHAKESPEARE

Praise the LORD! O give thanks to the LORD, for He is good; for His steadfast love endures for ever! Who can utter the mighty doings of the LORD, or show forth all His praise? PSALM 106:1–2 RSV

IN THE QUIET of these few moments, dear Lord, I thank You for making it possible for me to call upon Your name, and for always being ready to listen and understand. How grateful I am for the many things You have done and still do for me. Because of Your mighty works, I sing my praises to You and recall Your glorious acts. My heart rejoices in light of the love and grace You bestow upon me. The miracles and wonders You perform, Your love for me so strong and true, I gladly receive them as one who returns Your love.

I look out the window and watch a steady rain. To me it symbolizes the bountiful showers of blessings You daily provide. I listen to the drops fall upon our roof and think of how numerous they are. So are the countless ways You have helped my husband and me, and our children during their growing-up years. I listen to the rain rhythmically gurgle down the drain spout near the window, and marvel how Your blessings are now trickling down to our grown children and grandchildren.

You were there through the easy times and the struggles, and You mercifully guided us through each one. How grateful I am that You are with us even today. Your blessings shine forth like a beautiful rainbow after the rain. Your promises to watch over us are as sure and steadfast now as when I first gave my heart to You. They shall remain with my family all the days of our lives. Even into eternity, we can count on Your faithfulness and direction through our future generations.

Thank You for granting me the time to sit here with You, dear Lord. You are truly my God and my dearest friend.

Now let your unfailing love comfort me, just as you promised me, your servant. Surround me with your tender mercies so I may live, for your law is my delight. PSALM 119:76–77 NLT

TRIALS BEYOND OUR control can become too much to bear. Circumstances might look so hopeless that we become discouraged and think they will never get better, and we simply give up. However, when we've done all we can, we're able to find comfort when we leave everything in God's compassionate hands. Wendy and I experienced this hard-learned lesson while teaching Samuel, a nine-year-old special needs student.

Samuel suffered from brain cancer. His illness, surgery, and treatments had taken their toll on him, but miraculously, he came through everything with a big smile. He radiates love to those around him, and he has a way of lighting up the room whenever he's at school.

At the end of one regular school day, Samuel waved good-bye and chirped a "See you later." The next morning, Wendy and I received a call from Samuel's mother saying that he had taken a fall the night before and didn't appear able to recognize anyone in his family. Soon after, he began slipping into a coma. After school, several of the teachers gathered in Wendy's classroom, where we formed a circle and took hands. One by one we lifted Samuel and his family's needs to God.

Samuel's miracle came. He made a turnaround and regained enough energy to return to school. He entered the classroom with his usual big smile. "I'm ba–a–ck," he said. He laughed and hugged us. We hugged him and thanked God for our answered prayer.

Whether our struggles be financial, emotional, or physical, we can always be assured that God knows the whole picture and takes our concerns to heart. Rather than giving up, we can learn to never say never, and to trust our all-knowing, merciful God to handle the rest.

I have set the LORD continually before me; because He is at my right hand, I will not be shaken. Therefore my heart is glad and my glory rejoices. PSALM 16:8–9 NASB

IN ADDITION TO physical healing, there's another kind of miracle many of us request: for our friends and loved ones to accept Jesus as their Savior. We pray and pray and see no change. Sometimes things become worse as the one we're praying for goes deeper into sin. All the signs lead to discouragement and hopelessness as there's no apparent chance of repentance. In our eyes, the situation looks impossible. We're tempted to give up, write them off, and say they will never change.

At that instant, we must shake off the doubts and never say never. Nothing is impossible when we trust God. It may take a long time, but God works through everything. He never gives up. He loves our friends and loved ones more than we are capable of loving them. Unlike us, He can talk to their hearts, and they can't escape His words. There's a spiritual battle going on for the souls of these dear ones. As we present our prayers to God, we can be assured of the One who wins over sin and destruction.

Some of our prayers may go unanswered while we're still alive. Praise God, our prayers to Him go on, even after our lives here on earth are finished! We can look forward to the answers being revealed when we reach heaven. When all is bleak and appears impossible, keep turning your troubles over to God. Never say never. Always say, "Forever, with God!"

The Lord's ways are marvelous. When we're weak, He's strong. When our faith wavers, He fills us with His loving assurance. No matter how gigantic our requests, He can handle them. Praise God for His promise to never leave those who trust in Him!

Now He who searches the hearts knows what the mind of the Spirit is, because He makes intercession for the saints according to the will of God. ROMANS 8:27 NKJV

HAVE YOU EVER faced a situation so difficult there appeared to be no way out? A serious financial need? A stressful or discouraging job situation? A child struggling in school? God knows, and He understands.

Have you felt defeated with nowhere to turn? Have you taken your needs to His throne of grace—one more time? As you pray, you can experience an unexplainable, calming peace. That's God working. His merciful Spirit is ministering to your heart. It may also be that someone else is praying for you.

The Bible tells us about intercessory prayer, the kind of prayer God places on the hearts of friends and family members or possibly others we barely know. Others may not realize what we're going through, but God knows, and He understands. When we're so weak that we're unable to tell Him our needs, the Holy Spirit intercedes for us and takes our concerns to the heavenly Father.

Take heart during these times, and do not be dismayed. Through a combination of the Spirit's silent coaxing, the prayers of the saints, and God's mysterious timing, things do work together for good. We can stand back in awe and thank Him for His blessings.

Lord Jesus, right now my family and I are being hit from all angles. Despite our efforts to solve our problems, nothing seems to work. Please help us.

I wonder if anyone is praying for us, Lord. Although overcoming these problems appears impossible to me, I'm once more placing our needs, big and small, before Your throne of grace. Somehow I sense You surrounding me with Your unexplainable peace. Thank You for Your blessing through prayer.

In everything give thanks. 1 THESSALONIANS 5:18 NKJV

SHOWING APPRECIATION TO the kind people in the church and community was important to the pastor and his wife. Doing for them was a part of life because the couple loved them so much. A good deed accompanied with blessings offered from the heart—that was their motto.

Even so, there were days when the pastor and his wife felt weary. Was what they were doing really making a difference? They prayed they were.

October rolled around. It turned out to be pastor appreciation month. One Sunday morning during announcements a church board member stepped up to the pulpit to say a few words. She expressed on behalf of the congregation how much her pastor and his wife meant to them then handed them a lovely homemade card containing notes and signatures from everyone in the congregation. After that, she read a poem she had written years before for the pastor's ordination ceremony. What could be more treasured than the heartfelt thoughts written by the congregation? Gold couldn't have outweighed their value.

At day's end it was told that the pastor read and reread the thank-you card then commented to his wife that perhaps they really were making a difference. He took the card and carefully placed it in a frame in his office.

It seems such a simple thing to say thank you and show appreciation now and then. It's typical for most of us to take for granted the blessings we receive and the hard work done by others. When we do say "thanks," we may think little of the action—until we're on the receiving end. Then it becomes a priceless thank-you blessing.

Gratitude: so freely given, so freely received.

A cheerful look brings joy to the heart, and good news gives health to the bones.
PROVERBS 15:30 NIV

IT'S EASY TO let our attitudes slip to discouragement and despondency. But God doesn't want us to dwell on negative things. Instead, let's think on His promises to watch over us and supply our needs. He also promises that He'll never abandon nor forsake us.

So let's count the marvelous blessings He graciously gives. As we keep looking up, we not only encourage ourselves but we bring some happiness to those who need it. God has a purpose for our lives. When we listen to His guidance, other people through us get a taste of His mercy and love. When we care about the concerns and needs of others, we in turn will feel fulfilled.

D. L. Moody describes spreading God's joy as something beautiful. The love of God does wonders because of the joy we pass on each day. He knew of an entire family that was won to the Lord because of a caring smile.

A life without the Lord spells hopelessness and despair. We are given the hope that those who don't know Him are searching for. So let's take our frowns and turn them upside-down into beautiful smiles for Him. Then watch and see how God begins working in their lives.

Are you ever burdened with a load of care?
Does the cross seem heavy you are called to bear?
Count your many blessings, every doubt will fly,
And you will be singing as the days go by.

Count your blessings, name them one by one;
Count your blessings, see what God hath done.
Count your blessings, name them one by one,
And it will surprise you what the Lord hath done.
—JOHNSON OATMAN JR.

Now may the God of hope fill you with all joy and peace in believing, so that you will abound in hope by the power of the Holy Spirit. ROMANS 15:13 NASB

THERE COME TIMES in our lives when we feel so overwhelmed by difficult or heartbreaking circumstances that we can no longer handle the problems. Perhaps you or someone you love is going through such a time. Anxiety and despondency can become so overwhelming that the sufferer might not even be able to sleep, or else sleep comes at the wrong times. Occasionally terrible nightmares jolt them out of bed. Little things become huge. Intense fear may creep in. The one who is hurting may feel like giving up and fading away.

We must remember that God is far greater and more powerful than the most serious of problems. He is the merciful Master Healer of our bodies, emotions, and souls. God tells us to take our burdens to Him. He lightens loads and helps make things easier when people pray and trust in Him. Moreover, He provides Christian pastors, counselors, doctors, loved ones, and good friends. Don't be afraid to lean on Him and accept love from others. We don't have to go through it all alone. He can help relieve terrible trials, grant His mercy and strength, and turn darkness into light.

God loves His children with an empathetic, gracious love. He cares, even when we are at the lowest ebb. He is a retreat, an ultimate security, and strength. He is *always* present—in the good *and* the bad. Through His power, God is calling those who seek Him to push out the clouds and see clear blue skies and bright sunrises. Lean on Him. Rely on His guidance. Look ahead as He brings joy, peace, and hope for the future.

Trust in Him, for joy comes in the morning!

November 13 | Rainbow of Hope

Be joyful in hope, patient in affliction, faithful in prayer. ROMANS 12:12 NIV

SEATTLE HAS A reputation for being rainy. We who live here grow webbed feet, so to speak. Kids play in the rain, and we adults slosh around in it as we scurry here and there. After a few days without a sprinkle, we sometimes wrinkle our noses at the smelly air. We look up, stretch out our palms, and say, "Well, where's that nice cleansing rain?"

I don't like the slow, drizzly rain; I love the shower bursts in the afternoons. The rain pours down like crazy as the sun slips toward the horizon. I often head to the window, the yard, or even the street to spot a flamboyant rainbow (or double rainbow) in the eastern sky. Sometimes I grab my camera. One more rainbow for my photo albums.

We all face discouraging times and occasionally get depressed when the long drizzles and gloomy clouds of life cast their shadows over us. We wonder if we'll be able to see past the haze and find sunshine again. Then the Son of God breaks through our gloom and apprehension and gives us a Scripture with delightful promises of His love and grace. One of my friends calls them God's rainbows of hope—just for us.

Like rainbows, we can't touch His promises. Sometimes we aren't able to visualize where life is going, but God filters through the haze and reminds us that He never leaves nor forsakes us.

The next time uncertain rains fall and you become discouraged or depressed, cling to the hope God gives and look for His rainbow of hope. Don't be afraid to move forward with God and follow His leading. After all, He's the One who purposefully made it all. His capable hands will provide you a sure future with hope and grace.

O Lord, what a variety you have made! And in wisdom you have made them all! The earth is full of your riches. PSALM 104:24 TLB

OF ALL THE entertainment we have at our fingertips, of all the material gifts we receive, what can be more satisfying and appreciated than life's simple blessings? Think of them. Then write them down, one-by-one. Here are a few of my favorites:

Yellow, orange, red, and rusty-brown autumn leaves leisurely floating through the air and gently landing in strategic spots—awaiting an ambitious person to arrive with a rake. Children wildly jumping in crunchy leaf piles, squealing with laughter. The first mystical winter snowflake silently landing on a windowsill. Snowmen. A puppy stepping into a snow bank for the first time. Snowball fights. Sleds flying down deserted streets. The first spring crocus daring to pop its head out of the protective soil. The sun shining through the rain. A rainbow draping itself in the western sky. Warm summer nights with the sounds of crickets filling the air. A family sitting in the back yard, watching the sun going down while sipping cool lemonade and just having fun.

Isn't it wonderful how God has a part in it all? It's all right to be busy, yet sometimes it's good to slow down and simply notice and enjoy the delightful little things God graciously provides.

This is my Father's world, and to my listening ears
All nature sings, and round me rings the music of the spheres.
This is my Father's world: I rest me in the thought
Of rocks and trees, of skies and seas; His hand the wonders wrought.
This is my Father's world, the birds their carols raise,
The morning light, the lily white, declare their Maker's praise.
This is my Father's world: He shines in all that's fair;
In the rustling grass I hear Him pass; He speaks to me everywhere.
　—MALTBIE D. BABCOCK

He gives us grace and glory. No good thing will he withhold from those who walk along his paths.
PSALM 84:11 TLB

LORD, AS YOU know, I'm the kind of person who is constantly watching out for others, but often I get so caught up in doing that I forget to take care of my own needs. I'm wearing down, Lord. I feel like You are reminding me to watch out for myself so I'm strong enough to be there for others. But that's easier said than done. Please give me wisdom and direction.

Lord, I give You my soul. Your Word teaches me that in order to be physically healthy, it's important for me to be spiritually healthy: "Dear friend, I am praying that all is well with you and that your body is as healthy as I know your soul is" (3 John 1:2 TLB).

I give You my mind. Guard my thoughts. Help me keep them positive and focused on You: "Listen carefully. Keep these thoughts ever in mind; let them penetrate deep within your heart, for they will mean real life for you and radiant health" (Proverbs 4:20–22 TLB).

I give You my body, Lord. Help me to eat wisely and exercise, to avoid bad habits and be morally pure: "Your body is a temple of the Holy Spirit.... You are not your own; you were bought at a price. Therefore honor God with your body" (1 Corinthians 6:19–20 NIV).

I trust You to lead me each day. Grant me wisdom to make wise choices: "Because of the LORD's great love we are not consumed, for his compassions never fail. They are new every morning; great is your faithfulness" (Lamentations 3:22–23 NIV).

Thank You for caring for me, Lord, and helping me to take care of myself.

God is our refuge and strength, a very present help in trouble. Therefore we will not fear.
PSALM 46:1–2 NKJV

EXPERIENCING SERIOUS ILLNESS is frightening, yet during such times God's goodness often becomes more evident than ever.

The bruise on Brad's leg appeared to be harmless. Being a father of four growing children, he often ignored his aches and pains. But before long, the discomfort was difficult to ignore. The next morning the bruise was hard, red-hot, and doubled in size. When he stood up, he nearly collapsed from pain and sudden weakness.

Brad went to the doctor. When he stumbled into the office, a red streak was moving up his thigh. He was sent to the hospital, where he was promptly admitted. He could barely sit up in bed. He knew his wife Carrie was already contacting family and friends for prayer.

Over the next several days, the redness edged toward Brad's abdomen and vital organs. Would he lose his leg or even his life? He refused to harbor the thought and kept trusting God. Large doses of antibiotics were pumped into his veins. Carrie took the children to see their daddy every day, and his parents, brothers, and sisters hovered near.

Test results showed Brad had acquired a rare bacterial infection through a hair follicle on his leg. Quick action prevented the infection from developing into a fast flesh-eating disease. Had he waited one more day to see the doctor, he might have lost his leg, and the infection could have gone to his vital organs.

Brad's family and friends were surprised at how he regained his strength so quickly. He believes it was more than the doctors and antibiotics that stopped the dreadful bacterial infection. It was the compassionate intervention and healing hand of God.

During out-of-control times in our lives, God's goodness remains.

And we know that all that happens to us is working for our good if we love God and are fitting into his plans. ROMANS 8:28 TLB

ISN'T IT WONDERFUL how God answers our prayers? We're especially happy when His response is yes, but we know He handles our requests in His own way and time. Let me tell you about the most surprising answer to prayer I ever received.

It was October and the home Bob and I had owned for thirty years needed a new roof. We'd managed to save fifteen hundred dollars toward replacing it, but we knew that saving enough would take too long.

I recall sitting in my office one morning when I brought our need to God in prayer. I only asked once. One November night a massive wind and rainstorm hit our area. A fifty-foot oak tree stood near the south side of our home just outside my office window, the same window I enjoyed looking out of while I prayed. Around one in the morning, the tree crashed down on our roof. Its roots ripped out our gas meter, so we had to evacuate our home for three hours. During that time, it steadily rained through my office ceiling.

When daylight came, we discovered eight-inch tree branches poking through the roof and ceiling of most of the house. Surprisingly, my computer and the majority of my books weren't damaged. Our insurance company put on a beautiful new roof and redid my office walls and floor. There was some extra cost involved: it came to fifteen hundred dollars, the exact amount we had saved! Did God cause this storm? I don't believe He did. Still, I believe He used the circumstances to provide an unexpected way of answering my prayer.

Faith is deliberate confidence in the character of God whose ways you may not understand at the time.
—OSWALD CHAMBERS

Yet the Lord still waits for you to come to him so he can show you his love; he will conquer you to bless you, just as he said. For the Lord is faithful to his promises. Blessed are all those who wait for Him to help them. ISAIAH 30:18 TLB

THINK OF THE most frustrating answer to prayer you can get. Certainly it isn't "yes." Is it "no"? Could it be "wait awhile"?

I have a lot of patience, but I like to get things done ahead of schedule—microwave style. It's clear to see my greatest test of patience is to wait on the Lord to answer in His way and time. While I'm forced to wait, He reminds me that He really does know best.

After the oak tree fell on our house, workers repaired the damages, but we were responsible for removing the tree. Thankfully, friends jumped in and helped us for several weeks. When we were finished, we had enough logs for our wood-burning stove to last for at least five years; however, we also had logs two feet across by two feet high that we couldn't remove from the yard. No one would take them.

The first year I prayed for help. Two more years went by without an answer to my prayer. Last year a big pine tree in our backyard split from an ice storm, and we had to remove a smaller tree from the front. Now our entire backyard was filled with wood. By now my prayer had turned into whining. I just couldn't take any more.

About that time, our friends Jeremy and Kristi and their large family moved to a home with a fireplace. We found out Kristi's parents, Vern and Laurie, also used wood heat. The exciting thing was that the families had access to a wood splitter! In just a week, Vern removed all the large logs. What an answer to prayer.

Now I marvel at God's gracious timing. As we waited on Him, God helped provide for the needs of three families instead of just ours.

Then you shall call, and the LORD will answer; you shall cry, and he will say, Here I am.
ISAIAH 58:9 RSV

WHEN WE PONDER the amazing, omnipotent ways of God, we may find it impossible to comprehend that He isn't limited to only one place at a time. He is everywhere.

We often hear incredible stories of family and friends who prayed for men and women stationed in other countries as missionaries, peace-keeping volunteers, and soldiers. Later the prayer warriors learned that God powerfully intervened and protected the lives of the ones they prayed for.

Many of us have experienced the urge to pray for a friend or loved one. At the same time we prayed, God mercifully stepped into a crisis situation and intervened on that person's behalf. When we later visit those we've prayed for, we're astonished by the miraculous ways the Lord guided us into times of intercessory prayer for them.

At other times we are the ones who urgently need the prayers, phone calls, or notes. After we pray for help and encouragement, we might be surprised when someone contacts us and says, "God has laid you on my heart. How are you?"

Isn't it a comfort to read in Philippians 4:6–7 how God watches out and cares for us and those we are praying for? "Do not be anxious about anything, but in everything, by prayer and petition, with thanksgiving, present your requests to God. And the peace of God, which transcends all understanding, will guard your hearts and your minds in Christ Jesus" (NIV).

As God hears our prayers for others, He causes His unlimited miracles to sail across the miles or simply go right next door.

Lord, on Thee our souls depend;
In compassion now descend:
Fill our hearts with Thy rich grace,
Tune our lips to sing Thy praise.
—CHARLES WESLEY

"These things I have spoken to you, that in Me you may have peace. In the world you will have tribulation; but be of good cheer, I have overcome the world." JOHN 16:33 NKJV

MANY OF US pray for military troops serving around the world and for missionaries and chaplains at home and abroad. We also pray for the police, firefighters, and volunteers who help keep us safe.

Others who need our prayers, whom we brush shoulders with each day, are the family members who are left behind. While playing the parts of father and mother, they keep the "home fires burning," waiting for their loved ones to return home safe and sound.

My heart was warmed when a friend of mine told me about meeting a cute little three- or four-year-old boy who was with his mother in a local post office. He was dressed in army camouflage pants and fireman's boots. It was obvious that he was keeping his mother on her toes. As it turned out, his daddy was stationed in Iraq. Perhaps the father also served as a firefighter when at home. Either way, this little boy and his mother showed their love and support while waiting at home by remaining strong and being proud of their loved one.

Father, we pray for those who put their lives on the line in order to help others to be safe. Thank You for Your promise in 2 Chronicles 7:14: "If My people who are called by My name will humble themselves, and pray and seek My face, and turn from their wicked ways, then I will hear from heaven, and will forgive their sin and heal their land" (NKJV).

Dear Father, may Your love through us win over hatred. May Your kindness win over heartlessness. May Your understanding and compassion win over misunderstanding and skepticism. Grant us mercy, Father. And may You shed Your grace on our world.

The LORD appeared to Solomon by night, and said to him: "I have heard your prayer, and have chosen this place for Myself as a house of sacrifice [to Me]." 2 CHRONICLES 7:12 NKJV

ISN'T IT GOOD to know our churches around the world make up the marvelous, all-inclusive family of God! Whether we worship in beautiful buildings, in simple chapels, or within the walls of Christian homes, God graciously dwells among us.

Some of us as believers aren't able to worship the Lord in a public place but are forced to do so in secret. We can be thankful that the church, the wonderful family of God, isn't just limited to a building. The Bible says we all are part of God's church when we know Christ as our Savior. The place we meet doesn't matter. We can be thankful that the Lord always honors us with His presence when we worship Him with our whole hearts.

There in His presence, we can seek His forgiveness, mercy, and favor. There we can share our problems and praises, our concerns, defeats, and victories. We can be free to unlock the hidden corners of our souls and lay our burdens and worries at His feet. Each time we worship the Lord, He picks up our loads and carries them for us. He graciously surrounds us with His compassion and strength. How good it is that we can communicate with Him, friend with Friend.

Let's faithfully hold up our brothers and sisters in the Lord in prayer throughout our country and world. How grateful we can be for God's love for His church and His mercy and grace. Jesus is the head of our church, and no matter what the future holds, His church shall remain forever. May the Lord help those who love and serve Him, and may He grant us His mercy and strength so we can be spiritual lighthouses in our communities, our countries, and our world.

Thanks be to God for his indescribable gift! 2 CORINTHIANS 9:15 NIV

THANKFULNESS IS USUALLY wrapped up in thinking about what we've been given, yet there's another element of thanksgiving that provides as many blessings: giving of ourselves to others.

Roger, Charlene, and their children weren't rich, but they were blessed with enough to be comfortable. Only a week before Thanksgiving one year, bills were high and incomes were low. Both of them had experienced cuts in working hours because of a recession, but shortly after payday, Charlene figured the budget and was able to come up with a modest Thanksgiving meal she knew her family would be happy with.

As she started to write out her menu, she felt God urging her to pray for a family she knew whose husband had lost his job. As she prayed, she felt God leading her to use a third of the grocery money to buy a gift certificate for them and also invite them for Thanksgiving dinner. She prayed for guidance as she obediently laid aside the money for the gift certificate. Adapting her menu to include mostly homemade dishes, she was surprised by how much of what she needed was already in the cupboards and freezer. As she shopped she found sale after sale on the food items she needed and even ended up with money left over.

God blessed both families that Thanksgiving. Warmth and love filled the air as blessings of selfless giving and gracious receiving went full circle.

Not what we give, but what we share,
For the gift without the giver is bare;
Who gives himself with his alms feeds three,
Himself, his hungering neighbor and Me.
　—JAMES RUSSELL LOWELL

He will guide you into all the truth. JOHN 16:13 NASB

SOMETIMES IT'S HARD to find the right course for our lives in this overwhelming world. We try to figure it out on our own, yet when we finally turn to the Lord for His direction, He patiently leads the way.

The morning sun shone through the window of my friend Mary's hilltop home and crept across the Auburn valley. I had spent the night at Mary's house and awakened before anyone else. Restlessly I gazed out the window, pondering my future. I had recently graduated from high school and landed a job as a stenographer at the Renton Boeing plant. I should have felt a sense of satisfaction, but something was missing. I'd asked Jesus into my heart when I was seven, but since then I'd experienced spiritual ups and downs.

I thought about my Christian grandma and how she never minced words with me.

"Anita, you might be a Christian, but you aren't a dedicated Christian. Pray it through. Give your all to God." At the time, her words made me angry and frustrated. Now they were beginning to make more sense.

I heard Mary's mother moving around in the kitchen but paid no attention. Then she approached the window. She stood beside me and put her hand on my shoulder. "Look down there, Anita," she said, pointing toward the valley. "That's the Green River winding through the countryside. Your life is like that. You're beginning a brand-new adventure. Let God help you make the right choices. His mercy and grace have brought you this far. If you choose the right course with the Lord guiding you, all will be well."

I knew what my choice must be—to invite Jesus to be my Guide.

Be simple; take our Lord's hand and walk through things.
—FATHER ANDREW

I guide you in the way of wisdom and lead you along straight paths. PROVERBS 4:11 NIV

MAKING IMPORTANT DECISIONS can be difficult—especially when choosing a new course for our lives. I pondered giving my life completely to the Lord for a long time. A few months after my conversation with Mary's mother, I knelt one night beside my bed in prayer. There, alone, I rededicated my messed-up, yo-yo life to the Lord. Immediately I felt a huge weight lift from my shoulders. New joy that I'd never expected filled me through and through. Later I learned that enthusiastic new presence in me was God's cleansing, freeing Holy Spirit.

The new adventure began immediately. Before, I was afraid or ashamed to tell people I was a Christian. Now things were different. I was so excited about what God did that I told everyone who would listen. God seemed to roll out a map, His holy Word. He charted a new course on my river of life.

After all these years, I still sense His faithful hand on my shoulder as He guides me through each adventure. Now and then the river is as smooth as glass, yet frequently I face rough waters. God has to remind me to be careful when life goes my way. He teaches me to follow His direction. He reminds me to not panic when life gets rough.

He heals my hurts. He transforms my temptations to triumphs. He frees me from fear. He cares about my concerns. He opens doors I never dreamed possible and remains near. For this I'm always grateful.

Perhaps you're at a turning point in your life, trying to decide which way to go. God has a wonderful adventure in store for you. Just place your life in His capable hands. Choose the course He has planned for you, then trust Him to lead the way.

If you want to know what God wants you to do, ask him, and he will gladly tell you, for he is always ready to give a bountiful supply of wisdom to all who ask him; he will not resent it. JAMES 1:5 TLB

YOU AND I just made it through another tough time, Lord. I didn't expect financial disaster to strike like this. I felt like everything crumbled around me. In turn, my emotions went into turmoil. It seemed like there was no way to prepare for such a crisis.

Thank You for showing me how to pare down my spending and teaching me to eliminate some of the luxuries and credit payments. I realize making careful and wise choices according to Your will brings a feeling of security and peace of mind. All the possessions I've longed for aren't nearly as important as putting my financial and emotional life in order.

After I adjusted my lifestyle to cope with this catastrophe, it seemed like help came out of thin air. Air, that is, of Your doing. Thank You for taking over and meeting my needs. Thank You for those who reached out and helped me. Remind me, I pray, to be generous to others in return.

Thank You for helping me to focus on You and draw from Your wisdom and strength. The next time disaster strikes, I will not fear. You are the triumph over my problems. Help me bear in mind that You are always with me and graciously guide me. Whether I have much or little, it's all in Your hands.

My heart is fixed on You, Lord. How wonderful is the way You show me Your favor each time I submit my will to Yours. Thank You for showering me with Your mercy and blessings.

Even when I don't have many material possessions, I feel rich, for I am a child of You, my King. You know my needs and my heart's desires. You also know what's best (or not best) for me. You are Lord over all.

But true praise is a worthy sacrifice; this really honors me. Those who walk my paths will receive salvation from the Lord. PSALM 50:23 TLB

WITHIN THE STILLNESS of these quiet moments I have with You, O Lord, I just want to praise You. I want to celebrate the marvelous glories of Your holy name. How good, how great are You, my God.

Here I bow before You, sensing Your refinement, Your indescribable loveliness, the purity of Your most exalted cleansing Holy Spirit. How I adore You, dear God. How I praise You and feast upon Your Word. All is in vain if You are not Lord of my life. You are the ultimate Maker and Author of every fiber of my being.

Many of my prayers to You are filled with my requests and burdens. But this time, O God, I just want to praise You. I want to give you a gift from my heart that You haven't already given me—an offering of my sacrifice and praise. Every exaltation of glory and honor I give to You.

Praise You for changing my darkness of despair to brightness of a brand-new day. Thank You for awakening my heart to Your marvelous wonders. Thank You for restoring joy to my life. What endless concern and kindness You show me. Your palms spill out Your thoughtfulness and grace. Your works are immense. Your thoughts are immeasurable. I delight in Your loving care throughout my days and nights. Your lovingkindness is brighter than the morning sun.

Praise You for keeping me safe in the folds of Your almighty arms. In You I take refuge and draw from Your strength. Thank You for being my God. Take my life. Mold me. Use me. May all I do bring glory and honor to You!

To You in all things be adoration, respect, and praise.

Wait on the LORD; be of good courage, and He shall strengthen your heart; wait, I say, on the LORD!
PSALM 27:14 NKJV

WAITING ON THE Lord may be one of the most difficult things God asks of us.

I like to get everything done ahead of time. Because of this tendency, I used to sometimes beg and argue with the Lord and explain why He should immediately answer my prayers—especially when they were important and urgent. I'd fervently pray and tell Him what I thought was the best plan of action for my prayer. When I finally ran out of words or energy, God patiently encouraged me to wait. It was then that I asked His forgiveness and submitted to His will. Like me, many of us learn over time that God really does know what's best for our lives.

The Bible tells us how Hannah waited on God to answer a serious prayer. She and Peninnah were both married to Elkanah. Having to share her husband with another woman must have been difficult in itself for Hannah, but what made matters worse was that Peninnah gave Elkanah several sons and daughters while Hannah's womb was barren. Peninnah often provoked Hannah to the point where she would weep and not even want to eat.

Hannah's husband loved her dearly and couldn't understand her sadness. He tried cheering her up by saying, "Why are you downhearted? Don't I mean more to you than ten sons?" The poor man must have not realized that didn't help much.

Hannah kept waiting on the Lord. How soon would He answer her prayer? We, too, must remember to wait on God's will and trust Him to work everything out in His own way and time. When we do, we will come to see His blessings unfold.

"My heart rejoices in the LORD; my horn is exalted in the LORD. I smile at my enemies, because I rejoice in Your salvation." 1 SAMUEL 2:1 NKJV

AS WE WAIT in prayer, we draw closer to the Lord. He replaces our anxiety with surety and peace in Him.

Every year Elkanah took his family to Shiloh. They ate and drank, then went to the Lord's temple. Every year Hannah longed for God to give her a child. One time when she didn't feel like eating, she went to the temple alone to pray. She wept bitterly before God, asking Him to see her affliction and remember her. If He blessed her with a son, she promised to give him to the Lord all the days of his life.

Eli the priest noticed Hannah praying, but he couldn't hear her speak. He thought she was drunk. Hannah explained that she was asking God for a son. Eli gave her a promise that God would grant her petition.

Hannah knew God would answer her prayer. A year later she gave birth to a son and named him Samuel, which means "because I have asked for him from the Lord."

Hannah faithfully kept her promise to God. After Samuel was weaned, she brought him to the temple and presented him to Eli. Her heart was filled with great joy as she offered a prayer of thanksgiving. Even as a child, Samuel ministered before God. Each year when Elkanah and Hannah came to the temple, Hannah brought a robe she had made for Samuel to wear. Eli told Hannah and her husband they would have more children. Sure enough, Hannah was blessed with three sons and two daughters!

As Samuel grew, God provided him with much wisdom. None of Samuel's words went to waste. Because of Hannah's obedience, God used Samuel to prophesy to all of Israel. He served God all of his days.

Give thanks to the LORD, for he is good; his love endures forever. PSALM 106:1 NIV

MANY OF US value the simple act of someone saying thank you. These thoughtful words have a way of bringing smiles to our faces and lifting our spirits.

As a pastor's wife, I enjoy a group of caring ladies in our church who watch over and encourage me as dear sisters in the Lord. Truly, I am blessed. One particular week, the responsibilities seemed overwhelming. My body was weary, my spirits low. So I asked God to give me strength and encouragement.

That day I received a note in the mail from a lady in our church who said thank you and offered her help where needed. God used that lady's sensitive thank-you note to answer my prayer and give me the oomph I needed for that day.

Jesus frequently expressed His gratitude to His Father. Saying thank you was important to the Lord. One day, Jesus and His disciples arrived in Jerusalem. He noticed ten men with leprosy a distance away, who were crying out for Him to heal them. Without even touching the men, Jesus told them to go and tell the priest they were healed. Their leprosy disappeared.

A short time later, one of the ten men Jesus had made well (a reviled Samaritan) returned and fell before Jesus with his face to the ground, thanking the Lord for his healing. Jesus asked where the other nine men were, but only the Samaritan had returned to say thank you.

The Lord turned to the man and said, "Arise, go your way. Your faith has made you well" (Luke 17:19 NKJV).

How thankful we can be that the Lord showers us with His love and grace and places people in our paths who care about us. May we also remember to appreciate and encourage those we come in contact with.

Then will I go to the altar of God, to God, my joy and my delight. I will praise you with the harp, O God, my God. PSALM 43:4 NIV

LORD, DURING THE hurry and scurry, the calm and peaceful, the good and bad of my life, I find surety and comfort in knowing You as my God. What strength I gain when I commune with You. Thank You that each time I come to You in prayer You fill my soul—my entire being—with Your powerful, cleansing presence.

You are the One, dear Lord, whom I can count on all the time, day or night. When I call on You for help and direction even during the most trying and chaotic times, You cut through the confusion that presses in around me. You send forth Your light and truth, then You gently, yet firmly, lead me. I'm grateful for the way You calm my emotions and show me what I need to do next.

I praise You for being my Savior. I thank You for snatching me from sin's deadly snare, pulling me to safety and setting my wobbly feet on Your solid foundation. You are everything I need. You are my greatest love. There is no one else whom I love more than You. At times when I choose to stand up for You and what is right, and run the risk of being ridiculed or mistreated by others, I know You are my Shield, my Defender. You go before and behind me and help to make things right.

In all circumstances I bow before You, asking You to keep my focus centered on things that are pleasing to You. I can only do so as You are there to hold me up. Thank You for honoring me for being faithful and spreading Your table of blessings before me.

In You, O Lord, I take delight. You are my all in all.

A cheerful look brings joy to the heart. PROVERBS 15:30 NIV

THINGS SEEM TO come in streaks—especially bad things—and they can bring out the best or the worst in us. Sadly, the stress may cause us to lash out with sour attitudes toward the people we love most. We can certainly be grateful for their love and forgiveness.

My friend Jan has a way of caring and listening to others. She encourages them to let go of their problems, take them to the Lord in prayer, and trust Him to work things out according to His will. Some circumstances may not change in the way we want them to, but God understands and helps us through when we release the controls and just trust Him.

Jan makes a delicious sweet pickle relish. Since I have a sweet tooth, a little enhancement makes otherwise sour pickles taste better. During the difficult times in our lives, we can think of Jan's relish, ask the Lord to sweeten our sometimes sour-pickled attitudes, and become His instruments of peace. When we do, we can be amazed how His Spirit is able to work things out for good according to His purpose.

Lord, make me an instrument of Your peace.
Where there is hatred, let me sow love;
where there is injury, pardon;
where there is doubt, faith;
where there is despair, hope;
where there is darkness, light;
where there is sadness, joy.

O Divine Master, grant that I may not so much
seek to be consoled as to console;
to be understood as to understand;
to be loved as to love.

For it is in giving that we receive;
it is in pardoning that we are pardoned;
and it is in dying that we are born to eternal life.
—SAINT FRANCIS OF ASSISI

"Forgive, and you will be forgiven." LUKE 6:37 NKJV

SOMETIMES WE FIND ourselves loving and caring so much that our good attitudes are stretched to the limit. Then when someone hurts our feelings or things don't go our way, we're tempted to get angry, pout, or get even.

Marty's Sunday school student Jasmine was one of the most unselfish girls Marty had ever met. She always helped her friends, showed them how much she cared about them, and tried in every way she could to do what was right. But Jasmine's feelings were easily hurt, and it was hard for her to forgive and show mercy.

One day she was alienated by her best friends. When they realized they had wronged her, they tried to make up for their thoughtlessness, but Jasmine wanted nothing to do with them. During Sunday school class the following Sunday, Marty told the story about Jonah and the whale. Her students were already familiar with the story, but they didn't know that after Jonah repented and the big fish spit him out on dry land, he told the wicked people of Nineveh to turn their lives over to Him—and they actually did repent!

But Jonah was angry and went off by himself to pout. Why didn't God destroy them for all the bad they'd done? God reminded Jonah that He loved and forgave Nineveh the same way He had forgiven Jonah.

Jasmine and the other students got the picture. If God could graciously forgive them of wrong attitudes, certainly they must forgive each other. Hearts were healed. Friendships were mended. The power of forgiveness was seen by Jasmine, her Christian friends, and her unsaved friends.

Keep My commandments and live, and My teaching as the apple of your eye. Bind them on your fingers; write them on the tablet of your heart. PROVERBS 7:2–3 NASB

ONE DELIGHTFUL WAY of prayer journaling is to get away with the Lord. Sometimes we can find a quiet spot or go for a walk or hike. With paper and pen handy, we can tell the Lord our innermost secrets and experience His gracious presence.

One late winter afternoon I had the chance to enjoy some time with the Lord while trekking through a riverside wooded area at Flaming Geyser Park. As I climbed from my car, a chilly breeze forced me to zip my jacket and pull on my hat and gloves. I trudged up a hill to an old geyser. Natural underground gasses fed the one-foot-high flame. In years past, it was much bigger. I wondered if its flame would eventually die out.

At the water's edge I met with God. We talked with each other—and listened, just God and me. Trees lined the shore. Their roots sank deep and drank the pure water. Soon spring would come and tiny buds would appear. The river's whitecaps moved endlessly, sounding like refreshing laughter.

Brisk winds cleared my mind of distractions. I thought of difficult times in my life. In spite of hardship's chill, the Son of God's warm, merciful love restored my joy and strength. I pulled a small tablet and pen from my pocket and began to write:

Thank You for caring for me, Lord. Rather than following aimless paths, I will sink my roots deeply into Your Word and drink of Your living water. Rather than allowing the enduring flame that You placed within me to fade to nothing, may You graciously, ever so mercifully, fan it into a powerful fire, always to burn for You.

May you find solace with God and be blessed during your quiet times with Him.

Peace I leave with you, My peace I give to you; not as the world gives do I give to you. Let not your heart be troubled, neither let it be afraid. JOHN 14:27 NKJV

SEARCHING FOR PEACE during times of war is an age-old struggle; yet the peace mankind has sought can only be found in the comforting knowledge of God's merciful loving-kindness and unending grace.

Henry Wadsworth Longfellow was no stranger to the sufferings of war. During the Civil War near the Christmas of 1863, he found out that his son had been injured in battle. How could he bear being so far away from his son on Christmas Day when he desperately wanted to be at his side to help and comfort him?

In spite of his despair, Christmas bells penetrated his sorrow and made him aware of God's gracious love—a love that could be with him and his son at the same time. As he listened to the chimes, he penned the words to "I Heard the Bells on Christmas Day":

I heard the bells on Christmas Day
Their old familiar carols play,
And wild and sweet the words repeat
Of peace on earth, good will to men.

Then pealed the bells more loud and deep:
"God is not dead, nor doth he sleep;
The wrong shall fail, the right prevail,
With peace on earth, good will to men."

No matter how many wars are fought, no matter how many battles are lost or won, God is near, helping, comforting, and guiding those who trust Him. There is no limit to His powerful healing and grace. There is no measure to His love. Perhaps the greatest lesson to be learned during such troubled times is that Jesus truly is our Lord of lords, our Prince of Peace.

For thus says the LORD, *"Behold, I extend peace...like a river."* ISAIAH 66:12 NASB

LORD, I GET so frustrated about all the fear, turmoil, and confusion I see everywhere in this world. I wish it would go away. It's reached the point where I don't want to watch or listen to the news. If I'm not careful, I pick up on the negative mind-set and become of no use to You. Help my outlook. Let me experience the calm You promise.

Lord, please grant peace to this hurting world. Help those who suffer and are at war. Show them Your love. Place within their hearts a hunger for You and an assurance of Your peace that passes understanding. Bring to me Your goodness so I can do Your will and help pass on Your loving-kindness and comfort to those with whom I come in contact. Make me what You want me to be. Let me glorify You in all I say and do.

Bless my family and friends, Lord, and grant them Your perfect peace. Keep me within the boundaries of Your will, I pray. Each day as I serve you, show me Your graciousness and cause Your face to shine upon me. As I walk life's road with You by my side, I thank You for showering me with Your loving mercy and providing Your grace and peace. In Jesus' name, amen.

"Come unto Me!" It is the Savior's voice,
The Lord of life, who bids thy heart rejoice;
O weary heart, with heavy cares oppressed,
"Come unto Me, and I will give you rest."

Weary with life's long struggle, full of pain,
O doubting soul, thy Saviour calls again;
Thy doubts shall vanish, and thy sorrows cease;
"Come unto Me, and I will give you peace."
—NATHANIEL NORTON

Praise be to the Lord, to God our Savior, who daily bears our burdens. PSALM 68:19 NIV

DO, YOU EVER wonder if God hears our prayers when we cry out to Him for help? Is He really listening? Does He care about what's happening to us or the ones we love? For most of us our days are filled with struggles, multiple problems, and uncertainty about the future. As a part of life, we manage to deal with these things on a regular basis, but when needs are great, when things become urgent and stressful, when the stakes are high, we can become discouraged enough to question God's understanding presence when we need Him the most.

Sometimes life crashes in and there seems to be no way out of our problems. Our minds may whirl with jumbled thoughts of sadness, depression, anxiety, and confusion. How we long for some glimmer of hope. In times like these, how can we feel His needed presence? Why doesn't He send us an angel to help us in these times of need? Can't God bring about one encouraging thing during the day in order to remind us that He's really with us?

God truly *is* near. Trust Him. "Put God to the test and see how kind he is!" (Psalm 34:8 TLB).

Along with our needs, we can also bring Him our praise for what He has already done for us. Praising God helps break down the barriers of distrust and draws us closer to Him. When we praise Him, we can let *go* of everything and let *in* His merciful, loving presence. He's been here all along. He graciously allows us anytime, anywhere, the privilege of walking into the very Holy of Holies and communing with Him. As we talk with Him and *listen* to Him, He replaces our daunting doubts with His unconditional understanding, wisdom, and love.

I am not worthy of the least of all your loving-kindnesses shown me again and again just as you promised me. GENESIS 32:10 TLB

FATHER, I'M IN a quandary as to why You love me. Your grace goes beyond my comprehension. I can think of many times when I didn't even love myself.

During the years I wandered aimlessly through life, I had no clue that You personally loved and cared for me. I thought of You as Someone high in the heavens viewing Your creation as a bunch of little ants running around. I thought at the most You might have heard my two-minute nighttime prayer ritual before I went to sleep. I'm grateful for the way You kept whispering to my heart, assuring me that You actually did, and still do, love me. I could relate to the words in Psalm 8:4: "I cannot understand how You can bother with mere puny man, to pay any attention to him!" (TLB).

The more You talked to my heart, the more I learned to recognize Your voice and acknowledge Your promise in Jeremiah 31:3: "The Lord...said..., "I have loved you, O My people, with an everlasting love; with loving-kindness I have drawn you to Me" (TLB).

Now I know You love me because I belong to You. Even though I've given You my heart, I see there's no way I can possibly earn Your love. I'm thankful that You love me through Your grace and have made me Your child. Thank You for Your promise in John 15:9–10: "As the Father has loved me, so have I loved you. Now remain in my love. If you obey my commands, you will remain in my love" (NIV).

Every day, I love You with my whole heart, soul, and mind, and endeavor to live within Your will. Thank You for mercifully loving me during my good and not-so-good days. How I treasure Your personal love for me.

December 8 || Welcome Home

In My Father's house are many mansions.... I go to prepare a place for you.... I will come again and receive you to Myself; that where I am, there you may be also. JOHN 14:2–3 NKJV

DO YOU EVER wonder what heaven will be like? When I think of heaven, a deep, homesick feeling stirs within me. Perhaps it's because my heavenly Father has already prepared a place for me. There's an overpowering love drawing me to run and fall into my Father's arms.

Like Mary, I want to sit at the feet of my Lord and ask all the questions I've accumulated during my stay on earth. One by one, I believe He'll help me understand the answers. Perhaps many of us feel this way when we know the Father well. We communicate with Him daily and sense His loving presence. Although I love my husband, family, and friends here, there's a deeper, fuller love I feel for my Father in heaven.

What will heaven be like? The Bible says there will be no more sin or violence, sickness or pain, tears or grief, which we often grow weary of fending off. We long for a carefree, eternal life with God in heaven. What a delight it will be when we get to see our Christian loved ones and friends who have gone home before us!

But there is more to heaven than this. The glorious, awesome Trinity of God the Father, God the Son, and God the Holy Spirit is there. Heaven will be more than an energizing revival, women or men's retreat, or camp meeting. We will actually get to meet Him face-to-face!

As I fall before Him in reverence, I can imagine Jesus, my Savior, stepping forward, bending down, and taking my hand. As He helps me to my feet, I may hear Him mercifully say, "It's all right, My child. I paid the price for your sins and made you My own. Welcome home."

December 9 || Hearing His Voice

To him the doorkeeper opens, and the sheep hear his voice; and he calls his own sheep by name and leads them out. And when he brings out his own sheep, he goes before them; and the sheep follow him, for they know his voice. JOHN 10:3–4 NKJV

ONE OF THE ways the Lord blesses us is when He makes it possible for us to hear His voice at any time of the day. Even above chaotic or frightening circumstances, we're still able to recognize Him speaking as He guides and protects us.

The weather didn't look threatening when I took my elementary students outside for recess. My class joined the others in enthusiastic play, shouting and laughing. I was pleased that they were able to run off some energy.

Halfway through recess, black, threatening clouds worked their way toward us. Then the sky opened up with pelting rain pushed by hard winds. The children aimlessly dashed in every direction. From under the school's eaves, I shouted their names and told them to follow me. I was amazed how my voice cut through the noise of wind, rain, and screeching children to reach each child's ear. It wasn't long until they followed me inside to warmth and safety.

I used to wonder how our high school basketball players could hear directions during the games. Spectators scream until they are hoarse. Drums bang. Horns blow. But the trusted coach calls out, and the team members recognize his voice and follow his lead.

In our walks with God, we pray and read His Word. We listen as He graciously strengthens, comforts, and guides. The more we stay close to Him, the more we recognize His voice. When the storms of life and confusion blow and people aimlessly run here and there, we know to fine-tune our spiritual ears to His instructions. His peace and order surround us when we listen and obey. Before we know it, He has lovingly brought us under His protection into warmth and safety.

Beloved, let us love one another, for love is of God; and everyone who loves is born of God and knows God. 1 JOHN 4:7 NKJV

DOES THE LOVE you want to express to someone in your life fall short of your intentions? Take your need to the Lord and allow Him to work. When we ask Him, God accepts and transforms our love into that which is unlimited and holy. He alone can communicate that love to the mind and soul of another. He is love. He is all-encompassing. He is the answer.

Lord, how can I love others with a love like Yours? No matter how much I try, I don't measure up. Open my heart, Lord. Reveal my hidden thoughts. Cleanse me. Renew a right spirit within me, and grant me Your salvation.

How grateful I am, dear Lord, for Your mercy and compassion. How incredible is the way You manifest Your loving-kindness and forgiveness toward me. Thank You for sending Your only Son into the world so I can be as one with You.

You show me in Your Word that because You love us, we should also love each other. Even though I've never seen You, I know that You live in my heart and are with me all the time. Take this imperfect, bungling love of mine, Lord. Make it pure through the cleansing power of Your Holy Spirit so You can use this love I long to share to glorify You. Thank You for the way Your love abides in me, Lord, and my love abides in You.

Your love fills my soul. How precious it is to me.
Your love makes me whole. How gracious You are to me.
Your love calms my fears. It quiets my mind and soul.
Your love dries my tears. You comfort and make me whole.

[Love] always perseveres. 1 CORINTHIANS 13:7 NIV

THERE'S A STORY that I heard on the radio many years ago about a woman who wondered if she still loved her husband. What she did might be an encouragement to you or a friend, if this issue is a familiar one.

Jenny was sixteen when she became pregnant by her eighteen-year-old boyfriend Chad. Both sets of parents requested that the two do the honorable thing and get married.

Jenny soon realized that her husband felt saddled with her and their baby boy. And even though he was kind to his son, Chad became increasingly obnoxious toward Jenny.

Jenny once thought she loved Chad, but her love for him dwindled to nothing. Out of desperation, she decided to take her son to church. Before long, she went to the pastor for counseling. She told him she no longer loved Chad and asked for his advice.

The pastor told Jenny to treat her husband as though she loved him and to persevere with that love every day. Jenny did, and she was as kind and thoughtful as she could be. At her pastor's advice, she also began to thank God for a love that would grow.

In a few weeks, the couple's love began to blossom. Their family drew close and strong. After awhile, they dedicated their family to the Lord. This came about because of prevailing prayer and a love that persevered.

Should your love become mundane and you wonder if there's even love at all, love anyway. And keep trying. When love begins to spark, fan the embers with more love. And keep trying. When years go by and you both wonder how you could ever bear to be apart, love endearingly. And keep treasuring.

"Peace, peace, to those far and near," says the LORD. *"And I will heal them."* ISAIAH 57:19 NIV

WHAT CAN BE more challenging than trying to solve the stressful situations we often face in the workplace? We regularly spend six to eight hours a day at our places of employment. The people we work with may know us almost as much as our own family members do. They learn to pick up on our body language and sense what we're thinking, and they certainly know what our mood is on any given day.

Even more challenging than trying to untangle problems is daily reflecting the love of Jesus through what we do and say. Whether those we work with treat us with respect or look for ways to push our emotional buttons, we can learn to step back and say a silent prayer during difficult times. Then we can remember to take a deep breath, allow God to help us, then once again attempt to complete the job at hand. When we do, the Lord provides a sense of peace we urgently need. Like a jumble of puzzle pieces, He has a way of helping us sort them out and put them back into place.

The Bible has some great promises that can help us during our strenuous work hours: "You will keep him in perfect peace, whose mind is stayed on You, because he trusts in You" (Isaiah 26:3 NKJV). "Therefore humble yourselves under the mighty hand of God, that He may exalt you in due time, casting all your care upon Him, for He cares for you" (1 Peter 5:6–7 NKJV).

The next time things become too stressful at work, try stepping back a little, praying, taking a deep breath, then allowing God to help solve the problems.

If we do all we can do, then call on Him for help, He will do all we cannot do.

For if you forgive men when they sin against you, your heavenly Father will also forgive you.
MATTHEW 6:14 NIV

SOMETIMES WE MAY wonder if the Holy Spirit is using our act of forgiveness to impact the heart of the one we forgave, but no matter what, our sincere obedience lies in the hands of the Lord.

The Bible tells how Saul stood by while Stephen was stoned for being a Christian. As the stones flew toward him, Stephen looked up toward heaven and cried: "Look! I see the heavens opened and the Son of Man standing at the right hand of God!... Lord, do not charge them with this sin" (Acts 7:56, 60 NKJV). Stephen knew those stoning him didn't change their hearts, but he forgave them and prayed for their salvation anyway. Although Saul didn't acknowledge he was wrong at that time, he most likely never forgot what Stephen said that day. In addition to Jesus speaking directly to Saul (later to become Paul) on the road to Damascus, Stephen's sacrificial forgiveness may have had a part in changing Paul's life forever.

Though our hurts aren't nearly as bad as the ones Stephen suffered, it's still difficult to forgive and let go. May the Lord help us to forgive as He forgave us and thereby touch the heart of another.

When you're burdened with hurts from the past, when your heartaches engulf you with pain, seek the touch of love's forgiveness that only can come from God. When wrongs from the past can't be righted, when there's no way to turn back the clock, try the touch of love's forgiveness that only can come from God. Loads are lifted and joy reawakens. Hearts are mended and souls are set free! It's the touch of love's forgiveness that truly has come from God.

But He gives more grace. Therefore He says: "God resists the proud, but gives grace to the humble." James 4:6 NKJV

WHEN WE ARE wrongfully judged in the workplace, we're tempted to bristle, mutter behind backs, or try to get even. One local restaurant manager chose to respond to injustice with a godly attitude.

It was a regular workday when a state food inspector in her early thirties strode briskly through the restaurant door. She moved like a whirlwind as she darted from station to station. At one point she dropped her thermometer in a container of sauce. Then she brushed in front of an employee cutting lemons and charted in her report that the employee left the cutting board unattended. At the end of her inspection, the young woman ruthlessly wrote up a state report, recommending that the restaurant be shut down.

Every employee must have watched to see what the manager's reaction would be. His response surprised them all. Rather than retaliating, he quietly praised her for trying to do the best job she could. Yet he urged her to relax in her work rather than try to prove herself despite her youth. He told her if she did this and learned compassion, she would go a long way.

His right attitude certainly paid off. The evaluation must have been moderated, because the restaurant remained open for business.

When we're faced with injustice, may the Lord help us not to retaliate. By His grace we can keep our attitudes pure and our intentions in line with His will. In so doing, we trust Him to bring about good.

Men may spurn our appeals, reject our message, oppose our arguments, despise our persons; but they are helpless against our prayers.

—J. Sidlow Baxter

For the wages of sin is death, but the free gift of God is eternal life through Jesus Christ our Lord.
ROMANS 6:23 TLB

HAVE YOU EVER received money in the mail without knowing where it came from? That happened to me several years ago. It was surprising how the anonymous gift was exactly what I needed at that time.

Recently I was thinking about that act of kindness and wondered what I could do to encourage someone else. I decided to pull five dollars from my purse and attach a sticky note to it saying, "Please give this to the next person in line." No signature. No explanation.

I felt a little giddy as I took it to the local grocery store where I often shop. The clerks there know me, and I hoped they would pass on my gift. It was a busy time of day, and I didn't look at the person behind me. After I paid for my groceries, I handed the note to the cashier and put my finger to my lips. I quickly rolled my cart away and didn't look back. That would spoil the fun.

Far greater than the acts of kindness we receive and give is the way Jesus took our debt of sin and carried it to the cross. There it was paid in full. He freed us from our past and gave us a life filled with His abundance and grace.

The moment He died on the cross, there was an earthquake. The thick veil in the temple separating people from the holy of holies (where only the priests were allowed) was torn in two from top to bottom. There was no way any human being could have done such a thing. From that moment till now, the Lord has made it possible for us to come directly to Him and pray. Our debts were paid in full!

Our old history ends with the cross; our new history begins with the resurrection. —WATCHMAN NEE

"Though it [the mustard seed] is the smallest of all your seeds, yet when it grows, it is the largest of garden plants and becomes a tree, so that the birds of the air come and perch in its branches."
MATTHEW 13:32 NIV

IN THE PREVIOUS devotion, I told how I handed five dollars and a sticky note to a grocery store clerk. The note said, "Please give this to the next person in line." I know this clerk; she's a dedicated Christian, so I felt confident that she would do as I asked, even though she appeared perplexed and taken aback.

After a few weeks, I was fortunate enough to have her again as my cashier. I had a bunch of groceries so we had a little time to chat while she rang them up. She told me that since the person behind me that day purchased only a bag of ice, she'd decided to save the note and gift for a man who was next in line. She said the man's face lit up with a smile, and he appeared to be surprised and delighted.

I felt God's warm approval flood my soul a second time. I wondered if this man had been in need or was having a bad day. Perhaps he had prayed that the Lord would give him some kind of evidence of His love and care.

We don't know the answers to our speculations, but we can be assured that God uses the ripple effect like a pebble dropped in a pool. We can have faith that "all things [really do] work together for good to those who love God, to those who are the called according to His purpose (Romans 8:28 NKJV)—whether we are the ones giving or receiving.

Perhaps our acts of kindness turn into secret seeds planted in the hearts of others, and grow into more small acts that are planted—and grow.

Try planting a secret seed. It's kind of fun!

December 17 || Just Ask

Ask, using my name, and you will receive, and your cup of joy will overflow. JOHN 16:24 TLB

DURING THE LAST retreat I attended with some ladies from our church, I was deeply saddened by how many tragic prayer requests were turned in. Some were recovering from drug and alcohol addictions, others felt abandoned by broken marriages and relationships, while still others struggled to keep roofs over their heads. The retreat prayer team and others held these ladies up in powerful prayer. We listened to concerns and gave help wherever possible. These serious requests weighed heavily on my mind throughout the retreat. The world felt like a dark place. What more could I do?

The final night at retreat, I whispered my question to the Lord in the stillness of the night. *What can I do, Lord, that I'm not already doing? This world appears so hopeless to some, like the total darkness I'm in right now.* I drifted off to sleep with the question still whirring through my brain.

In the middle of the night, I awakened to a bright light flashing back and forth across the ceiling. Although it was tiny, it pierced the darkness of the room. I soon realized the light came from my upper bunk partner's flashlight as she tried to straighten her bed.

Just ask, I felt the Lord whisper back to me. *Keep asking Me what little things you can do. You are the light that makes a difference.* The Scripture in Matthew 5:16 came to my mind: "Let your light shine before men in such a way that they may see your good works, and glorify your Father who is in heaven" (NASB).

Whenever you are burdened over the sadness around you, just ask God what He wants you to do that day.

Doing little things with a strong desire to please God makes them really great. —ST. FRANCIS DE SALES

For the ways of man are before the eyes of the LORD, and He ponders all his paths.
PROVERBS 5:21 NKJV

HOW I LOVE You, heavenly Father. I'm grateful that You love me like a faithful parent does a child. You are everything to me. You are complete. You are holy. You are perfect. You, Father, simply *are*.

You know me better than anyone else. You understand my peculiar ways. You recognize my likes and dislikes. You, Father, know what I'm thinking even before I speak. You see my weaknesses and pick me up when I fall. You identify my strengths but remind me to not get ahead of You.

You open the doors in my life that You want me to go through and close some that aren't best for me. When I struggle to follow Your leading, You take my hands in Yours and help me along. When things go wrong and I'm afraid, You wrap Your arms around me and hold me fast.

Thank You for being my Teacher, my Counselor, my Listener, my dearest Friend. Thank You for keeping my heart right and true, for filling me with Your wisdom that's sufficient for each day. I feel as though You are proud of me, Father, when I manage to do things right. The very thought of Your approval fills my heart with gladness.

Thank You for how Your presence is with me all of the time. With You as my heavenly Father, I will never be alone. By day, You walk along with me. By night, You protect and keep me close. Thank You for loving me as Your child, dear Father. Thank You for adopting me to be Your own. Keep me near to You, I pray. As was said in a prayer by David, "Keep me as the apple of your eye; hide me in the shadow of your wings," from this day forward and forevermore.

Charm is deceitful and beauty is passing, but a woman who fears the LORD, she shall be praised. Give her of the fruit of her hands, and let her own works praise her in the gates.
PROVERBS 31:30–31 NKJV

DO YOU FEEL like you're beautiful? Most of us have trouble answering this question. Sadly, we can only think about our flaws. Yet we may see our children and grandchildren as being absolutely delightful. Whatever flaws or faults they may possess go mostly unnoticed in our eyes.

Isn't it amazing how God created us in His image? That means He planned us to look the way we do. As we strive daily to make ourselves prettier through diets, makeup, and clothing, God often reminds us that He doesn't look at our outward appearance, He looks into our hearts.

The Lord delights in us when we honor Him and place our hope in His love. Throughout the triumphs and trials of life, God has a wonderful way of turning the beauty within us into something even more valuable than refined gold. Years pass and our bodies change. How many times do you look at an elderly Christian lady and see her as the most beautiful woman in the room? Thinning gray hair, age spots, and twisted fingers and toes fade from view as we see the comeliness in her eyes, her smile, and her cheerful voice. Most beautiful of all is the gentle spirit within her, radiating God's presence in her soul.

As we walk with the Lord each day, we are beautiful in His sight, and often in the sight of those around us. My prayer is that I will be beautiful for the Lord and that He would help me to take good care of myself and try to look my best. May I remember to dress modestly so I can reflect Him in my life. I pray that He would cleanse my heart and grant me His holy presence so I may reflect a beauty that comes from Him.

But let all who take refuge in You be glad; let them ever sing for joy. PSALM 5:11 NIV

SHORTLY BEFORE CHRISTMAS one year, the phone's shrill ring at one thirty in the freezing cold morning jerked Pastor Charles from a sound sleep. The voice on the other end sounded urgent. "Pastor Charles, this is Sergeant Lance. I'm sorry to awaken you, but there's been a shooting at our neighboring city's community center and a man was killed. We've had people stranded outside in the cold for quite a while. Can you help?"

The church was only a few minutes away from the crime scene. Charles didn't hesitate. "Meet me at our church. I'll have the doors unlocked." He quickly dressed and prayed as he drove to the church, *Lord, help me to help these who are in need.*

When Sergeant Lance and other officers arrived with a police van, Charles was shocked to see about twenty-five people pour out of the van and stumble up the steps to the church. They looked cold, bewildered, and tired. Many were in nightclothes. Some wore no shirts or shoes. Quite a few were women and children.

"There was a party in the community center," Sergeant Lance explained. "Someone outside fired eight shots through the window and killed a man inside. The gunman reportedly fled to a nearby house, which made the house a crime scene. Everyone inside had to vacate the premises. They've been stranded outside for quite a while." He sighed. "I'm glad I could reach you."

"No problem," Pastor Charles said. "I'll do everything I can to help."

Danger lurked as the investigation continued, but that night God mercifully protected everyone sheltered in the little church.

Can we not follow His footsteps, filled with His Spirit, to finish the task appointed, with heart aglow and hurrying feet?
—DR. V. RAYMOND EDMAN

"For I was hungry and you gave Me food; I was thirsty and you gave Me drink; I was a stranger and you took Me in." MATTHEW 25:35 NKJV

WHEN DISASTER STRIKES, God often brings out the best in us. Our compassionate instincts kick in and motivate us to help in any way we can. It was that way when people found refuge in the church that night of the tragic shooting.

A few people had trouble warming up. Babies cried. Some of the children were coughing from exposure to the cold. Pastor Charles wasted no time making hot drinks and cooking up a huge batch of pancakes. Some of the officers went out and purchased milk for the babies and medicine for the ailing children. Next they borrowed blankets from the hospital and brought them to the church. At three a.m. the sergeant and the other police officers told Pastor Charles they had to return to the crime scene and that he couldn't be left without help. Anyone could see in through the windows.

So Charles called Dave, one of his faithful friends. Dave arrived in minutes and pitched right in. Everyone seemed grateful to have a safe place to rest. Steady breathing soon filled the building as children and adults quietly slept on the carpets.

By daybreak, the weapon was located in the vacated house and the shooter was arrested. The family members thanked Pastor Charles and Dave before returning to their homes. The church had provided sanctuary for about six and a half hours.

What would have happened if no one had been found to take those families in on that cold winter night? Would God's compassionate love have ever had a chance to be shown when it was most needed?

Love one another. As I have loved you, so you must love one another. JOHN 13:34 NIV

CHRISTMAS IS A wonderful time, but as we prepare to celebrate Christ's birth, we often get caught up in so many activities that we neglect our loved ones who need our attention the most. This happened to youth leader Derik Nelson.

Shortly before Christmas one year Derik received a phone call from his father asking if he could join his father and mother for Christmas Eve service at their church. Derik had already committed that night to setting up for a Christmas program at his own church on Christmas Day and had to say no. His dad sounded disappointed and Derik's heart sank. Once again he'd overextended himself and was neglecting his parents.

After praying about it, he asked some older teenagers to help him Christmas Eve afternoon. They got everything done in record time, and Derik drove straight to his parents' candlelit church. He knew his mom and dad would already be sitting near the front.

Derik's parents broke out in big smiles when they heard his familiar voice whisper, "Got room for one more?" As he enjoyed the service, Derik remembered a saying: "Christmas is made for us to love one another." He silently asked for God's forgiveness and vowed that he would always keep his parents at the forefront of his busy schedule.

Don't wait to say you love me. Don't wait to sing my song.
Be quick to let me know, I may not be here long.
Don't think there's still tomorrow. Do something nice today.
In life's most hectic hour love must find a way.
Let me know you love me. Show me that you care.
While the clock is ticking, keep me in your prayer.

Don't wait to show you love me. Don't let the present fly.
Build now the loving memories before life passes by.

[The Magi] departed; and behold, the star which they had seen in the East went before them, till it came and stood over where the young Child was. MATTHEW 2:9 NKJV

HARSH GUSTS OF freezing wind shook the small trailer. Inside, my son Dave and I took turns selling Christmas trees to raise funds for our church youth group's upcoming mission trip to Mexico, where we would do volunteer work and tell children about Jesus.

Dave burst inside. "All right!" he announced. "I just sold three more trees." I smiled at my son and tried not to show how cold I felt as I shivered under a coat and blanket. I was glad to help but wished I could be home.

As night approached, fewer customers came onto the lot. Dave drifted off to sleep on a couch. I began to wonder if we'd be able to meet our goals, and I began to pray, "Lord, please help us." Out of the corner of my eye I noticed a shadow outside the window. It was a cloud steadily floating across the sky, revealing a round silver moon and one bright star. In the stillness, the scene made me think of the star of Bethlehem. I wondered how Mary and Joseph felt in the stable so many years ago. Our small sacrifice paled in light of their act of faith that changed the course of time.

"I'm sorry, Lord," I whispered, "for inwardly complaining about this small task You've given us. Nothing I do can begin to compare to what You did when You came and gave Your life for us."

Dave roused from his short nap. "You okay, Mom?"

I felt pleased that my son was looking out for me. "I'm okay. Here comes another customer. I think it's my turn." For some reason, the moon seemed brighter and the air not as cold. "Happy birthday, Jesus," I whispered again. "Thank You for Your love and grace."

December 24 | What Can We Give Him?

Through Him then, let us continually offer up a sacrifice of praise to God, that is, the fruit of lips that give thanks to His name. And do not neglect doing good and sharing, for with such sacrifices God is pleased. HEBREWS 13:15–16 NASB

WHAT A COMPASSIONATE God our Lord is! Consider for a moment a few of the countless blessings He showers upon us. How might we repay Him for His goodness? What can we give Him that He hasn't already given to us? Our lives? He created us. Eternal life with Him? He paid the price. Food? Clothing? Shelter? Money? He provides these. Love? He loved us first.

The only offering we can give is our unconditional sacrifice of praise. It's easy to be thankful when everything is going smoothly, but it's much harder when life takes a wrong turn. When our problems seem impossible to solve and we're at an emotional low, we cry before the Lord, asking Him to rescue and intervene. Is there an element of love we can pull from the storehouse of our souls and simply give Him our heartfelt sacrifice of praise?

Whether we're dealing with bumps and potholes in our walk with Him or experiencing an unusually smooth ride, we may consider stopping what we're doing and tell Him how much we love and adore Him—with no strings attached.

As we nestle in the arms of our Father who knows us best, we can tell Him how dear He is to us. We can thank Him for making us in His image, for sacrificing His only Son to save us from sin; for adopting us as His children; and for loving us as His own. We may want to thank Him for when His presence seems to be closer than the air we breathe. We can thank Him for how He shares our joys, carries our burdens, and protects us from evil and harm.

How good it is that we can tell Him, "I really love You, Lord."

And going into the house [the wise men] saw the child with Mary his mother, and they fell down and worshiped him. MATTHEW 2:11 RSV

WE WORSHIP GOD the Father, God the Son, and God the Holy Spirit, but we may seldom think of worshipping Him as our Savior when He came to this earth as a pure and holy, innocent little baby. Let's acknowledge Him for leaving heaven and being born in such uncomfortable surroundings—He who would be pursued by King Herod, He who had to rely on a God-fearing mother and stepfather to keep Him safe.

Imagine what it was like for Him to humbly learn from the scholars and grow in wisdom and stature. Think of how He overcame earthly temptations and remained pure and holy. I wonder how He felt, knowing He would some day give His life for you and me.

As we think of Jesus the holy Child during this Christmas season, let's thank and adore Him for coming to this earth and being our Savior and Lord.

CHRISTMAS ON BENDED KNEE

When I think of Christmas, Jesus comes to mind;
A babe in swaddling clothes,
A manger so sublime.

How could a Savior lie that way, amidst the stench and straw and hay?
How could His Father, God, permit His child, so precious seen,
By lowly ones, the shepherds there, dirty, worn and mean?

And kings, the three, road weary they, for a Savior lying upon the hay?
Gifts, gold and frankincense and myrrh, fragrance, power and grace;
But taken by our Wise Men three, to such a humble place?

Maybe yet I'll understand how Christ must come to be,
A lowly birth, a humble life,
To end upon a tree.

For the Savior born and Savior died, I find on bended knee,
A Christmas gift from God above,
With Him, eternity.
—ROBERT DONIHUE SR.

But from everlasting to everlasting the LORD's love is with those who fear Him, and His righteousness with their children's children. PSALM 103:17 NIV

AFTER ALL THE years spent raising children, the time comes when they're ready to be on their own. We know this day is approaching from the day they were born, but I usually tried not to think about it, instead focusing on what time we had together.

When they're gone, fond memories come to mind: rushing to activities; hearing everyone talk at once; enjoying their infectious laughter; watching their wrestling matches; teasing and playing practical jokes. Some memories may be of praying together at the front door before school, around the dinner table, or at bedtime.

It's hard to let go. When the hubbub is gone and the house rings with silence, loneliness may feel almost unbearable. Yet it's part of the maturing process. We might ask ourselves what we did right or what we could have done better. When we recall our shortcomings, we can go to the Lord in prayer and ask His forgiveness. And we may need to also ask forgiveness of our children.

It's strange how we once had confidence in ourselves as we were growing up, yet we now tend to worry about our grown offspring and ask God to bless them with protection and wisdom. Our conversations with them now might change from our correcting and assuming responsibility for their actions to our listening, understanding, and assuring them that we are proud of them and believe that they will do well. Without a doubt, God made our children out of good stuff and He's constantly watching over and helping them.

Now I count the days until our children and grandchildren get together. Best of all, I love it when I'm talking with any of them and they say, "Let's pray together." Just like we did in days gone by.

"I am leaving you with a gift—peace of mind and heart! And the peace I give isn't fragile like the peace the world gives. So don't be troubled or afraid." JOHN 14:27 TLB

IN OUR JOURNEY with the Lord, we go through days that are smooth as glass. We're amazed how everything can be so perfect during these times. Other days can be so bumpy that we feel like life is out of control. Sometimes it can be downright scary. We may strive to hang onto our most valued possessions, allowing our trials to distract us from what is really most important: the priceless love of our Lord Jesus Christ.

Nita and LeeAnn were traveling down a remote washboard gravel road in Nita's little sports car. They were chatting about all sorts of things when a large moose bolted out of the woods and hit the driver's side. Both ladies were shocked at first then noticed the moose staggering down the road in the opposite direction. They discovered he had knocked off the side mirror. The moose appeared to be all right, so there was no need to report the accident to the authorities.

Nita got out of her car, checked the driver's door for damage, then reached down to pick up her mirror from the shoulder of the road. LeeAnn glanced out the back window and suddenly shouted to Nita to leave her mirror, jump in the car, and take off—full speed ahead. The moose was charging at the car from behind! The two ladies never knew they could go so fast on the washboard road. They escaped to safety and later retrieved the mirror.

When troubles charge at us and cause us to tremble with fear, we may need to relinquish everything to the Lord and trust Him to take control and bring us through. Our Lord means more than anything or anyone in this world.

One thing I do, forgetting those things which are behind and reaching forward to those things which are ahead, I press toward the goal for the prize of the upward call of God in Christ Jesus.
PHILIPPIANS 3:13–14 NKJV

DO YOU HAVE a special wish or dream you want to make happen? Wishes and dreams that turn into prayers can become realities when our central focus is on the will of God. When He is the director of our dreams, we can work hand-in-hand with Him and see them come true.

Well-known author Colleen Reece experienced a remarkable answer to prayer in this area. As a young child, she learned to read by kerosene lamp. One evening she told her parents she wished they had a magic lamp and a magic carpet like Aladdin. They were quick to explain that her lamp was an "Aladdin" lamp and that the books she loved were her magic carpet. Colleen vowed then and there to someday write a book of her own.

Her wishes turned into prayers. In 1977, while working a government job, she felt led to write for the Lord. In an amazing way, God used a passage from Emilie Loring's *There Is Always Love* to call and encourage her to write: "There is only one common-sense, [sic] move when you don't like your life. Do something about it. Get out. Go somewhere. Follow a rainbow. Who knows? You may find the legendary pot of gold at the end of it."

This was God's confirmation for Colleen. She quit her job and went into writing full time. It took a lot of hard work, prayer, and dedication, yet with God's help, she has written over 140 inspiring books.

Don't be afraid to write your dreams and wishes down and bring them to the Lord for direction and help. As soon as He gives the go-ahead, set your goals, roll up your sleeves, and work hard to make it happen. You just never know until you try.

"If you love me, obey me; and I will ask the Father and he will give you another Comforter, and He will never leave you. He is the Holy Spirit, the Spirit who leads into all truth." JOHN 14:15–17 TLB

AS WE WALK with the Lord, we get to enjoy His marvelous presence and the blessings He bestows on us. Our main focus is our relationship with Him and trying to live a Christian life that's pleasing to Him. But there's more. Before long, we want to draw closer to the Lord and ask for His Holy Spirit to fill our lives. We want to sense Him talking to our hearts about what He wants us to do for Him and those who need to hear about Him. With each step we take, He gives us a calling or challenge. The key is to trust Him and obey what He asks us to do.

No matter the challenge He places before us, may we wholeheartedly follow. When the task becomes difficult, let's pray for Him to go before us and give us courage. Though we might not feel brave, He is strong where we're weak. With enthusiasm and vision for the future, let us show mercy, then go forth and follow Him.

THE MASTER'S CALL

Behold, the Master now is calling for reapers brave and true;
The golden harvest fields are waiting, but laborers are few.
Go, bid the poor with joy and gladness the feast of love to share;
And He the Bread of Life Eternal will make them welcome there.
Go forth, with patience, love and kindness; and in the Master's name,
The blessed news of free salvation to all the world proclaim!

—JULIA STERLIND

I plead with you to give your bodies to God. Let them be a living sacrifice.... Be a new and different person with a fresh newness in all you do and think. Then you will learn from your own experience how His ways will really satisfy you. ROMANS 12:1–2 TLB

MANY OF US dream of making a new start in our lives, but our dreams may be hampered by roadblocks from our poor choices; we can't find the new life of joy and purpose God offers.

Ben grew up attending church regularly. He knew how to talk the church talk—but he didn't take God's lessons to heart. While in college, he and his girlfriend Cheryl enjoyed partying. He considered himself the "best drinker there ever was." He figured that no matter what he did or said, God still loved him.

They went to Ben's home church on occasion—both before and after they married and moved to their own home. All along, Ben's parents and church family faithfully prayed for them. God answered their prayers when Ben became friends with Jason, the new young minister. After awhile, the couple made a commitment to follow the Lord.

God gave their lives a new direction. Now they tell everyone about God's love and grace and the change He mercifully provided them. Ben is currently a trustee in the church and has gone on a mission trip to Haiti. Cheryl enjoys serving God in several different areas of the church—and the couple has recently been blessed with their first child, a son. Ben and Cheryl experience lives that are now abundant and free in Him!

It's never too late to make a fresh start. When we ask, He removes the roadblocks and shows us an exciting turn of direction with Him.

Leo Tolstoy described this when he said, "When I came to believe in Christ's teachings, I ceased desiring what I had wished for before. The direction of my life, my desires, became different. What was good and bad changed places."

"I am the Alpha and the Omega, the Beginning and the End," says the Lord, *"who is and who was and who is to come, the Almighty."* REVELATION 1:8 NKJV

LET US THANK God for His unfailing faithfulness. Because of His mercy, we know that whatever fiery trials we might face, we will never be consumed. No matter how alone we feel during life's uncertainties, He'll never desert us. Instead, He makes Himself known by His gracious presence, for He is constantly by our side—as close as the air we breathe. When we struggle and fail and struggle some more, and are to the point of giving up, the Lord is with us. When life seems unstable like sinking sand, He truly is the solid Rock on which we can stand! When all else fails, He gives us hope, just when we need Him the most.

How thankful we can be that God is always with us. Each day as we wait for His direction, He sheds new light upon our unfamiliar paths. Each night when we lie down to rest, He provides us with portions of His everlasting peace and joy.

God will bless us with His everlasting faithfulness all the days of our lives. His mercies shall unceasingly remain. His goodness and grace are with us now and forevermore.

GOD'S BLESSINGS BE UPON YOU

May you lift your gaze to the heavens and hunger for the Lord your God.
May your help come from Him, the Maker of all creation.
May He not let your feet slip outside of His Holy ways.
May He keep you safe day and night, for He never rests.
May He encompass you as you go out and come in.
May the Lord be your shade by day so the sun will not harm you.
May He be your shelter when the moon shimmers by night.
May He protect you with His mighty hand and
   watch over you—now and forevermore. Amen.

My sincere appreciation to Janice Lewis Clark
for her faithful friendship, prayers, encouragement, and help
during the creation of *Glimpses of God's Grace*.

Ellie Claire® Gift & Paper Expressions
Franklin, TN 37067
EllieClaire.com
Ellie Claire is a registered trademark of Worthy Media, Inc.

Glimpses of God's Grace 365-Day Devotional Journal
© 2015 by Anita Corrine Donihue
Published by Ellie Claire, an imprint of Worthy Publishing Group, a division of Worthy Media, Inc.

ISBN 978-1-63326-049-8

Scripture references are from the following sources: The Holy Bible, King James Version (KJV). The Holy Bible, New International Version®, NIV®. Copyright © 1973, 1978, 1984 by International Bible Society. Used by permission of Zondervan. The New King James Version (NKJV). Copyright © 1982 by Thomas Nelson, Inc. Used by permission. The New American Standard Bible® (NASB), Copyright © 1960, 1962, 1963, 1968, 1971, 1972, 1973, 1975, 1977, 1995 by The Lockman Foundation. Used by permission. *The Living Bible* (TLB) © 1971. Used by permission of Tyndale House Publishers, Inc., Wheaton, Illinois 60189. Used by permission. The Revised Standard Version of the Bible (RSV), copyright 1946, 1952, 1971 by the Division of Christian Education of the National Council of the Churches of Christ in the USA. Used by permission. The Holy Bible, New Living Translation (NLT), copyright 1996, 2004. Used by permission of Tyndale House Publishers, Inc., Wheaton, Illinois.

All unattributed material is by Anita Corrine Donihue.

Interior design by faceout studio | faceoutstudio.com
Typesetting by Thinkpen Design, Inc. | www.thinkpendesign.com
Cover photo by Shutterstock | www.shutterstock.com

Printed in China.

4 5 6 7 8 9 10 – 20 19 18 17 16